Goldoon

and

Professor

*Memoirs and Reflections of a
Bicultural Marriage*

Jackie Shahzadi

Bahman Shahzadi
Jacqueline Buckman Shahzadi

Contact the authors at bshahzadi@yahoo.com or in care of Trafford Publishing.

Printed in Victoria, Canada

Note for Librarians: a cataloguing record for this book that includes Dewey Classification and US Library of Congress numbers is available from the National Library of Canada. The complete cataloguing record can be obtained from the National Library online database at:
www.nlc-bnc.ca/amicus/index-e.html
ISBN 1-4120-1231-7

TRAFFORD

This book was published on-demand in cooperation with Trafford Publishing.
On-demand publishing is a unique process and service of making a book available for retail sale to the public taking advantage of on-demand manufacturing and Internet marketing. On-demand publishing includes promotions, retail sales, manufacturing, order fulfilment, accounting and collecting royalties on behalf of the author.

Suite 6E, 2333 Government St., Victoria, B.C. V8T 4P4, CANADA
Phone   250-383-6864   Toll-free   1-888-232-4444 (Canada & US)
Fax 250-383-6804   E-mail sales@trafford.com   Web site
www.trafford.com
TRAFFORD PUBLISHING IS A DIVISION OF TRAFFORD HOLDINGS LTD.
Trafford Catalogue #03-1609   www.trafford.com/robots/03-1609.html

10   9   8   7   6   5   4   3

Contents

Preface   1

Chapter One   Culture Shock, or Not   3

Chapter Two   Marriage against all Odds   11

Chapter Three   Teaching, Learning, and Driving   60

Chapter Four   The Fruits of their Labor   92

Chapter Five   A Place to Call Home   125

Chapter Six   S-E-X   142

Chapter Seven   Out and About   145

Chapter Eight   Dollars and Rials   167

Chapter Nine   Trying on Zoroastrianism   174

Chapter Ten   The Pets among Us   183

Chapter Eleven   The Fun Times   189

Chapter Twelve   Touched by Revolution   211

Chapter Thirteen   Ending and Beginning   222

Chapter Fourteen   Leftovers   230

Epilogue   238

Chapter One

Culture Shock, or Not

In her first letter home, Jackie wrote:

Sept. 10, 1967 I had a nice plane ride by Pan Am to Tehran. The plane was 50 minutes late, but we arrived with no trouble. Bahman met me at the airport—how wonderful it was to see him again after 6 months! You can't imagine two people happier than Bahman and me. We have been so busy the last two days, rushing around Tehran looking for a place for me to stay and trying to find me a job. The American Embassy was no help—they could only tell me about a few open secretarial positions. Finally we discovered, through the Iran Tourist Organization, the apartment I am now in. Actually, it is only one room, and I share a kitchen and a bathroom. However, no one is now living in the other two rooms of the house so I have the kitchen and bath to myself. We bought food at an America-style supermarket, and I do my own cooking.

I am still looking for a job—I will probably teach English. Every place I ask wants to see my "documents" and so—this is very important—would you please make copies of my H.S. Diploma, my B.A. from Drew and my M.A. from Wisconsin and airmail them to me as soon as possible.

Tehran is a different, unfamiliar city, but not necessarily unpleasant or bad. Everything is going O.K. for me, so far. When I have been here longer, I can tell you more about the city.

On Friday we are planning to take a picnic lunch and drive to the mountains where it is cool. Fridays are the holidays here instead of Sundays.
P.S. Bahman says "Hello" and not to worry about me!

So it seems that finding a room to rent for her wasn't that hard even though it turned out to be a continuing problem; she had to move several times in the space of four months. On the other hand, what had occupied their mind and effort long before this time was whether and what kind of job may be available for her. While in the U.S., she had inquired from many sources and companies without much success. However, as it turned out, while she was in Tehran, a job opportunity which was sort of natural for individuals like her presented itself to her. Here are parts of her letter home ten days after the first one.

Sept. 20, 1967 Let's see, when I wrote you last I think I had found my apartment but didn't yet have a job. Well, I still need to show them my "documents" to prove my education, but I have accepted a nice job at the National University of Iran. My official title will be "Assistant Professor of English," and I will be teaching first year college students beginning Sept 23, which is "Mehr 1st" on the Persian calendar. I will be teaching mostly English pronunciation and sentence structure for English conversation. The National University is new and modern, in fact, parts of it are still being constructed. It is located away from the city, up towards the mountains. It is so high up, it has a wide view of the city and countryside. In back of the U. of course is a clear view of the mountains. Unlike the University of Tehran, where Bahman teaches, National University is a private university not under government control.
After being here now about two weeks I can still say that Tehran is not such a bad place. Of course, there are bad things here too. The streets are hot, dry, and usually dusty. The traffic is perhaps the worst thing I have seen: cars make three lanes where only two should be, they cut in front of each other, and dare each other at intersections. People jaywalk everywhere, fearlessly, it's amazing. I like to walk

with Bahman in the city at night. It's beautiful then with lots of flashing neon signs everywhere and lots of street vendors who come out at night to sell things on the sidewalks. All the shops are open in the evenings too. The evening breezes are cool and nice. One evening we ate at Café Naderi, a large outdoor garden restaurant where there is a modern band and dancing. It was wonderful.

I still do most of my shopping in American style supermarkets, drugstores, and department stores. I also live on lots of imported items like British sugar, Dutch butter, U.S. orange juice, and German hairspray; but everything is available here.

I expect to join the Iran American Society soon. So far we have been to two lectures on sociology (about literacy) in English at their cultural center, and I went on one of their tours last Sunday to the Ministry of Cultural and Fine Arts. I met a bunch of Americans on the tour. We saw native Persian craftsmen making mosaics, rugs, brocade, ceramics, wood panels, and silver trays. The work is so beautiful.

Last Friday, Bahman, another Persian friend, and I went hiking in the mountains. We even hired donkeys and rode part of the way up the mountain. Then we hiked for hours, but also spent hours sitting eating our picnic lunch.

I am healthy and happy and hope you all are too.

Reflecting back on these experiences, from the perspective of the year 2003:

Jackie: Our very first hike was quite memorable. We arrived by bus in the village of Evin at the foot of the mountains where the end of the paved road was marked by a large statue. This was no statue of a weekend hiker, but one of a fully outfitted mountaineer, ready for the task of rescuing lost hikers. We knew it was possible to spend several days hiking, staying in mountaineering huts along the way, but the dozens of people who showed up for hiking on this day wore everything except mountaineering gear. A few women seemed to have just left a social gathering with the whim of taking a hike, and we wondered how they could manage to hike in such inappropriate shoes. So many families were headed upwards on the trails that one had to hike in line!

At the beginning of the trail were a bunch of mules handled by very small boys who appeared to be as young as six years old. I couldn't believe those small boys would be able to control balky mules on those trails. But mule riding was an adventure that I wanted to experience, so we bargained for two mules and climbed aboard. The mules climbed slowly and steadily, and it was not too different from a steep horseback ride. But very soon we heard the jeers of some youngsters hiking near us on the same trail. "They are teasing us," you said! They are saying, "What kind of hikers are you that you ride up the trail on the back of mules!" Well, the mule was fun, but I wanted to be a real hiker, so that was the last time we rode mules.

Bahman: Well now, on to more serious matters. So you landed the job of English teacher. Do you want to elaborate on it? Do you remember how it happened?

J: Hold on! Before answering that, I (and maybe the readers) would like to know why we are not using our nicknames?

B: Well, I don't see any logic in using nicknames here. By the way, I'd like to declare here and now that I wasn't in favor of having that title for our book. It was all your idea, implanted in you by your daughter and son-in-law!

J: Oh well, we think it is an interesting and attractive title. And after all you agreed to it, remember?

B: Yes well, I can always claim it was under duress! It is as though you think people are going to judge the book by its cover, ha?!

J: It doesn't hurt to have a catchy title, does it?

B: All right, but I don't think we can keep using the nicknames throughout the book. For one thing, my nickname has been in retirement for a long time, just like myself.

J: OK, you have a point. But I'd like to point out, for the record, that the term "Goldoon" is still alive and well and I often hear it from you.

B: All right. Now, can we go back to real issues? The question was about how you got your job, remember?

J: Oh yes, those foreigners I met in Tehran had said it was easy to work as an English teacher for the Iran America Society, but the IAS interviewer said just then it was hard to get work permits for non-citizens. However, he then said, National University has no problem getting work permits. We went in the next room where he introduced me to the head of the National Univ. English Dept. I was hired right away, because I had an M.A.—any M.A.!

B: OK. Now I have a couple of specific questions to ask and discuss. First, among the complaints and inconveniences you mention about Tehran, traffic stands out as the most notable. And it is rightly so because this is what visitors to Tehran cite as the most astonishing and frightening phenomenon. Now, looking at it sociologically, how do *you* explain it?

J: Well, I wish I had a good sociological or psychological explanation, but I hear traffic is bad in lots of developing countries. I must say I was disappointed to see in our visit back in 2001, that Tehran's traffic had not improved in 34 years! Isn't that enough time to get it right?

B: Well, I have an "engineering" explanation and that can be expressed in three words, *lack of infrastructures.* That includes not only streets, roads, traffic signs, parking spaces, and other physical things, but also education of the public on how to deal with the "new" technology. No wonder we didn't see any improvements after so many years, because the same underlying causes still exist. And by the way, similar problems occur when any new technology is introduced into a culture that . . .

J: Wait a minute. You are not going to bring up your favorite issue of finding problems with new technologies, are you?

B: OK, maybe this is not the place for it, but we'll hopefully get a chance to discuss it some time. Instead, let's go back to my second question. In your letters you seem to be looking at a glass of water more than half full! Do you remember whether you were really so cheerful and optimistic as you sound in your letters? Or, were you expressing so much optimism because of your folks?

J: Of course, there were problems and hardships but as a whole I felt good. I'm an optimist and I was determined not to let culture shock get the best of me. Of course all these new things were *exciting* and interesting. My letters to my Mom had to focus on the good things—remember at that time my Dad was dying of cancer—a very sad time for her.

B: Yes, your subsequent letters also show your uplifting mood. However, later you wrote to your mother:

Nov. 16, 1967 I got your Nov. 4 letter a day ago and it sounds like you're really upset about the few worries I wrote about. Honestly, things aren't so bad here as you think. I only wanted to give you an idea of some of the kind of problems I have so you won't think that *everything* is cheery and rosy here. I didn't mean to emphasize the negative. Really things here are even better than I expected. I wish I could see those relatives from Trenton again so I could tell them how wrong they were. No one is beating me or robbing me or cheating me. There aren't even any slums here in the *northern* part of Tehran, and I can walk alone on the streets in the evening safely. I have most of the conveniences of the US, I have a good job, a cozy apt. with a refrigerator, hot water, heat, etc., and many nice friends— Americans, British, and Persians. This past week I bought a good radio that has 3 bands (one medium wave and two short wave)--it's all transistor but can also be plugged into an outlet. I even have a violin here, since Bahman fixed his old one up for me to play. Yes, I'm pretty comfortable and happy.

B: Do you remember what your mother's worry was and what caused it?

Culture Shock, or Not

J: I think it was mostly about my apartment hunting and moving. You remember how much trouble I had with my first landlady. Also the problems we had with your family's resistance to an interfaith marriage.

B: So, is it fair to say that you really didn't have a significant "culture shock?"

J: Well, at least not in the negative sense. I have learned that I actually thrive on the disorientation and stimulation of discovering a new culture. That's why I love to travel so much.

B: Looking back, what factors would you say contributed to this relatively smooth transition?

J: I think it helps if a person who wants to get married and live in another culture has at least taken a course in sociology. My studies seemed to help me expect the unexpected. It was also helpful to have *you*, so willing to bridge the parts of the culture I couldn't deal with so well (the language and the laws for example).

B: Now I want to take this opportunity to discuss another aspect of cultures. This is something that comes up often especially when the issue of human rights is discussed; and it touches on the question of "right" and "wrong." How do we judge whether a certain action or behavior in a given culture is wrong and should not be tolerated?

J: There are some recognized "universal human rights" and the abrogation of those should cause anyone to be concerned. On the other hand, "right" and "wrong" for most issues occurs within a context, and if you don't fully understand the context it is better to suspend judgement, at least for the time being.

B: I can't disagree with you! And I'd like to complete your answer with an example. Wearing *chador* or *burka* by women is okay only if it is voluntary, right?

J: I can't disagree with you either! I would assume that according to democratic principles the term *voluntary* makes all the difference.

B: OK, this chapter will be complete after adding the following cute excerpt from a letter you wrote to the *Reader's Digest* magazine for possible publication, which I don't think happened.

Feb. 7, 1978
Dear Sirs,
Kissing one another in greeting and departing is an old Middle Eastern habit. But some foreigners tend to misinterpret it. The worst case of misinterpretation was an American housewife, anxious not to offend local custom, who kissed the local garbage collector at his daily appearance. After several weeks of this, she learned she was the only one observing the garbage man's interesting new version of an ancient custom.

Chapter Two

Marriage against all Odds

Marriage was the reason that Jackie went to Iran and marriage was the reason that Bahman had to struggle to overcome the obstacles. Their original plan was for Bahman to go to Iran early March and pave the way for the marriage, which they assumed shouldn't take more than a few months! Jackie would visit Iran in early summer and hopefully like it, or at least wouldn't dislike it! Then they would go to the U.S. and get married and return to Iran before schools start. However, as we'll see, there were so much changes in the process that one can say the only thing constant was to get married—and they did. All other intentions and plans were changed completely.

Here is how things started unfolding. After Bahman had been in Iran about a couple of weeks and after a couple of other letters, on March 26, 1967, he wrote to Jackie, who was in Washington, DC.

He: 3/26/67 Since Friday noon we are having a more or less miserable time around here—since the time I broke the news. Since moving to a new apt. might not happen these days, I thought I should start telling the news. After a few days of preliminary talk (other people who have got married, how to find a girl, how to "know" her, etc.) with my mother, I told her and my sisters and showed them your pictures. The first and most critical objection is the religion. They say we'll lose all our reputation, which presumably I've earned recently, among relatives and

Zoroastrian friends—to them it is a crime or something. I realized that their "fire is too hot" so I planned to play it cool for a while. We have had little conversation, even ordinary one, in the last two days. I'm thinking of finding some effective tactics to use after a few days. As I have told you, it *is* going to be a very unconventional, radical event for my people, but it has to happen anyway. It needs patience and a lot of courage.

To which she replied with some encouraging statements such as, "I wish you all the courage and patience I can wish you, so that you can convince your people of the 'rightness' of our plans. This is certainly a good test of diplomatic skills for you! I wish I could be there to encourage you personally, but this is a battle you must fight alone. You know you have all my love there with you, if that is any help." Meanwhile, he is trying to find intermediaries to help solve the problem. One in particular is Dr. Yaganegi, a prominent member of the Zoroastrian community and a good acquaintance who is now in Europe. A few weeks later, he writes:

He: 4/22/67 Yes dear, I finally talked to Dr. Yaganegi—and his wife was there too. The result was neither too favorable nor discouraging. He believes, in short, that marriage is one's own decision to make and he never interferes with this kind of things. He said, but I should get my mother's consent. On the other hand, at some point he said that we should have got married and then come home (maybe he wasn't too serious)! At least he doesn't disapprove of it and that is good enough. Now I'm thinking of telling some other closer relatives and ask them to talk to my folks—not necessarily to take my side, but just make a ground for a sensible communication channel between us. Because such a communication hardly exists now. When we can talk sensibly, then they'll see the bright side of the picture too—at present they all see the dark side. Even though my letters sound unhappy—and it is not an exaggeration—I'm not pessimistic anyway. I am not worrying much, but thinking and making different plans to solve these "terrible problems." Yes dear, I expect you not to worry much either. Things will come out fine.

A day later, as a postscript to the letter, he says: "My folks seem 'softer' today, after a rather sensible talk, and their talk to Dr. Yaganegi's wife later." But a week after that he writes:

> He: 4/29/67 I don't have good news. My judgement that they were softer wasn't correct. For about 4 or 5 days their behavior misled me—it seemed favorable. We hardly discussed anything in this period. Finally on Thursday evening I started talking, hoping to receive favorable response. But it turned out that they were the same objectionists. Friday was a bad day. Since sometimes they used to say that I should have stayed in the U.S. if I had this plan in mind, I finally thought of giving them an alternative—me going back to the U.S. and staying there. Apparently they prefer this—but I doubt if it is not a superficial judgement. Anyway, the atmosphere has been calm since then. What I'll try to make happen is to convince them and others that I want you even if I am obliged to go to the U.S. Then, convince them, through other people, that this is not the best for them and the misconceptions they have about us staying here is not all true. Well, let all our plans still remain valid now.

Meanwhile starting around this time, Bahman's folks decide to communicate directly with the source of trouble; i.e. Jackie and even her parents. This was easily possible because they knew the address from the mail coming from the U.S. The first letter was in Farsi and dated April 19. Let's hear it from Jackie telling her parents:

> May 2, 1967 It looks like I may not be too welcome in Iran. I received a letter in Persian from Bahman's mother (he didn't know she wrote it)! I just had it translated, and it explains her belief that persons of different religions and nationalities should not marry. She asks me not to even write to Bahman any more. I can just imagine the problems Bahman is facing there trying to convince her. It will take all the diplomacy I can muster to write her a kind answer, explaining *my* beliefs.

That Farsi letter was followed in a few days by an English letter to Jackie and one to her parents, using the same address. The English writing, which was pretty good, was done, it was learned later, by a relative who had studied in England. There was nothing much new in them; except saying the same things over and over again. Jackie's letter to him of May 5 included her reply to the Farsi letter. After explaining how she had to mail it to a Persian friend in Madison, Wisconsin to be translated (he wrote her not to be discouraged), she writes:

> She: 5/5/67 I realize this must be only a small example of the opposition you are facing, and I am *so* sympathetic. I have drafted an answer for your mother and I think it would be a good idea for you to write out a Persian translation for her. Of course, you are free to change any part of it since you can better judge what effect it will have on her. It may be better to translate the spirit of my letter rather than the exact words—I leave it up to your diplomatic skill.

> "Dear Mrs. Shahzadi,
> I have asked Bahman to translate this letter for you because I do not yet know enough Persian to write directly. I received the Persian letter you sent me, and a Persian friend recently translated it for me. However, I did not get the English letter you mentioned—perhaps it is still in the mail.
> I am happy to get a letter from you which tells me honestly how you feel. I have always heard that Zoroastrians are very honest people, and I am looking forward to meeting you. I agree that you are right: in most cases two people make a better marriage if they have a common background. However, Bahman is an unusual Persian (as I am sure you already know) and we are sure that we share a great many important ideas that will give us a successful marriage which will be stronger and happier than most other marriages.
> I am planning to live in Iran because that is Bahman's wish for me. Again you are right in saying that there will be many problems for me to leave my country and live in a land which is foreign to me. I will certainly need *your* help

in order to adjust to Iran and to the ways of the Zoroastrian people. I have very much to learn from you, and I very much want to learn the correct things. I want to live happily and peacefully as a good daughter-in-law for you and a good wife for Bahman. I think you and your daughters will be my best teachers in Iranian life. I am also sure there will not be too much trouble for me to live with Zoroastrians, because people who believe in 'good thoughts, good words, good deeds' must certainly be kind and friendly people.

My parents have met Bahman and approve of our marriage plans. The wedding is planned for Aug.19, but before that I would like to meet you and your daughters and the other relatives. I have bought a ticket to come to Iran on June 8 and visit Tehran for 17 days. Bahman will have to translate our conversations since I know only a little Persian. I think that you and I will become good friends when we meet, and that we will live happily together as relatives in the future."

My goodness—now that I have written the letter down it seems very long, but I don't know how to shorten it (?) I hope you have time to translate it all.

Bahman's response a week later was, "Last night I translated your letter to her—more or less what you have written except the part about your visit and the wedding date. She later gave me a paragraph of Persian to translate it for you, but there is nothing new in it. They want us to stop correspondence!" And this seems to be an appropriate point for a dialogue.

Bahman: I wish I could remember at least generally of how I translated your letter, especially all those flattering remarks, and what happened at that meeting. Unfortunately, I don't remember an iota of it! Also, in contrast to their letters, which were harsh and threatening, your reply was understandably very polite, logical, and conciliatory. But I suppose those qualities don't count much in an emotionally charged atmosphere. That aside something intrigues me. It seems to me that the main wishes you express in your letter, came to pass, albeit they took longer with some twists and turns. Looking back, how do you evaluate it?

Jackie: Well, I was prophetic, wasn't I? Although I was off on the wedding date by five months. Looking back so many years, I don't remember even writing that letter, but I remember the emotions. It seemed at the time that changing your mother's mind was the key to our future happiness. I did the best I could, just trying.

Now, going back to the main course of events, here is what he wrote her on May 5:

He: 5/5/67 As I had guessed, the alternative of my going to the U.S. was not to their liking either—I am not in favor of it either. But I thought I could use it as a "threat" to make them like the original plan. But it doesn't work. The point is that I can't be too "brutal" to them. I have used all available techniques to make them softer, but I've failed. It is their conviction and belief that I must get married to a Zoroastrian. It seems to me like this: Suppose your father and the rest of your family were prejudiced against Negroes and you wanted to marry a Negro and *stay* with your parents. What would be their reaction? Moreover my mother is sick and I can't fight too much. She cries and swears and so on. She says they have raised me with so much problem and patience. They haven't seen a happy day so far. And she thought I would bring happiness to her when I came home. But it lasted for a few days *only*, and so on. Well, I can see these things are right. But I can't convince them that our plans should not cause unhappiness for them—or even they would enjoy a good life, after a short period of adjustment in the beginning. This is something I can't make them believe and I understand it. Don't think that I have changed my mind about you dear. I still love you and want you, and I will forever. The only thing is that we have to be more patient. Everybody whom we consult, the most favorable answer is "do it with the consent of your mother." And I can see that I can't rush her to accept it. During this past week we still had some bitter arguments. After some thinking, I realized that there is only one sensible door open, which is more or less a compromise. I told my mother that I couldn't forget you

16

and break with you (that is what they want me to do), but the only favor I can do for them is to put it off now and wait. This was last night and the suggestion seemed comforting to her.

This battle turned out to be longer than we expected. It might make us 20th century "Leila and Majnoon"! You'll ask "What will happen by waiting?" Many things can happen (we try to make it happen) in our favor. I am sure that finally "The seeker is the finder."

I can make them accept your visit to Iran—just as anyone else visits Iran (as far as they are concerned), but I am not sure if June 7 is the best time. We *might* have to change it to July 6 afterwards. I'll write you as soon as I can tell you more. I remember that the end of May is the deadline for the complete payment [of ticket refund]. You might lose *only* $50, right?

I wish I didn't have to write you these things to make you sad—one of us is enough to feel it. Please write me soon and tell me anything you want. Is there any possible solution that I have missed to use? Don't feel too sad my love. "To get honey one might get bit by a bee." I am sure I will finally get my Honey.

Looking at it now, this innocent-looking suggestion for modifying their plans seems pretty tame. However, to her at that point in time, it had sounded like a dashing blow to all her dreams and plans. Here is her response.

She: 5/9/67 I received your 5/5 letter today, and I have been crying almost constantly since I read it. I became so upset by the time I had read half of it that I couldn't hold the paper to read the second half. Perhaps it will take me all night to write this letter. My arms are rather sore from typhus and typhoid shots I received today—the doctor has scheduled me for 9 shots quickly, in order to recover from any side effects by June 7. I will continue to take the shots because I still have hopes to visit you then. I think the alternative is not to visit you at all, because I had great difficulty in reserving a connecting flight to NY from Wash., and I am sure most summer flights to Europe must be filled by now.

You are making me a great pessimist. I am sorry that your mother has won. You know that she accepts the "compromise" to wait because she expects you to eventually change your mind, just as you hope she will change her mind. If you try to plan to marry me again, she will "cry and swear" again because she knows that this method works. You are right that my parents would be equally upset if I tried to marry a Negro. My father became so upset at my plans merely to attend Howard University (swearing, yelling, etc. for a whole summer) that I decided not to mention controversial subjects to him, never to live at home for much more than a week at a time, and to live my own life by my own decisions. One of my own decisions is to marry my own choice, even if Negro.

I really did (and still do) want to marry *you* but it seems that in a situation where your mother and I are opposed, your mother can make you feel guilty and obligated enough to turn you against me. I do not think waiting is a true compromise, it is a tactic your mother hopes will work for her benefit. I do not see that there can be a true compromise in this situation—in a compromise *each* side must give a little to gain a little. I feel so sorry for you dear, I know you are in a very difficult position. I understand even more since I received the following letter, typewritten in English, from your mother yesterday: "2nd May, 1967 / Miss Jacqueline Buckman, I hope that you have changed your mind about this stupid and childish idea of getting married to Bahman. / I have written you two letters and I have also written to your parents; I tell you again that we are Zoroastrian and will not accept any outsider into our society. / You must stop correspondence with Bahman; the hope of Bahman's renting a flat is very slender; Bahman and I will live together in the present house. Whenever he wishes to get married, there are plenty of decent educated Zoroastrian girls ready for him to choose. It is for your own good to marry in your own country. / You will have to take this stupid idea of yours to the grave with you as we will use all our power, regardless of the consequences, to stop this nonsense. Should you be both stupid enough to get married together, we will make life unbearable and break your marriage in no time. / Bahman owes his education to his sisters as they have worked hard all their lives provided the facilities for his studies. We are all unwilling and wish to warn you of the terrible misfortune ahead of you if you do not change your mind. / Send us everything that Bahman has left with you as soon as possible. / Mrs. Banoo Shahzadi."

Apparently she would rather see me *dead* than married to you! Is your mother such a violent person? I am not bitter toward her though, because I am trying to understand her position. I spent last night drafting a polite, kind answer which I will write when I have more room in another letter.

I think your mother would find it easy to make life "unbearable" after we are married (though I hope she cannot destroy our marriage). You know that I am already somewhat afraid to move in a house with *any* mother-in-law . . . . and now one who *hates* me!

Dear, dear, sweetie, I am not willing to be a 21st Century "Leila and Majnoon." How long do you want to *wait*? You want me to give up my home, family, country, and job, which I agreed to willingly, because I loved you with all my heart. Now you want to postpone my greatest happiness indefinitely. I already suffer so much from missing you for two long lonely months. I want so much to be married and have children while we are still young enough to enjoy them.

My alternative idea, which I touched on in the last letter, is to be married as planned, but to stay temporarily in DC. We can send your mother enough money to live comfortably and she will soon realize that you are a man who makes strong decisions that are not changed by threats. Perhaps she will *soon* ask us to return to Iran and we should have been able by then to save enough money to provide her with some luxuries. Perhaps this way your mother will not try to *direct* my life too. One thing I cannot sacrifice is my right to be a free, thinking, deciding, acting, human being. *You* are the only boss I will tolerate (even that is modified).

B: My suggestion of postponing your trip to Iran seems to have caused a lot of disappointment, uncertainty, and pessimism to you. Why do you think it was so? Actually, I had mentioned your trip to be after July 6, which should have implied to you that the wait wasn't meant to be very long. But you seem to have taken it as the beginning of the end! And this becomes even more obvious in a letter you wrote two days later, in which you say; "Your last letter made me feel as though we may never actually be married and now I'm beginning to think I may never even see you again."

J: My pessimism certainly was evident, wasn't it! I guess I supposed if there was going to be a "beginning of the end" this is how it would start: postpone our plans, then postpone again. I began to think this is how someone would let me down gently, although I hoped with all my heart it wasn't so.

B: In other words, if we had a better faster means of communication, we could have saved a lot of your headaches.

J: That seems to be so. For instance, if we had easy phone contact as it is today, we would have cleared the misunderstanding quickly. But overseas phone calls weren't common and easy those days and moreover, there was no phone in your house.

B: Another thing is that you are implying in your letter, ever so slightly and politely, that I am a bit of a "mama's boy." But, of course, I know that you knew that in reality that was not the case at all. You already knew that in my whole life how much my mother and I had disagreements, arguments, and fights because both of us had strong wills and were strongly opinionated. As a matter of fact, when the other day our daughter asked me how I could have been so sure that I would win over my mother and marry you, my quick ready response was because I had done such things many times before!

J: I knew that. But your letters mentioned several times that the key was to marry *with* your mother's consent, according to those who advised you. I was in a bit of culture shock. It was hard for me to understand the influence of a Persian mother in her adult son's life. Now, I have a question. I think this *Leila and Majnoon* story deserves an explanation. All I know is that it is something like the *Romeo and Juliet* story. What else do you know about it?

B: Until now I didn't know more than that either, and it is fair to conclude that I didn't know any more at that time either. However, now that I consulted a site on the Internet, I learned that this Persian version of the story is also tragic, and Majnoon goes mad eventually. No wonder you didn't like the idea. Good that the fate of "Goldoon and Professor" didn't follow that route!

J: Right!

A week after his "shocking" letter of May 5th to Jackie and before getting her answer, Bahman writes another letter with more specific suggestions.

He: 5/12/67 The other day I talked to someone whom they had talked to first. He is a prominent old man (used to live in Yazd) who has married a Zoroastrian girl from *India*. We talked for a while. He basically had two points. First, about the problems involved in such a marriage—nothing new but a re-emphasis for me. Even he and she, both Zoroastrians, have been having problems—she and the children being sometimes here and sometimes in India, etc. Second, my family is so upset, and I should take that into consideration.
That night something came to my mind. As I had mentioned in my last letter, we have to wait for a while. Now, to make it sure and to convince *ourselves and others* that you can live here, we should arrange a longer stay for you in Iran. This will also acquaint them to you gradually. So, what I suggest is this: Find a job for you here— preferably through your Government in the US. Then, you come here and stay for several months, and when the time is appropriate we'll get married in the US. What do *you* think of this? In any case your visit in June doesn't seem

realistic now. They are not ready to accept you yet, even if you stay away from them.

Her answer to this letter is again full of unhappy remarks and complaints.

She: 5/20/67 I don't know if you realize exactly how unhappy you are making me. My whole beautiful world and all my lovely summer plans have collapsed. Life has always been so happy and good for me (especially since you became part of my life) that it is very hard for me to believe that such tragedy is happening. It would have been worth $1000 for me, just to see you again, but *if you* do not even want me to come, there is no use for me to make you angry by coming. I will try to cancel my ticket next week. The reason I paid for it already is that I thought my trip was a definite thing—that maybe I could affect your mother positively by meeting her.

I am very disappointed of course, and I feel very helpless and hopeless since you have vetoed both my trip and our wedding. I still believe that if you want me enough, you will do something to make it possible for us to be together and to be happy. But I am trying to prepare myself for your next letter in case it says that your relatives and Iranian friends have convinced you that our marriage is not realistic. That is the worst thing that can happen, but other terrible things I thought could not happen did.

It does seem that my only chance to see you is to work in Iran. I have applications for an Embassy *staff* position (if there is any open now or in the future?) and I will register for the Foreign Service Exam to be given in Dec. (oh, dear, that's *so* far away from now).

I still love you very much, but I'm not very patient. I want to be with you. It would be tempting to say "Forget it, a future, possibly-unhappy marriage is not worth such present unhappiness," but I still have enough faith to believe that marriage to you would be good for both of us.

In the meantime Bahman just received her stormy letter of 5/9 and is answering it.

He: 5/20/67 Your letter today made me so depressed and unhappy. Your comments on becoming a pessimist, feeling our marriage seem like a dream, made me so. I hope that these are because of the depressing mood you have been in dear, and you didn't really mean it. I don't believe that you become a pessimist and give up so soon dear. Of course I acknowledge the difficult and disappointing situation that you are facing. But please be patient and let's work out reasonable solutions.

The first thing I should say is that my mother is sick, and I cannot fight as severely as necessary. During the last whole week we didn't talk, but she was in a depressing mood and getting worse. She is a patient of nervous system and depression is her enemy. Finally yesterday we had to bring a doctor to her bed. He says her remedy is first in peace of mind and *then* in medicine. She is a bit better today. But she might become mentally ill easily—she had been in coma and in the verge of losing her mind for several days a year ago. That is why I have to be soft on and off, but this does not mean she has won.

After reading your letter several times, I got the feeling that "waiting" meant to you a "long waiting"—that is not so. To make it short, I think the plan about your coming and working here should specify it pretty well! I expect that with this plan you can be here before the end of summer and stay unmarried for several months. When I get better established—in job, house and in "ruling"—then there shouldn't be much difficulty in doing what we want. I am waiting to get your opinion on this.

There, finally they seem to have a practical workable plan. A plan that in retrospect turned out to be dandy! Now, in the midst of all these letters crossing in the mail, in a letter dated May 14, Jackie brings up a sociological argument, which deserves some attention and analysis. First, here is the related paragraph.

She: 5/14/67 After I wrote to you last week, it occurred to me that we are dealing with a classic problem in my own field of sociology: how to overcome prejudice. I don't think you will ever be able to convince your mother by talking because emotionally held beliefs are not usually changed through logic or reasoning, because the beliefs involved in issues like religion or prejudice are not originally arrived at through "reasonable" methods. Sociologists have shown that it is almost impossible to change someone's attitude first in order to have them change their behavior. The effective method is to change the *behavior* first and then the attitude change happens as a result. This is the theory behind the policy to *force* the South to accept integration by law in order that racial prejudice will be decreased. I don't know why I am such a theoretical sociologist that I cannot see a practical application of a social theory in order to help myself! My conclusion: marriages that are accomplished will be accepted more easily than marriages that are planned. Do you see logic to it?

At least I want to have the chance to come to Iran on June 8 (arrival time) and meet your mother. Even if your mother refuses to see me, I can still see the city of Tehran and most important, I can see *you* again. Your last letter made me feel as though we may never actually be married and now I'm beginning to think I may never even see you again. I intend to keep planning to come then, and unless you have a *very* serious objection to my trip I will arrive as planned. If you only have a slight doubt that this is a poor time to come, *don't* tell me not to come, I'll come anyway I think. It will be very difficult to rearrange my vacation at this late date. Please answer this letter quickly with your recommendation.

B: I am all geared up now to challenge your sociological theory! First, in my humble opinion, I don't think my mother's reaction to you should be called prejudice. Her feeling and objective was that her son must marry a Zoroastrian because that is the way it is done.

J: Maybe I should use "bias" or some other term to indicate the view of one who only sees one side of a situation and assumes the opposite side cannot even exist. Certainly your mother could not even think of me, either as a person or simply as a non-Zoroastrian, living peacefully in Iran with your family. This one-sided view, based on emotion and not experience, is what I call "prejudiced."

B: OK, you can characterize my mother with any term you wish, but one has to be careful when comparisons are made. For instance, I don't think our case is comparable with racial prejudice you talked about in your letter. My mother had nothing against you personally, only she didn't want you as her daughter-in-law. Everyone has a right to dislike something or someone, no?

J: In a manner of speaking, everyone has that right unless it impinges on someone else's rights. There's a classic test of the degree or level of prejudice that goes something like this: Would you mind having this person (of a specific ethnicity, nationality, or race) live in your neighborhood? How about living next door to you? Working for you? In your social club? Married to your son or daughter? If your mother had met me and rejected me on some personal characteristic, that would seem reasonable. But to reject me based solely on a societal label, such as non-Zoroastrian, still seems to fit my definition of "prejudiced."

B: You seem to have come close to the conclusion that I've had in mind; i.e., prejudice is not black and white (no pun intended) but, like most everything else, covers a wide range. At one end is a "benign" or relatively harmless prejudice, like my mother's, and at the other extreme is the kind of harmful prejudice harbored by the likes of the Ku Klux Klan. Do you agree?

J: Well, yes, except your mother's "harmless" prejudice was about to affect me in a very significant way!

B: I'd rather call that an unintended consequence of her behavior. In any case, let's now look at another side of the issue: The remedy. This may be helpful in distinguishing the two examples. Your solution of changing the behavior first does not seem to me to apply to our case. Tell me, whose behavior should be changed and how?

J: Well, here the theory could take the form of getting married first and presenting the inevitable afterwards.

B: I don't think "presenting the inevitable" is similar to passing anti-discrimination laws and enforcing them on southern whites. But let's not belabor this point anymore. Instead, I want to add in passing that I am not sure the theory of "getting married first" would have worked in *our case.* A worst case scenario I can imagine is that my mother, who was in poor health, could've been fatally shocked!

* * * *
* * *

After a long aside, let's go back to the succession of events. We left the two lovebirds a bit less unhappy and with a new plan of action. In their consequent letters they will have to work on the big changes in their plan. Here is Bahman's letter, which is still trying to placate her.

He: 5/23/67 Yes dear, your sociological theory seems to be valid. Apparently, if we had done it first and then informed them—which I am not sure *yet* I would do if it were now—we would have had less problems. But that time has passed now, or has it? To me the next best is what I've suggested. You come here and stay for a while. Your short visit in June or July would not accomplish anything in many respects—you getting to know Iran and they getting to know you. Our apt. hunting might not start before June or July—I don't know when! My mother is a little better. She talks and goes to bathroom now. All these make me believe that you should postpone your visit, and make it a long one. On the other hand, you shouldn't get too worried for all these uncertainties. "Life has cycles; peaks and valleys." Things will get fine.

In the meantime, she has found a new source of amusement and consolation. Mohammad, a good friend of Bahman's and an intermediary for him while in Tehran, has just arrived in Washington, DC and is planning to attend a graduate school in the U.S.

She: 5/23/67 Mohammad phoned me last evening, as you told me he would. I drove into DC to see him. He had a room at the YMCA . . . I drove him out to my apt. He seemed to like my "beautiful" car and my pretty apartment. I "introduced" him to my cat and explained how sometimes Americans treat cats almost like children.

Well, I wonder what his impression of American girls is after meeting me (if he ever tells *you*, let me know). I hope I didn't shock him any. He did shock me in a way: I asked about his wife, and he said she would be coming here after *4 or 5 months.* Then later he showed me his wedding picture and said they had been married only about a month! The Persian attitude toward marriage continually surprises me. My goodness, dear, once *we* are married I don't think I will let you out of my sight (well, *maybe* I will let you go teach classes by yourself!). After we have been married a month, I will still be following you so closely you will think you have two shadows! I am going to make up for all the time I am missing you now.

We talked about you and your mother a lot. He thought, also, that it might have been best to have gotten married first. He said (and I think he mentioned it to you) that teaching English privately in my own classes would be a good job for me. Talking to him made me feel better and somewhat more optimistic again. I'm glad he came.

B: I am surprised that you were surprised about the Persian attitude toward marriage. I am sure that you would find similar attitudes even in this country if you go back a few decades in time.

J: Yes, it was probably true that Americans endured separations as newlyweds in earlier days, but I wasn't thinking of that practice being current in any country.

OK, going back to the letters now, we see that after all the emotional roller coaster of the month of May, it was time to "kiss and make up!"

He: 5/28/67 The first thing I'd like to say is to appreciate your understanding and cooperation. I realize that I am causing you temporary unhappiness and all that, but my state is not better than yours—I am not less unhappy and lonely. I want you to be here with me right now as much as you do. The only difference is that the difficulty originates here in my side and I am "in" it, but you are only a recipient through the medium of my "writing" which is far from conveying all details and events. That is why you might feel that I am not doing my best or I may change my mind or so on. On the contrary, I am always trying to find sensible and effective ways to get closer to our marriage. Anyhow, I sympathize with you and I am so glad that you are a sensible and reasonable sweetie. Be sure that whatever plans I suggest are what I feel to be the best for both of us and our future—so trust me dear (and you do). I'll do my best "to make it possible for us to be together and to be *happy*." Without going out with other girls, I already "realize how really wonderful you are."

My mother is better now, close to being as she was when I came. We have not talked about "us" in the past 2 weeks, and we might not do that for a while. I am trying to analyze and understand their feelings and reasons of opposition (in their hearts). For one thing, she thinks that I am a kid—"I don't have a grain of wisdom." It is not only for this matter that she says so, but in general she thinks I am not mature enough. She has to be shown, by experience, that she is all wet! And I am mature enough to run my life. Secondly, they believe, I think, that in case of our marriage, they might be forgotten, and you'll get *all* my attention. My disobedience of marrying you is enough a reason for them to think so. I have to convince them that this is not so. Also, I am not still well established in salary, in house, and in household. Now, I expect all these to be solved in a rather short time. And then other things like religion and other people's attitude can't be real obstacles. Do I make sense *aziz*?

5/29—I got your May 23 letter today. I am glad that you feel better. Say hello to Mohammad. I would have guessed that you'd be surprised by Persian attitude in marriage (and other things for that matter). On the other hand, I am sure you spoke *for* me too when you wrote ". . . I don't think I'll let you out of my sight . . ."!

She: 5/28/67 Dear "Professor," (for that is what Mohammad says you have been nicknamed for a long time.)

I am *so* sorry, dear, --sorry your mother is so sick and sorry I have written you such unhappy letters. It is not fair for me to add to the worries you already have, and I *know* you are trying hard to arrange a good life for us. I think those letters were written out of pure emotion. Having you postpone our wedding and cancel my trip was the most disappointing things that have ever happened to me, and I wrote you how I felt. I think I began to be afraid I was losing you, and I cannot think how I would live in the future without you. I am glad you mentioned the end of the summer as a possible time for me to come—it is now something I can plan for and look forward to. Can you find some alternative in case I cannot find a job?

Well, as you know I have been seeing a married man lately!—Mohammad, of course. Actually he did not phone me all last week so I thought he might have found some friends or been busy or something. Finally I called him on Sat. night and he said he didn't phone me because he thought he would be bothering me! Well I explained that I am rarely busy. Today I drove into DC to see the rooming house he is at and we went walking in the National Arboretum for a while. We talked lots. We also drove around the Iranian Embassy and actually went inside the beautiful Islamic Mosque. I am certain that he approves of me and thinks that I will be good for you. He said it will be nice when he, his wife and you and I can get together. He sends his regards to you, Professor!

On the third of June he wrote a letter to her, which was long as usual but includes nothing of much interest for us here! On the other hand, she was still seeing the "married man" and the following letter has some interesting news!

She: 6/8/67 Afternoon of May 30 was the last time I saw Mohammad (has he written to you?). This time he served me an apple "American style" (last time it was peeled and cut—then I explained how *we* eat it!). We went sightseeing—up to the top of the Washington Monument and to the History and Technology Building of the Smithsonian Institution.

Somehow he was surprised that a girl like me could walk as long as we walked that afternoon (!), he didn't seem to think that most Persian girls would do it. He could not see how I could live "alone," even with a roommate and a cat. This leads me to wonder how I will be able to work and live alone in Tehran, where it is *not* a usual custom for females—??

She goes on to say that she and a few friends went for four days to Montreal to see Expo '67. Then, "We spent yesterday driving back to Conn. and now I am just relaxing around home before I return to Va. on Sunday. Unfortunately my father still has the idea that you should come back to the U.S. to live."

At the same time, he sends a postcard to her saying, "Trapping (?) seems to have been contagious. Last night Reza told me that he is on the way to it! The situation is similar to that of Mohammad." And about the postcard: "This is just a view of a street in Tehran in winter, and a note to you." So, now Reza, another college classmate is going to get married, ha! Anyway, when she receives the postcard, she is ready to answer it in a long letter.

She: 6/13/67 I received that nice snowy postcard (6/8) today, and this morning I had sent one to you! So Reza is getting married, too! his *first* wife? another teenage girl? When Mohammad was telling me that he thought he was getting old and it was about time to get married so he got married, I thought he was kidding but I guess it was mostly truth! Your description of his marriage was fantastic and sociologically intriguing. Perhaps I will write a book on Persian marriage and family customs—there are so many books on other countries. Perhaps under such a tradition, it is a *good* idea to have four wives—after so many tries a man ought to learn what qualities he is looking for in a good wife, and at least one out of four ought to be a success. Is the Persian philosophy that *any* two people ought to be able to make a happy marriage? or is there less emphasis on being happy as long as they have a large family? or what is it that makes this "marriage of strangers" so hard for me to understand from an American viewpoint?

Unfortunately, my being home for a few days meant my father had a chance to warn me again and again how much I will dislike Iran, and how you should come to the U.S. if you want to marry me. He is still without a job, and sitting around all day with nothing to do for months seems to have made him an extremely bitter, discontented, and argumentative person. My mother has amazing patience with him. . . .

By the way what happened to my future career as a sociologist, particularly a research sociologist? I'm not doing it now, and if I teach in Iran I won't be doing it there either. Must I *not* be a sociologist and just be something that earns money now? I have been wondering about this lately.

In the Iranian pavilion at Expo. I saw a modern fancy-designed Isfahanian refrigerator with a lock on the door. Tell me, how can I live in a country where you have to have locks on refrigerators!?!

He: 6/19/67 Oh dear, I got *four* pieces of mail from you last week—very nice. I'll try to answer and make comments.

The letter I received from Mohammad was for three other friends to read too! So, there were only a couple of lines about you. He said you met each other and then he "praised" me for my "good taste" (i.e. in selecting you). This is not anything new to hear, but I'm proud of you dear. I checked with the Iran America Society. They said, in the summer you can get a teaching job almost for sure. For the rest of the year, they can't promise, but it is very likely to get a job. Also you don't need no (!) knowledge of Persian language. I'll try to get in touch with some other American agencies for other possibilities.

I am glad you enjoyed your trip to Expo—in the company of your friends and family. But I hope you didn't "kill" your feet too badly.

You wonder how you could live alone here? No dear, don't worry. You won't be alone—*I* am here, you know.

I don't exactly know what the real meaning of "mother-bound" is. But as much as I understand, I don't think I am mother-bound—unless it means fighting & arguing with each other! Yes, you worry too much.

Your comments about men getting several wives were oriented only in men's favor—strange. How are girls supposed to "learn what qualities they should look for..."? Writing a book about customs? Well, that is swell, but you are to see and learn much more. So far it is just "a drop out of sea!" (But I don't mean to frighten you, there are good customs too, you know.)

"Marriage of strangers" is not totally understandable to me either. But at least I guess that under this tradition the couple doesn't share many important things: each has his own "world."

Locks on refrigerators? Well, I was surprised to realize that they have locks on the cover of the gas tank of cars here—otherwise the lid would get stolen!

"There are many things in common life which are equivalent to each other, and when they have been mentally listed as similar situations, experience which has been secured in handling one case can be quickly applied to treating the equivalent problems. It is the ability to recognize new setups, to which old procedures can be applied, which enables some individuals to accomplish so much more in life than others." Quoted from "Communication Engineering"—a technical book teaching philosophy! This might not seem very significant, but it got my attention because occasionally I have thought of and tried similar philosophy.

B: It seems that in this "philosophical" statement the emphasis is on the ability to recognize what can be applied where. This reminds me of the well known "prayer" that says: "Give me the serenity to accept what cannot be changed, the courage to change

what can be changed and the wisdom to know the difference."
I've always liked this "philosophy" and quoted it often in my
conversations and writings, even in Farsi and in my letters to Iran.
But I have always emphasized that the last part, i.e., having
wisdom, is the most important part. That is where most of us fail
the test. What do *you* think?

J: That is commonly known as the prayer of St. Francis of
Assisi, and it is an interesting philosophy. There is a bit of
passivity implied in the desire to accept what "cannot be
changed." Of course figuring out which things *cannot* be changed
is devilishly difficult, so that's where the wisdom comes in. Not
only do most of us *not* have that wisdom, but we'll never ever
really know what "can't be changed" until we have actually tried
it!

B: About that refrigerator lock! Maybe it was a primitive
version of the high-tech devices and alarms now available for
those who are on diet!

J: Very funny. What you didn't tell me was that maids and
servants are common in Persian households, and quite likely the
family was a bit suspicious of their honesty.

His next letter to her would unfortunately become the source of
another misunderstanding and much misery. But before getting to
that, it is necessary to tie up a few loose ends. Here are a
composite of some questions, answers, and comments.

She: 6/27/67 Do you understand what I meant by living
"alone"? If I move there sometime soon and stay unmarried
for a while, certainly I will be spending much of my time
without you. No? Where can I live (safely)? Can you find
me a place?
You noticed that my comments on multiple-marriage were
male-oriented because my American upbringing conditions
me to see no benefits for the woman in such a marriage. Yet
there must be some benefits. A recent magazine had an
article on Fundamental Mormons in the U.S. and it says
their religion believes a man needs more than one wife.

There are more than 30,000 Mormons practicing bigamy in the US, this article claims. Of course, their multiple marriages are kept secret, since they are illegal here.
Your letters have been more encouraging (especially about job possibilities for me) lately, and I am much less depressed. In fact, enough optimism has returned that I have gone back to my study of Farsi again, after a long break.

He: 6/29/67, 7/15/67 About you staying here "alone", well I'll see you as often as possible. We'll find you a good place to stay. I enclose a sample of apt. ads. I saw an ad somewhere about room and board—this might be a good idea. Don't worry about these things. The important thing is your arrival.
It so happened that Reza didn't get engaged. In other words, their attempt was a failure. Why? Well, it was about getting [to get] materialized (using new words!). They had a couple of dates and he had some talks to her family. But meanwhile he learned that her family and relatives have occasional parties—playing-card type, i.e. gambling! Apparently, it is not too strange. Many families seem to hold this kind of parties. It is one way of entertainment and killing time (and themselves!). Anyway, since he is not this type, gave her up. Even though he could ask her not to join them after marriage, but this could mean a partial separation from her relatives. Now they are looking for some other girls. Meanwhile he is getting ready for a business trip to Europe in about 20 days.
Finally, today we agreed upon renting an apt. It is located on the second floor of the house in which Reza is living on the 3rd floor! It has 4 fairly big rooms, kitchen, phone, etc., and we can sign the contract and move in toward the end of next week—hopefully. On the first floor, a German lady is living with several dogs! Reza said that the dogs have a schedule for barking—every morning at 9:00 they all bark and after a few minutes the "symphony" ceases!

She: 7/9/67 I hope your family and you enjoy your new apartment. Perhaps I can be more enthusiastic about it if and when I ever see it. Can you draw me a diagram of the apt. indicating approximate size and shape of the rooms? Whatever happened to the plan for a 2-section house that you wrote me about? I am hoping that your letter to me this week will explain why you decided it was necessary to move *now*, especially since our plans for me changed and it is no longer necessary that you have a place for me after Aug. 19. It could have been possible for me to help you choose a new apartment under our new plans (?) or have plans changed again? Let me know what plan you are using now, OK?

I guess you will enjoy living near Reza and family. How many of them are there? Your description of Reza's almost-engagement was beautiful! If he is an educated company executive, then he is probably what Americans call "a good catch," marriagewise, and there must be plenty of girls willing to marry such a fellow. Isn't it strange that two of your friends suddenly decided it's time to get married? Are they feeling old?

OK, now let's confront another storm in the making. It all started because of a "typo" in his letter of June 24 to her.

He: 6/24/67 It is good that you rewrote the part of the last letter about children and religion. Apparently we still have to learn about each other's beliefs & ideas. I thought I more or less knew your views on religion, but I am not very certain now (maybe you feel the same too). I say I don't want to be fussy about religion mostly because I want you. Although I am not fanatic in my religion and prejudiced about others, I do believe and accept lots of the principles of Zoro. But most of our problems arise because of the environment we are going to live in. I don't think I can agree to call our children Zoro. *[the culprit]* from birth if we are to live in Iran. If we were to live in the US, then it would be much different. Actually, to be realistic, I quote your own sentence: "It is probably true that since our children will be under continuous Zoro. influence . . . , they'll choose to become Zoro. . . ." Now please, don't feel that I want to use this "weapon" against you. This is more or less a

35

natural phenomenon. We should look at religion in a much broader sense. Religion is a means to a good and happy life, not for causing trouble and worry.

She: 7/3/67 Your 6/19 letter gave me hope and optimism, but this recent letter took it all away, and I cried while reading it. It seems that you are not too happy with me and that makes me sadder than anything. I think perhaps you copied a sentence wrong. You wrote: "I don't think I can agree to call our children Zoro. from birth if we are to live in Iran," but from the context I think you mean "I don't think I can agree *not* to call . . . etc." [*wrong!*] This is the most important sentence in your letter. Have we reached a point where neither of us is willing to compromise? and will this make marriage impossible? Think seriously dear, are we fooling ourselves by thinking this "international" marriage can succeed? I am having *serious* doubts now. I told you once before that a marriage cannot succeed where one partner makes all the sacrifices. I will have to give up the sociology career for which I am trained so you can follow *your* career. I must live in *your* country, stay in the same house with *your* family who dislikes me, live with *your* customs and culture and language, give up my hobbies and sports and friends, and learn to accept *your* country's government. I am even willing to raise our children in *your* religion *if* they choose it themselves and it is not forced up on them. It seems that your life will be nearly "normal" and my life will be as changed as possible. I have always believed that you love me and want me near, but do you love me enough to make some sacrifices for a happy marriage? If you want everything in your life "normal" then you will have to marry a Persian girl who will follow your orders because then I am not good enough for you. I love you enough to sacrifice many things for you. I have never stopped loving you—but I cannot become completely Persian. When you "postponed" our wedding I was really shocked because I have heard that "postponing" a wedding is not a single action but a *process*. I have nothing definite to anticipate now, and even now it does not seem likely that we ever will be married. I began to love you two years ago for your quality of tolerance and open-mindedness, but it seems now that you are not "tolerant" in your ideas of raising children. This will cause constant arguments I guess. I should decide whether I will be unhappier *with* you than I am now without you. Is there no chance for happiness?

I wonder how you have changed in the last 4 months you have been away in Iran. I wish you had let me visit you in June. Do you miss me or is your life pretty well adjusted without me around? Am I still *needed*?? Our communication by letter is so inadequate; I want to see you.

I got a letter today from my former roommate Carole, too. She thinks it is not a good idea for me to move to Iran and take a job because then your mother will think I am a very "forward" American girl, "chasing" her son all the way to Iran because I can't find a man in my own country! Even my good friend Carole doesn't sympathize with my plans— it's disappointing.

So, she is understandably plenty upset again; and all because of the nefarious mistake he made in writing a single word wrong (Wasn't Freudian something or other, was it?!). Don't you wish they had discovered the telephone right away and cleared the air? Well, it didn't happen; instead the air only cleared after a long 16 days, which probably seemed to her like an eternity.

He: 7/12/67 I was going to write a long letter, mostly about the events around here—new apt. But when I got your 7/3 letter today, I am now answering *this* first, and at the end or another letter I'll write my own reports!

Your letter today was going to make me real sad and even angry if I was to take it all a serious letter. But realizing that it was written under "intense emotion" and that some misunderstanding has occurred, I'll try to be reasonable and calm, and clarify things. I definitely agree that "our communication by letter is so inadequate" unfortunately. And this is the source of most of your problems and worries.

I can assure you that I have *not* "changed in the last 4 months" I've been in Iran. As a matter of fact, I very often remember the comment my friend Dr. Rostam in Chicago made—that I'll change later—but thank heavens that it didn't apply in my case.

Apparently, the basic problem which made you sad and pessimist to write this letter, was the subject of children and religion. My "most important" sentence had an error unfortunately, and you interpreted it wrongly. It should read like this: "I don't think I can agree to call our children *Christian* (this solution was mentioned in your previous letter) from birth if we are to live in Iran." And this is quite different with your interpretation: "I don't think I can agree *not* to call our children *Zoro. . . .*" Our original agreement was to leave the choice to the children. But two problems arose. First, in order to avoid one more point of opposition by my family, I suggested only to *call* the children Zoro. Secondly, you brought up the psychological problem involved in leaving the choice to them. Now, in short, if you prefer, we would follow our original agreement and cope with the two problems—hopefully successfully. In any case, I'd like to emphasize again that the subject of calling children Zoro. is not new, but I brought it up in DC (I am defending my opinion of not changing since leaving you!).

I very much sympathize with you, because almost no one sympathizes you with our plans, because you alone are making a big decision which might seem risky, because we can't talk and discuss things freely to clarify things and avoid misunderstanding, and finally because you are to sacrifice a lot of things. I certainly see how much you are sacrificing and appreciate it. But, I'd like to remind you that I can't expect "everything in my life to be normal" either. My biggest problem is to "pacify" my family and then to stand & "nullify" the reaction of my society. But I am definite that you are worthy of all these problems.

If you don't mind, let me call your questions of the sort; "Do you miss me? or "Am I still needed?" very silly! Whatever I think and do, the plans I make and wherever I go, all include *you*. I guess the beginning of Sept. is a good time for you to come here; no matter if you apply for a job there or not. I'll write more about this later.

By the way, Carole's comment about your visit to Iran is not out of place, i.e. I've certainly thought of that too. But remember that it is not only your decision to come here. *I* suggested it to you. I'll make my family to believe this *fact*: *You* didn't chase me, *I* asked you to do it!

Hopefully that letter is going to make her happy again. Now, since he wrote another letter three days later and she would get both of them at the same time, let's see this one too before her answer.

He: 7/15/67 I got a letter from Mohammad including a letter for my mother. He asked me to say hello to you—he'll write a letter when he knows enough English to write a good letter! In his letter to my mother, he expresses his understanding of our situation: "They love & want each other; but they also want your consent; it is not a good idea to oppose them—causing him to remain a bachelor perhaps forever."!

Now about the apt. 1) As you know it wasn't easy to live in that house. The living condition was very low and it was a temporary place for me to stay since I arrived. 2) In my calculations (!) postponing your visit from June to Sept. did not mean postponing our moving until after you arrived. In other words I want to receive you in a nice place. 3) Most important of all; in my opinion moving out was the first step toward the rest of our plans—to get the consent of my folks. I have to show them some power, decisiveness, organization, manhood (!), etc. I have to get control over things & be the boss—and this was a big try & a *success*.

No dear don't worry, *I* have organized the apt. as *I* wanted & you'll have your share when here. In the past week I've been organizing & purchasing some *essential* things like refrigerator, bookcase, chairs, and so on. And of course I am always having you in mind; there will be so many things and occasions for you to have your choice. The idea of getting a 2-section house was brought up before our plan changed, i.e. I could do that if they knew you would become a part of the family. But under the present condition there was no excuse to look for such a place. On

39

the other hand the lease is only for one year, being able to cancel it after 6 months by paying one month of extra rent.

A "by-product" of living in this house is the existence of Reza & his mother's temporary stay here. This might turn out to be of great value to our plans. He is living alone here; with a man & his wife living in another room and taking care of Reza. His mother sometimes visits here from another town & helps to find a girl for him. So it is not a "sudden decision" to get married. Now, apparently they are tired of so much trying here and they wish they had an opportunity to pick up a European girl! His mother is even more enthusiastic about this! He'll leave here in a couple of weeks & will stay in Europe (mostly in Germany where his brother lives) for about 2 months. Half-seriously they talk of him going there & perhaps finding a girl—maybe with his brother's help!! So you see that his parents are so liberal— although not very "modern." Now, without any reference to myself, I had told my folks about Reza and his situation. A few days ago his mother came down to visit us and get acquainted to my family. Very soon the conversation got around marriage & Reza. After a while I left & they still talked. To use a diplomatic tool, I had told Reza's mother not to mention you & me & our plans (she knows about it), but just try to enlighten them indirectly by talking about Reza. Even though this doesn't cause an immediate change, in the long run it should be effective.

All schools here start on Sept. 23 and I can be at your service more and better before that time. By the way, you may and should stay here for at least a couple of weeks before getting busy with a job, to get acquainted with the surrounding. So you should plan to be here about Sept. 1, OK? Are my (our) plans clear now? Of course I am not using any plan without you knowing it, dear.

So everything seems to be in place for her to become her hopeful and jovial self! And it certainly becomes obvious when we read the following letters.

She: 7/21/67 Thank you for the two long, wonderful, comforting letters which arrived one day after the other.

You want me to come on Sept. 1st! I am happier than I have been for the past 2½ months, and I am beginning to "believe" again: to believe that things will turn out good for us. I realized that I have only 6 weeks before Sept. 1, and there is a great deal for me to do before I finish life here in the U.S. and try to start it in Iran.

Are you very sure the beginning of Sept. is all right? I do not want to be so close to coming and then be disappointed again. Especially when, this time, there will be so many "doors" I will be "closing" that cannot be opened again: leaving my apt. by Aug. 31, selling my car, and quitting my job. I need to know some more answers right away—please write quickly! How long do you estimate it will be from the time of my arrival until we can leave together to come to the U.S. for the wedding? If it is less than three months I will need only a regular visa; if it is more than three months I will need a residence permit and an exit permit when leaving. Which kind should I get? Also, shall I buy a round-trip ticket from here or a round trip ticket when we leave (perhaps that is better) Iran together? . . . My powerful, decisive, organized (*and* reasonable *and* calm) man—I need your guidance in directing my life now. . . How excited I am!!!

He: 7/28/67 I hope you had a good experience in surfing. Very often I regret why we are not together to do things and go places. I often feel lonely and *miss you very much.*
It is about 8 p.m. now, and, with Dural [Company] people, we are going to see a movie. I am impatiently waiting for Sept. 1st and you to arrive, so that I don't need boys as "dates!" I love you very much aziz [dear].

Finally! A good ending for now. By the way, in her very long letter she lists a host of other questions of what things to bring to Iran, how much money, what kind of clothing, etc. etc.. She also explains how she is going about resigning from her job, looking into finding a job for Iran, and commenting on a sketch of the apt. he sent her! Most of all, she comments on the fact that her father's health may become a serious problem.

* * * *
* * *

In the next four to five weeks, their primary concern and effort is preparation for her trip to Iran. Here is a composite of questions, answers, and comments.

She: 7/30/67, 8/2/67, 8/8/67 One thing I think I will buy especially to bring is the library book I am now reading: *Sociology of Development, Iran as an Asian Case Study* by Norman Jacobs. This book is fascinating and frightening! You *must* read it also, even if I must explain it to you paragraph by paragraph: In a sociological analysis, it explains not only *what* is wrong in Iran that causes serious problems, but also *why* these things are the way they are. The author is highly critical and his tone can almost be called sarcastic, but he is really *explaining* and not just *complaining*.

I also found out something surprising—for the price of the airline ticket to Iran, I am allowed to make as many stops along the way as I want! Here is a great chance to see Europe for only the added cost of hotels! In fact I am surprised that *you* never stopped to tour on your way back or forth (?!).

I don't know of anyone who really thinks it's a good idea that I will be leaving the United States, sometimes not even me! . . . But I am definitely planning to come to Iran in early Sept. You know that *you* are the most important reason, and, also, I have a great curiosity to see your country. I guess curiosity is stronger than being afraid, and love is stronger than my need for security.

On the basis of your letters, I have taken steps to quit my job. I started yesterday by going to talk to a man in the personnel dept. I was very nervous and uncomfortable, I didn't know how he would react. He teased me a bit saying that if I was marrying a Persian prince, I wouldn't have to work in the future, and was I sure I wasn't becoming part of a harem? I wanted to practice telling *somebody* because I was too nervous to tell my boss. But today I pulled together enough courage to tell my boss. Again, I was extremely nervous, but he was so sympathetic I almost cried from relief! He said people are not machines and they must follow what they think is in their best interests. He said I was starting a great adventure.

I don't know how any woman can live with only 44 pounds of luggage, especially if it is heavy fall and winter clothes. . .

He: 8/6/67, 8/10/67 For the past couple of months you have almost been out of our discussions. I am planning to keep your visit a secret, until after your arrival. This time I am using the method "Do it, say it"! Want a tutor? Well, in the beginning I won't let you have time for an *extra* tutor. Then, if you need it later, we might find someone. Don't worry about finding a job. It is not so mandatory to have a job right away—you can have a vacation for a while. I will not only support you "moneywise" but all other "wises"!

Yes, I knew it was easy to visit Europe "in route" to the US, but I never had time for it, or never planned!

Reza and Henrik have told me again & again to ask you to bring a couple of girls along—sister, friend or so on! What do you think?! Reza is still here, should leave in a few days.

I certainly understand your fear of coming to Iran, but I strongly suggest you to have courage and faith. Trust me dear, it won't take long before you get used to the surrounding. I'll do my best to make you feel comfortable and happy.

The more I look at your picture, the more I believe that you have a particular talent of your own for smiling. I looked at a mirror and tried to smile as you do but I failed!

She: 8/15/67, 8/20/67, 8/28/67 How excited everyone in my office gets when I mention that I am leaving and moving to Iran! One girl, about my age, was particularly interested when I told her my future plans. She then spent about a half an hour telling me a fantastic story about her past life that I hadn't known before. She said she married (and everyone in the office thinks she is *single*!) an African and moved to Tanzania. She got an accounting-clerk job with the Tanzanian government, and apparently, she and her husband had their own apartment and entertained important people often. However, her marriage and stay there lasted only 4 months—she couldn't take it any longer. She told me some of her bad experiences. Her husband was the most educated man in his district and was being mentioned for political office, but his friends kept telling him how bad, politically, it was to have a white American wife. Some of their mutual friends were Christians (as he was) but were very fundamentalist and criticized her to him because "she must be a very bad woman because she *owns* jewelry." The worst weekend she had was when she was sick (though her husband wouldn't believe how sick she was and gave her no sympathy) and her mother-in-law came to visit. Her husband just got tired of translating and walked out, leaving her alone with several Swahili-speaking relatives and guests while she was too sick to entertain them. She is now in the process of getting a divorce. Strangely enough her present boyfriend is from Rhodesia! I guess the most relevant lesson from her story is that you must be prepared for a *great deal* of patient *translating* in the beginning or else find me an interpreter.

Also, I was talking to a man who had worked for the Agency for International Development (AID) in Turkey and Nepal. He tried to discourage me: In Persian households (*homes*), the husband's word is *law*, wives are not consulted." "Iranian men are very dependent on their mothers, though." "Iranians are not 'logical' by American standards." "They say 'yes' to everything, even when they mean 'no' just to make you happy," etc. He told me a few interesting stories I will relate later.

When I read that you are not telling your mother about my arrival yet, I wondered about that. But I guess you can judge her reactions best. At least she will not have a chance to plan any bad things to do to me. Will she be angry about your not telling her, when she finds out? It is the kind of "trick" I would get angry about, for example.

I laughed out loud when I read Reza and Henrik's "request." Do they know any American girls? Mohammad, for instance, was surprised to see how *independent* we are. Some Persians, I think, would not like such a quality in women. (Even some Americans don't like it.)

I guess everyone in my office knows I am leaving to go to Iran. They stop by my desk and ask me all about it. There was an intern coffee hour on Thursday, and I absolutely shocked a couple of my intern friends by explaining that I was leaving soon and why. I'm getting used to making my private plans public now. On Friday night my boss had a cocktail party at his house for our staff and there the wives of the staff members had a chance to ask me about my plans. Even at a meeting last week, one staff member from my office announced that I was leaving, so of course everyone wanted to know where and why.

My flight is Pan Am 114 which arrives in Tehran at 8:20 p.m. on Sept. 8. And you will meet me with a Mercedes Benz--how elegant!

He: 8/16/67, 8/23/67, 8/26/67   I am sure you were kidding when you said if you should take a bus from the airport into town! Not only I'll meet you at the airport, but I'll also drive you into town myself—yes, I am driving a car (someone else's!).

Yes dear, I don't know how any woman can live with only 44 pounds of luggage either! This is a puzzle.

Finally Reza left here for Geneva (for a day) yesterday. Meanwhile he left his car, an old Mercedes Benz, with me. His trip will take about two months. So the car is a good opportunity for us.

You don't need to overfeed yourself with milk dear, you'll of course find enough here—only, people don't drink it as much as you do.

Of course my mother will be upset, to say the least, about your visit. But still this seems to be best policy. I remember you wrote me "change the behavior first, then the attitude will change" or so. This is more or less what we are going to do.

I sympathize with your office-mate. It certainly is worth to hear other people's problems—to get prepared for it. Of course I do expect a lot of translating—among other things—in the beginning, before you get to know enough Persian.

About what that "AID" man told you: Well, in *general* it is not incorrect, but you'd better judge yourself when here.

By the way, Reza saw me a couple of times reading your letters. He then told his mother: "This professor (!) used to read the difficult college books *once* (he was of course exaggerating) and he was the top student. But now, he reads Jackie's letters *several* times (and he *was not* exaggerating), again and again! He also was amazed to see your letters, all written tightly and with no blanks.

B: A couple of points seem to need a bit of a review. How do you now view that "AID" man's comments?

J: I find it, now, surprising that someone trained to be tolerant of intercultural differences, such as the AID fellow, would be so full of negative remarks. And my office-mate, Sydney, was another who wanted to warn me of what I might be getting myself into. So many people wanted to "warn" me of the dangers! There weren't many like my boss who saw it like I did—an adventure, and the biggest adventure of my life. I guess my fallback plan was that, if I didn't like it, I could just come back. Did you know that quitting my job with the federal government, a job that was not easy to land, was a signal of my commitment to making all our plans work? Many people advised me to just take a leave of absence and go to Iran and look it over, but I wanted to cut my ties completely in preparation for *staying* there.

B: My other point is about what you called a "trick." It appears that playing the trick on my mother by not telling her about your arrival beforehand was okay but you wouldn't like such a thing for yourself. In other words, it's good for the goose but not for the gander, ha?!

J: Ha! You are just too perceptive. I plead "no contest."

* * * *
* * *

OK, now let's follow the events as they developed. One remark about the change of pattern is in order. As soon as Jackie is in Iran, obviously there won't be any exchange of letters between them; only what she writes to her parents. This may result in a one-sided story at times. But not to worry, we'll supplement her letters with comments and dialogues when necessary.

After visiting her family on Labor Day weekend of 1967 in Darien Connecticut, she started her adventurous journey overseas. As planned she toured London, Paris, and Rome for five days before arriving in Tehran in the evening of Sept. 8. She stayed in a hotel for a couple of nights and then moved to an "apartment."

A week later she signed a contract for teaching English at a university starting Sept. 23. (There went the sociology career!) And finally, she wrote her parents about the issue of utmost importance to them.

Oct. 3, 1967 I haven't met his family yet. First, we wanted to get me well-established here. As it turns out, my landlady is *very* bossy and mean and keeps adding "extras" to my rent. So, I am moving out at the end of this week— I'm not sure where though.

The process of getting to meet his family is a slow delicate process. Today Bahman arranged a "discussion" with his sisters and a distant aunt to announce that I was here. Now, *they* know. Of course *they* were upset, but the main problem is his mother. It is almost certain that such a severe shock will cause her to become mentally ill; she has been sick on and off for so long. Bahman has a great problem in finding an easy way to tell her that we will be married in spite of her objections. I don't know how long it will take, but we have to be optimistic. So far, so good, I guess.

B: "We will be married in spite of her objection," ha? That is the way you put it, but I wouldn't have put it so harshly. I think I would've said we'd be married after getting her consent.

J: Same thing! We'd get a consent, though maybe a reluctant one after overcoming her current objections.

B: I don't think they are the same in all respects. The conclusion may be the same but the effect on the other party (i.e., my mother) could be vastly different from one approach to the other. Of course, one can't be certain that the "consent" would be finally obtained, but usually "the seeker is the finder."

J: Good heavens! I never thought of the possibility that we might *not* have gotten married if your mother never gave in!

B: And I never thought of the possibility that she might *not* have given in!

Oct 30, 1967   I haven't met Bahman's family yet, but negotiations for such a meeting are underway. We have an unofficial mediator now, a friend of Bahman's who delivers messages between the family and me. Up until yesterday Bahman's mother wouldn't speak to him and refused to meet me. Now she is getting used to the idea of his wanting to marry a foreigner (thank goodness), but the sisters are making trouble by putting conditions on the marriage (like paying them money, and insisting on a Zoroastrian marriage ceremony). Bahman is becoming more and more optimistic, but things don't seem so favorable to me. There is still a lot to be worked out.

Of course the mediator as we now know was Reza (and his mother).

Nov 9, 1967   I am under a legal contract to the University to teach for nine months. I can't get away until we have a vacation and the first vacation (two weeks) is in March. This awful schedule is preventing Bahman and me from getting married any sooner than that too. I am planning to beg for one more week off so we can come to the U.S. to be married as we had originally planned. Things are in a mess right now though, because Bahman's family is insisting that our wedding be a Zoroastrian one, held here in Iran. Also, Bahman's two youngest sisters are saying that they sacrificed for years to pay for Bahman's education and now he is going to become a disgrace to the family by marrying a non-Zoroastrian. So they are demanding $1,500 each as a price for having raised him. I got very upset when I heard this because we don't have enough money for plane tickets, for a wedding, and for them too. Bahman says, though, that he doesn't expect them to get around to actually asking for the money. He says it's just a threat.

Some good progress has been made though! And it's almost a miracle. Last Friday morning, Bahman's friend, who is a mediator between the family and me, arranged a meeting at his apartment. So at last I have met some of Bahman's family! At the meeting was Bahman, me, the mediator, Bahman's mother, his oldest sister, and his niece (14 years old), and a distant aunt. The aunt was very nice; she brought me flowers and asked me how I liked Tehran. We had tea and cake. The entire conversation was in Persian so I couldn't understand or participate. Sometimes it was embarrassingly quiet because no one knew what to say. Mostly they talked about their other friends and relatives. Bahman's mother didn't speak to me, not even "hello" or "goodbye." Bahman later told me that when his mother saw me she said "She is skinny!" (Maybe skinny by Persian standards, but I weigh 132 now.) The meeting lasted only about an hour. I still have two more sisters to meet. Bahman is planning now to bring me to his house for dinner some evening.

In the above letter, and in response to her mother, Jackie ponders on the deterioration of her father's health and the inevitable fact that she couldn't be with the family at the time of crisis. The two-week vacation in March refers to *No-Ruz*, the Persian New Year, which starts on the first day of spring.

Nov 16, 1967   I'm not worrying about Bahman's family much anymore either. What they say is mostly emotional because, of course, they are very upset. I'm learning to understand the situation, but it's hard to explain to you since you're not here. Certainly Bahman's mother depends on him (she has no pension, no life insurance, no income, no social security) more than you depend on your only son John; but, for example, how upset would *you* be if John said he was going to marry a Negro and bring her home to live with you? I know Dad would be *very* emotionally upset and make threats—no matter how good-looking, intelligent, well-educated, etc. the girl was. My fault here is not that I'm a Negro, but that I'm *not* a Zoroastrian or even Persian. Maybe you can understand this way: Suppose the girl John wanted to marry was not only Negro but also a Catholic (more upsetting, at least to Dad) and on top of it all suppose she came straight from Africa and couldn't even speak your language! My situation is something like that. Now, one more supposition. Suppose John said he wasn't marrying this girl because he loved her, but because she was rich. You would say you can't understand why he would do such a thing. In Iran it is not a tradition to marry for love. Two families arrange for a son and daughter to meet each other, and it is good enough if they don't *dislike* each other before marriage, since it is assumed they learn to love each other *after* marriage. Bahman's family cannot understand why he would do such a thing as marry a foreign girl because he *loves* her. Another fault against me is that I don't have any family in this country. Usually, here, a marriage brings two families close together to help each other. Can you understand why they're so upset and making empty threats?

But things are progressing very *very* well. Already his family has been more welcoming to me than Dad has ever been to Patricia's husband, Rich! Last Friday Bahman took me and two Persians to his house for lunch. This was the first time I saw his apt. His sister cooked lunch, and then surprised me by welcoming me to the house in Zoroastrian tradition. She put candies and small fragrant leaves from her hands to my hands and then sprinkled some of them on both my shoulders. She said "welcome" in Persian, and I really felt welcomed. Since then I have been over his house three more times—twice for dinner.

As a matter of fact, it is now Nov. 17, Friday, and I am now at Bahman's apt. finishing up this letter waiting for lunch!

If you could see Bahman these days, you'd have no doubt that he loves me as much as any man could love a woman. I've had lots of boyfriends, but none has been as devoted as he. Since I've known him more than 3 years now, I don't think I'm wrong. He is going to be such an ideal husband, and I'm very happy with him. If he has any fault, it's that he's too kind. He doesn't want to hurt anybody. He realizes that he has already shocked his family, so he is trying to make things as easy as possible for them so they will learn to like me. Things are getting better now, so we are both optimistic for a happy future.

I hope things are not too hard for you at home. Bahman has been saying how nice it would be for us to get married sooner, but, as I wrote in my last letter, it will probably be March before we can come back to the U.S. to see you again.

B: I probably shouldn't tell you this, but, believe it or not, every time I read that letter, and I've read it many times, I get tears in my eyes!

J: Me too. That letter seems to have been the beginning of good news from us and for us. However, in the midst of all this activity in Iran, life in the U.S. took a sad turn. On November 13, my father died from Hodgkin's Disease. My mother sent a telegram to inform me (phone was still not a common means of communication). The telegram arrived two weeks later on November 26, making it the saddest birthday of my life.

Jan 1, 1968 Of course, my nicest Christmas gift this year, I haven't mentioned yet. On the evening of Dec. 24th, Bahman and I went to a fancy Tehran jewelry store and picked out a diamond engagement ring! Most rings for sale here seem to be big fancy ones with many stones, but we managed to find a diamond solitaire that we both think is pretty. The setting makes it look like a star or small flower. After that we went to a Christmas service at St. Paul's Anglican Episcopal Church. On Christmas day we had a little "engagement party" by taking two friends, Reza and Edik, out to dinner at the new Chattanooga Restaurant. Bahman and I ate coq au vin (chicken in wine sauce).

Now that I have a ring, Bahman and I consider ourselves really engaged and it would be nice to have the announcement in the papers back in the US. Unfortunately, it doesn't seem that I will have time soon to take an engagement picture, so maybe you can just put the announcement in the papers. I'm not sure how you go about it but I think you send the announcement with all the information and let them make it shorter if they want to. So I wrote a long announcement that might be used: . . . "A late January wedding is planned."

Well, are you surprised by the last sentence! So am I! I always wanted a big wedding and reception in the First Methodist Church, but now it doesn't seem possible. Bahman's family is still extremely upset about our marriage plans, but they say at least we must be married in a Zoroastrian ceremony. Since Bahman himself would also like to have his identification papers marked that he was married as a Zoroastrian, I finally agreed. Since we are to be married here, there's no reason to wait until March. After the university semester ends, about Jan. 18th, Bahman and I will travel south to Yazd, Iran to have the Zoroastrian minister sign the legal papers. I would like to have a Christian ceremony too, so we are planning to have a ceremony in one of the small churches in Tehran about Jan. 19th with a reception afterwards to invite my friends on the University faculty. We might have a short honeymoon, but we are planning a long "honeymoon" for next summer to come to the U.S. and to stop off in Europe.

These plans are probably better for *you* too. Now you won't have to plan a big wedding for me by mail, with all the other things you have to arrange these days. The only thing I'd like you to do now is to look around for a not-too-expensive printer since I'd like you to send engraved wedding announcements to *all* our relatives and friends in the US. I'll send more detailed instructions later, O.K.?

Also, please tell people *not* to send us presents since import customs taxes here are about 100% the cost of the item, and we just can't afford it! Anyway, I'm pretty excited about getting married!

Jan. 10, 1968 Just a very short note to tell you the news. Bahman and I were married last evening! I was surprised that we had it so soon, but on Monday night Bahman told me the Zoroastrian priest had come to Tehran from Yazd and wanted to perform the ceremony quickly and go home again so we were to be married the next day!

We had the ceremony in the house of some Zoroastrian friends. On Friday, Jan. 19th we will have a Christian ceremony of blessing in the Community Church and a small reception. I'll write to you soon to tell you what to print in the wedding announcements.

We're very happy to be married!   Love,

Jackie (Mrs. Bahman Shahzadi!)

B: Wow! Getting married seems to have happened very fast and suddenly. But of course lots of things were happening during that short period. To start with, I think, the single most important factor that helped and guided us in the days before marriage was the discovery of a Zoroastrian young man and his new British bride. What do you remember about them?

J: Yes, I remember them, the Abadanis. They had been faced with the same dilemma we had in trying to arrange an interfaith marriage in Iran, where there are no civil marriages, only religious ones. In addition, Iranian law did not allow for marriage of two persons with different religions. One had to convert, and Zoroastrianism forbade conversions! The strangest thing about the Abadanis wedding was that the groom and his father went to see the priest in Yazd (One of a few cities in Iran with a relatively large Zoroastrian population—several thousand!). While they were there, the priest performed a marriage ceremony with the father-in-law standing in for the bride! I certainly did not want to be married by proxy, but the discovery of such a liberal maverick priest, willing to marry two people as if they were both Zoroastrian, was a godsend for us. You contacted that priest, and he was the one who married us.

B: I still have his old letters. He states his philosophy as "if two people want to get married, it is my duty to do it."

J: With all your relatives refusing to attend our wedding, and the necessity of arranging a ceremony on short notice, we were married in the Abadanis living room. Their family and servants signed our wedding certificate as the official seven witnesses. I had thought that, not knowing Farsi or the ancient Persian language of our Zoroastrian ceremony, I might not feel "really

53

married." But no! The long (45 minutes) Zoroastrian ceremony really worked: I felt "This is it—this is really getting married!" It was so funny when you later translated some of the "vows" to which I had agreed. One was promising not to overburden my donkey!

B: All these wedding problems seemed almost funny in light of the family secret we learned some months later. Here it is the way you tell your Mom.

May 10, 1968 A funny thing happened last week. Bahman's brother-in-law has an uncle, about 35 years old, who sometimes lives with them and sometimes travels to Germany on business or pleasure and stays there. For years now, he's been traveling between Germany and Iran. Last week, he returned from his latest trip to Germany with a German wife! So there is another Zoroastrian in our family who has married a foreigner! Not only that, but it seems that he has been keeping his marriage a secret for about 5 years now, and has a 4 yr. old daughter who will soon arrive here from Germany! It's quite a topic of conversation in the family, since of course it is quite a shocking thing for a Zoroastrian to marry a foreigner. I'm glad Bahman and I aren't the only ones now.

But that passage of course is quite a few months ahead of current events of the time. So, let's go back to where we left off.

Jan. 19, 1968 Enclosed is one of the invitations we sent to people to invite them to the Christian ceremony we had today. About 25 people came, and we had a nice reception afterwards. Tomorrow we expect to leave for a week of honeymooning is southern Iran, perhaps to Isfahan, Shiraz, and Ahwaz.
I wore a pretty wedding dress today. It was lace over satin (I think) with lace sleeves, and it reached to my ankles. The front was embroidered with a kind of tear-drop pearls and these were also on my white shoes. On my head was a band of white flowers (not real ones) with pearls and there was a short veil that reached to my shoulders and a long one that

was the length of my dress—both had embroidered scalloped edges. It was a nice dress and at a very reasonable price, since we went shopping in a less expensive district than the one we live in.

However, it cost about $10 to have my hair done at the hairdressers and have the veil fixed in place. We went to the photographers right after the hairdresser's, and I hope to send you some pictures in about 2 weeks.

It's been a pretty hectic day today, but I wanted to send you a note before I went off on the honeymoon.

J: This is obviously my opportunity to expand on our Christian wedding and ceremony. The Christian minister announced at our second ceremony that it was a "celebration" of our recent marriage. I guess I had all those girlish dreams of walking down the aisle in a white dress and we did make them come true, with some changes. In the absence of my father and brother, we decided that *you* would walk down the aisle with me in the beginning! And there was no vocalist, but an organist who played for us.

The reception was cake and punch in the church hall. I remember that all your relatives boycotted our ceremony except for a (curious) brother-in-law who brought along our niece. Later I learned that the Zoroastrians got together and decided to give us no wedding presents as a sign of their disapproval of this interfaith marriage! We did get a few gifts from our guests, co-workers from the university.

Tues. Jan. 23, 1968 My goodness, it seems I just never have time to sit down and write you a complete letter. It is now the fourth day of our honeymoon and we are in Shiraz, Iran. Last Sat. we packed and took a train south to a small town called Ahwaz. We traveled "deluxe" on the train and had a nice air-conditioned compartment we shared with another couple. The seats were made into bunk beds at night (the trip was 15 ½ hours long). We stayed one day looking and walking around Ahwaz. Yesterday we spent 13 hours in a bus coming from Ahwaz to Shiraz. A lot of the journey was on rough unpaved roads and part of it at night was on steep and narrow mountain roads. All the Moslems on the bus were praying out loud for a safe trip (and this was our driver's first time on this route!) but, of course, we made it safely. We saw a lot of the scenery of southern Iran on the way, too—even some camels!

Today we spent touring Shiraz. We met an American lady at the Iran America Society, and she invited us to lunch at her pretty house. Tomorrow we are off again—to Isfahan. Expect to be back in Tehran on Friday. Will write more when I have another chance.

J: That was a rather unusual honeymoon trip, although it was nice to see various parts of Iran. I didn't write my Mom that the hotel in Ahwaz was poor and old—we hadn't checked it out first! I wonder why we didn't realize there were steep mountains between Ahwaz and Shiraz. Oh well, the important thing was we were married and together at last.

Feb. 4, 1968 Well, we got a letter from you the other day addressed to Mr. and Mrs. Bahman Shahzadi; so I guess you got at least the first note I sent you telling about the wedding. I guess so many people are already finding out about the engagement and wedding that I guess I'll give up the idea of sending out wedding announcements, it won't be necessary. We don't have the wedding pictures yet, but when we do we'll also send you some and you can put it in the papers. We'll also send you some address labels in Persian so you can send letters to our home address (and then they might arrive a day or two quicker). Meanwhile, keep using the Dural Co. address.

Of course, I've moved in with Bahman's family, but we are trying an experiment to see if we can live together for the few months left in the lease. When the lease is up, we may decide to move to a two-section house and live more separately. So far, life here is better than you might expect. As soon as we were married, Bahman's family seemed to realize there was no basis for opposition any more. They became much nicer, and even gave me an embroidered handbag and a broach as wedding presents. Living in our apt. is Bahman's mother, who is old and sickly and usually stays in bed knitting, his oldest sister, Morvarid (about 48), and Morvarid's 14-year-old daughter, Fereshteh, who is kind of shy and somewhat over-weight. The three of them share a large room where they eat, sleep, and sit usually. I don't know enough Persian to talk to them easily, but lately Morvarid has been talking to me a lot, trying to get me to understand. Morvarid does most of the cooking, though sometimes I do, or Bahman and I do. Bahman and I have been doing a lot of rearranging and cleaning, and of course a lot of extra shopping.

The honeymoon trip was so nice. Part of the time we toured the mosques and places of old Persia in Isfahan, and we toured the ancient ruins at Persepolis—very impressive. When we arrived back in Tehran (by bus) it was snowing hard, and lately the weather here has been quite cold. University classes began the second semester a few days ago, and even though Bahman and I are back at work again, we still feel like we're on a honeymoon!

Jan. 23, 1969 January 9th was our first wedding anniversary, and we spent the day feeling happy and lucky to be married to each other. The weather was bitter, so we didn't go out to celebrate, but Bahman surprised me with a few gifts including a gold-colored wrought iron bookcase to hold my books and a pair of gorgeous silver Persian earrings. We wished each other "happy anniversary" again on January 19th, the anniversary of our Christian service.

* * * *
* * *

So, they got married, had a nice honeymoon, and so far celebrated their first year anniversary, too! Now, it was time to get occupied with other things like jobs, children, moving, etc., and finally the preludes to the Revolution. These are all going to appear in the chapters to come. For now, however, we are going to look at a few interesting anecdotes, which could come up in any marriage. The following are exchanges between the two of them in the summer of 1976 when he returned from their vacation in the U.S. before she and the children did.

She: 8/3/76 Mom asked me if you were concerned that I wouldn't return, but I'm sure the thought never even occurred to you. I read an article saying that the mid-30's is the usual age of women running away from their husbands since many feel that's the last chance they have to make significant changes in their lives before they get too old. But don't worry, dear, being with you is still the best reason (maybe the only one) for abandoning the pleasures of America and returning to Tehran.

He: 8/11/76 By the way, don't read those brainwashing articles that women of 30 run away from home! I am sure you can find something better to read.
The only couple of reliefs I have these days: No one tells me how to drive, and bothers me about hair in the sink.

She: 8/20/76 Do you spray the poinsettia? Ever vacuum the house, etc.??
I guess this is my last letter. So be prepared, I'm coming back to you to tell you how to drive and other things!!

Hair in the sink?! Well, that is when he had let his beard grow and trimming it at the sink (where else?) would inevitably leave traces behind! And although he did not have a chance to answer her last question himself and in writing, what *she* wrote her Mom after arriving in Tehran *did*:

Sept. 6, 1976 Fortunately we saw Bahman right away at the airport and were able to get out of the crowds (I think 3 planes had just landed) right away. We got home to find the apartment spotless. Bahman had done a fantastic job of cleaning everything and everywhere. We're adjusting to sleeping at the correct times, and we're lucky the kids don't have to start school immediately. It seems the school building is in need of some repair and so the opening of school has been postponed.

May 14, 1978 That was funny about you calling and Bahman being home while I was out dancing. Bahman said you sounded surprised. He wondered if you realized it was

Scottish Country Dancing. (For square dancing, we go together; but we've had very little time for that lately, too.) Don't be surprised about Bahman "babysitting" either. We share taking care of the kids pretty equally and it's a good system for everyone. (Actually whenever he gets tried of them he can send them downstairs to visit Grandma and Auntie!) Bahman's especially good on the 3 nights a week (4-7 p.m.) that I go to university classes. I usually arrive home to find all three of them glued to the TV and not missing me at all.

Chapter Three

Teaching, Learning, and Driving

It was in the middle of May of 1967, when Bahman wrote Jackie about a change of plans and suggested to her to come to Iran and stay there for a longer time. This way, he argued, she would have a better chance seeing Iran, and together, they would have a better chance at getting his family's consent for their marriage. This plan, of course, would require finding a job for her to keep her busy and earn her living, and finding a place to rent and live on her own.

In her May 20, 1967 letter, she reluctantly accepted a change of plans and outlined different possible ways of securing a job in Tehran.

She: 5/20/67 It does seem that my only chance to see you is to work in Iran. I have applications for an Embassy *staff* position (if there is any open now or in the future?) and I will register for the Foreign Service Exam to be given in Dec. (oh, dear, that's *so* far away from now). I'm afraid the State Dept. will only decide that I am a security risk because I have close Persian friends who influence me. Anyway it would take several months to process my application and then there would probably be a *long* training program here in the U.S. before I could be sent out. I would *prefer* to stay with the U.S. gov't but I don't think I could find a Labor Dept. position there.
Yesterday I bought a trade list from the Bureau of International Commerce. It lists all the American firms which have subsidiaries or affiliates in Iran, mostly in

Tehran. There are about 80 on the list, it is dated Sept. 1964. My problem now is that I am not sure that I have any skills or abilities that I could offer these businesses. I don't see any place for a sociologist, so I may have to emphasize my experience in management and that's only been a year. Perhaps I could fit into some personnel dept. Most hiring for Iran is done *here* in the US. I might have to make several trips to New York for interviews but I will try it. I might have to wait until I can build up some more work experience. It might take several years for me to get a position this way! There is an Iran-American Chamber of Commerce in Scarsdale, NY that might be of some help. What else can I do?

Bahman: So it was sort of natural to look for a job first with the U.S. Government, and next, with American firms doing business in Tehran. Can you think of anything to add here?

Jackie: It's interesting, looking back, to see that I assumed it was absolutely necessary that I get a job. In some way that might have been tied up with justifying my education, all the way through my Master's degree. I also see now that it was naïve to think I could be a sociologist, though that was my goal. I was really trying to make some use of U.S. contacts to land a job—a task that proved fruitless.

B: And there is a little funny anecdote in your subsequent letter saying, "Today I went to my doctor to get cholera and typhus shots, and I told him my visit was to be canceled, but I was looking for a job there. He said that if I was in the health or medical profession he could get me a job in a day. I should have been a nurse." In any case, in your letters you frequently talk about your job and responsibilities in that period of time. How about giving a very brief summary of it here?

J: I really felt among the "elite" in government by having landed a job in Washington, DC as a Federal Management Intern! Maybe you remember the long test-taking process I pursued to be selected as being among the top 2% of applicants on the civil service tests. Then I had multiple job offers from federal offices—

very flattering. I chose the Dept. of Labor for interesting work and non-traditional position for a woman (though it really wasn't that). I even turned down a mental health position in Wisconsin, where I could have remained close to you during your graduate studies, in order to move to Washington and become an Intern. After a year in the Internship, I was promoted to Manpower Analyst, which because of my move to Iran only lasted a month. I felt good about my job and I hoped to maintain that feeling.

The first time teaching English as a job comes up is when Mohammad makes a suggestion to her and she writes to Bahman about it. And here is his answer.

> He: 5/28/67 Yes dear, I was going to ask you about teaching English here. Do you mean only private teaching, or along with teaching in an institute? Shall I inquire about it? Do you have any other suggestions? Anyway, you don't have to wait for years to get more experienced and then work here. You are much more than a typical Persian girl, dear, and you'll get a good job (the only barrier might be Farsi).

In her answer she wonders what happens to her dream of being a sociologist, saying, "By the way, what has happened to my future as a career as a sociologist, particularly a research sociologist? I'm not doing it now, and if I teach in Iran I won't be doing it there either." At the same time her thoughts explore other possibilities:

> She: 6/8/67 The U.S. Supreme Court, just last week, declared unconstitutional the law that said Americans would lose their citizenship by voting in a foreign election. I guess I will be able to vote in a Persian election! According to the newspaper, the only way now that an American can lose his citizenship is by voluntarily giving it up—it cannot be taken away by the government. This means, I guess, that it would be OK for me to be employed by a foreign government—in other words to work at the University of Tehran sometime in the future, or to teach English in any institute, government-sponsored or not. It wouldn't hurt for you to pick up some information on possible jobs. Of course

now I would only be able to teach in English, probably teaching advanced conversation or composition English to some who already know some of the language.

The issue of work permit also comes up. Bahman writes, "A friend inquired whether or not you'll need a work permit when here. Where he works, there is an American (I guess!) who said either you don't need it, or you can get it easily—they'll help." And all along in this period they are both looking for job possibilities.

He: 6/19/67 Today, I went to the U.S. Embassy to inquire about jobs. They said when you are here, you give an application for a job and wait. By this, one might get a job in some foreign firms and companies, but the chances are not very high, he said. On the other hand, they gave me a several-page list of American companies in Tehran to contact personally for a job—but I don't know how to start. Isn't this list what you acquired there? (Prepared by the Commercial Section, Am. Embassy in Tehran, April 67)

She: 7/21/67 Today I went to see the firm of management consultants called "Booz, Allen, and Hamilton" to inquire about a job (perhaps even as a management consultant trainee) in Tehran. They said that most overseas offices are staffed with 40% of their own American employees and 60% nationals—all secretaries are nationals. To apply, I must contact their New York office, which I plan to do soon.

She: 7/30/67 Today I spent all day preparing a 2-page resume of my work experience to send to companies when asking about jobs in Tehran. It has taken me over a week just to find time to sit and write it! I am afraid most companies will say I have to know Persian well before they hire me or I must complete a lengthy training program in the U.S. before going abroad, or both. I think it would be good for me to begin Persian lessons immediately when I arrive in Iran. Do you know a professional tutor? I discovered that there are college courses for teachers called "Teaching English as a Foreign Language" which might have been good for me to take if I had had time. Perhaps teaching English will be the best job for me. if all attempts fail at finding me employment—are you prepared to help support me? Any news on your promotion yet?

And of course we've already seen his answer, "It is not so mandatory to have a job right away—you can have a vacation for a while. I will not only support you 'moneywise' but all other 'wises'!" And finally in a letter a couple of weeks before leaving the U.S., she says, "I applied to three American companies with branches in Tehran. Only one replied, and he said "Sorry."

* * * *
* * *

As we have seen, a few days after her arrival in Tehran, she secured an English-teaching job with the National University. Teaching English turned out to be acceptable and enjoyable. Let's look at a few of the letters she wrote to her parents on this topic.

Oct. 3, 1967 Teaching English to first year college students is kind of interesting, in fact, it's rather enjoyable. It's easy to teach English as a "foreign language" because here I am "expert" in English! I teach 20 hours per week (a heavy load for teachers) and usually get home early in the afternoon. I have Thursdays and Fridays off. Most of the English teachers are from the U.S. or England and most are married to Persians! I can read Persian numbers so I am able to take the right busses (two of them) to and from the University. I commute about one hour in each direction. Busses are cheap—3 or 4 cents a ride! Yes, I teach more than Bahman does. Promotions in his University have to go through mountains of red tape, so until he gets his promotion, he is a lab instructor—part time.

Oct. 12, 1967 I'm still enjoying teaching English. Fortunately, I don't have discipline problems in my classes that the other new young female teacher has. She never taught before, either, and in the past 3 weeks she has gotten so disgusted she decided to quit. I especially enjoy the lunches from the University cafeteria. We get a big plate of delicious Persian food, lots of bread (flat Persian bread) and a Pepsi for only $.40! All the English teachers' offices are located together, and we have two or three servants who bring us tea between classes. The servants also deliver our lunches! The lunch is my biggest meal of the day.

I am tutoring English privately now, for free, 3 hours a week, for one of Bahman's friends who knows only a little English. He lives upstairs from Bahman and often lends him his car. His name is Reza.

Oct. 11 1968 (a year later) Up until last week I had planned to work only part-time at the University, but I finally changed my mind and signed a full-time contract. We have to be there from 8 a.m. to 12 Noon and from 2 p.m. until 5 o'clock, and the University is too far from the city to come home for lunch so we must eat there too. Altogether I teach 18 hours a week—I have two classes of first-year students and I teach English composition to three classes of third-year students. My other hours at the university are supposed to be office hours. I enjoy teaching my first-year classes best; the students are more polite and attentive when they are new in the universities.

J: I think I can add a comment here. The first subject area that I taught was English grammar. After a short period of time I became quite an expert at English grammar, and teaching became much easier. Over the years, I was able to teach other subject areas, usually due to lack of any other teacher available, but grammar was always my favorite. I remember teaching several courses on short stories. Every story was a conversational opportunity and a chance for me to learn from my students. One day the story was about unusual foods, and I learned that my students almost never ate the large, delicious shrimp from the Persian Gulf because, as one girl said, "Who wants to eat such an ugly animal?" I learned then that there were also religious prohibitions in Islam against shrimp.

B: So all this past academic year you were teaching English and all indications are that you liked it. Now, do you remember why you wrote your mother that you had been planning to work part-time before changing your mind?

J: Yes I did like the teaching, but why the part-time plan I'm not sure. It could've been that we were planning for a baby and the thought of teaching full-time while pregnant, could've scared me a bit!

B: But apparently you finished your second year of teaching, pregnant and all, without any problem or unusual hardship, right?

J: Yes, there were no special problems except for the morning sickness that lasted well past "morning." I remember once being so sick I had to get off the bus earlier than my usual stop. But my colleagues at the university were helpful—recommending a doctor, etc. and of course, I was delighted to *be* pregnant.

Sept.27, 1969 I was looking for a part-time position too, and found that experienced English teachers are in great demand. I was offered more work than I could handle. By the time that I was offered a very excellent position—high pay, small classes, and adult students—I had already accepted 18 hours of teaching and had to turn them down regretfully. This year I'll be teaching two courses at National Univ.—Department of Economics and Social Sciences—and three courses at the Pars Institute of Higher Education. I've arranged for all my teaching to be in the mornings so that I can spend my afternoons with Ramin.

B: I know we are going to talk more about baby Ramin, and the other, later, but the connection between children and jobs is something we can talk about here. So, Ramin was born in July and three months later you are off going teaching again. Well, maybe that isn't unusual in America but do you remember how you felt and were looked upon then and there?

J: I remember Ramin was a planned baby—precisely so that I could go back to work after the summer break. I know, though, that your mother and sisters thought I was a "different kind" of mother.

B: OK. In early July of 1970 you wrote to your Mom, "I have some problems in trying to plan a trip to see you this summer. First of all, not enough students registered to take my summer courses, so Pars College cancelled the courses and I am unemployed for the summer." So, this goes to show that you were going to enjoy being a housewife and mother for a few weeks before we visited the U.S.; which is going to come up in detail later.

Sept 23, 1970 School is supposed to start in Iran today, but the colleges and universities are usually slow to get organized. Pars College (which is where I'll be working mornings this year) doesn't even begin registration until this Sunday. Our 16-year-old niece, Fereshteh, is supposed to enter a hospital-nursing school today for a 2-year program to become a nurse's aide.

Nov. 14, 1970 Bahman has been offered a couple of extra teaching jobs. It seems there's a demand for his specialty now. One job he accepted. It is at Tabriz University, a few hundred miles to the north! So every *other* week he will fly there Wed. noon and fly back Friday afternoon. I guess they are desperate for teachers there—they'll pay him about $15 an hour to teach! That makes the plane ticket and hotel bill worth it. I tease him about being a jet-setter now that he flies four trips (2 round trips) per month.

Dec. 14, 1970 By the way, Bahman wanted to say that he's *not* so important for teaching in Tabriz. The fact is, that the University is desperate for teachers and it's quite a common thing for professors to fly there to teach. Most of them seem to get tired of the commuting after a while though.

April 9, 1971 Last week I went to a 3-day seminar for college English teachers put on by the Ministry of Science and Higher Education. It was quite interesting to meet

English teachers from all over Iran and to hear their ideas on teaching.

June 27, 1971 I accepted a "mini-job" to give me something interesting to do. It's only 6 hours a week teaching English to 25 employees at the Ministry of Water and Power. The class was supposed to start last week, but the Ministry won't be ready for another two weeks. It feels almost like wasting time to do housework and watch Ramin. I don't even have the car during the days now that Bahman goes to work . . . every day.

July 24, 1971 I began my 6-hr. a week summer job today. I am practicing English conversation with young men (10 in class today) in a management training program. The material they study reminds me of what I had in the Labor Dept. I had such a good time today, I ran over my 2-hour class time without even noticing!

Sept. 20, 1971 My 6-hr.-a-week teaching job at the Water Ministry will probably end tomorrow—2 months are over now. With such small classes (5 to 10 students) and high pay ($8 per hour) I felt like a real professional. Also the students were so pleasant I would have volunteered my time to teach them (maybe).

March 5, 1972 I don't get as much time to write now. I finally got a job about 3 weeks ago at the Iran Girls' College. The teacher who wanted to leave finally made up her mind and left! They phoned me to come to work the next day. I teach there for 16 hours a week and then I have four more hours of private teaching here at home, so I'm quite busy again. Anyway, I enjoy this more—I can't be just a housewife.

J: I've got to interject an explanation here about being, or not being, a housewife . . .

B: Sorry, you have to wait your turn! I've got more urgent matters to settle. Did you notice that the pattern is missing? We've gotten used to you writing your Mom every year toward the end of September on how your job and the school year was going to be. How come we didn't hear anything about this school year?

J: Oh you men! You didn't forget, I hope, that it was this November (1971) that our second baby was born. And of course I didn't work for a few months after that.

B: Of course! Of course! Now, what did you want to say?

J: You note from the previous letter that I return to a common theme—one that has marked my whole life: "I can't be just a housewife" and I need lots of activity in my life. And it was quite a revelation that I could actually teach. I had always assumed that teaching was the *last* occupation I would ever choose. I think the possibility of discipline problems had scared me off.

B: Yes! And that theme *never* changed!

April 23, 1972 The Iranian Girl's College where I teach has only about 3 weeks or less of classes left! Then there's a final exam and then I'm at home again. Such a short semester! I've started inquiring about a job at Pars College again for next year, since that school is close to Ramin's (future) nursery school and the work load is less.

May 14, 1972 It is possible for me to get a raise and still work only mornings next year apparently. I was expecting to go back to Pars College, but Iran Girl's College wants me to stay so badly that the president offered me a nice salary and even the possibility of a supervisory position if I want. Of course I said that there's no chance of me working full-time and also that I had to check back with Pars College and then let him know. But it is nice to feel that my work is appreciated.

June 7, 1972 I settled my employment for next year. Yesterday I signed a contract with the Iran Girl's College to work five mornings a week, during the time that Ramin is in nursery school.

Oct. 11, 1972 I teach 4 hours a day (mornings only) and get home for lunch pretty tired, especially this week with this cold. Bahman has some classes beginning at 7:30 a.m.!

* * * *
* * *

It so appears that the subject of teaching is becoming routine and other matters, especially children, are becoming more of a conversation piece for Jackie to write to her mother. That's why we don't have much of anything to report for a couple of years.

June 13, 1974 I signed another half-day contract for next year at the Girl's College. I got a 10% raise but I figure inflation will take care of that.

August 29, 1974 School doesn't start for me and the kids until Sept. 23rd. I wish their school would start sooner so I could really have some "free" time to get things done. This week I've begun giving English lessons to a Persian man who will be coming here three evenings a week. I earn about $6 an hour this way!

Sept. 25, 1974   School started this week, and today I met my first class. It's nice to be back at work. (Do you think so too?)
Did I tell you I'm taking a 4-hour a week job teaching English to nursing students during the kids' nap time as well as tutoring a Persian man 2-3 nights a week. Also Scottish Country Dancing has begun again.

Jan. 9, 1976   Last Wed. was the official inauguration ceremony to officially change the name of our school from Iran Girls' College to Farah Pahlavi University. Empress Farah herself came to "open" the university, and I got to see her close-up, in person, for the first time, since the staff was standing in line to welcome her. I was quite impressed that after her formal speech, she informally apologized to the audience for having arrived half-an-hour late! As I said to my friend, I always thought, "Being a queen meant never having to say you're sorry!"

J: This time I go first, no questions asked! That remark was a take-off on the line from Love Story--a popular movie just about that time. I wonder if I ever mentioned in my letters the fun we had going to the late show at Goldis Cinema to see movies in their original English version. If we arrived too close to the movie start time, we stood in a ticket line that seemed endless!

B: Well of course, ladies first (some time)! I really don't have much to say except to remind the readers that the remark about Scottish Dancing wasn't part of your job description—just happened to be there!

April 2, 1976 I got to do some traveling the week before [the Persian] New Year's though. After "persuading" my university for months, and then setting up substitute teachers for all my classes for a week, I finally got my university to send me as one of their representatives to the 3 ½ day Seminar for professors of English in Iran in Ahwaz (south Iran). With registration, etc. the conference stretched to 5 days. This was the first time I've ever left Bahman and the kids—but they seemed to get along all right without me! The conference was very interesting and informative. I also loved the extra benefits—the plane trip to Ahwaz, five nights in a swanky hotel, the chancellor's banquet at the Univ. where the conf. was held, and on the last day, a tour by bus of some of the very famous archaeological sites nearby. It was also nice to see the palm trees of Ahwaz after taking-off from Tehran in a snow storm!

J: Now here was a benefit of having live-in in-laws! I could go off and everything at home was well taken care of.

B: Not to mention a good husband! But seriously, when I read this portion, it occurred to me that some things *never* change. You are still "persuading" your university to send you here and there, aren't you?!

J: Naturally, that's the nature of university life—always learning (and for me always going somewhere in order *to* learn.)

May 9, 1976 The other problem that crops up again as it has been doing every spring is whether to sign another contract and continue teaching at Farah Pahlavi University. Every year they put pressure on me to sign a full-time contract though I enjoy working part-time and getting home at lunch (and afternoon nap!).

June 6, 1976 I've had a great time since I last wrote—3 dinner parties, 2 tea parties, two picnics and a wedding reception. But the best activity was this past week when I left Bahman with the kids again and flew off to the southern central city of Shiraz for 4 days of business (and pleasure). My university sent me there to check up and get information on a summer intensive English program. I worked hard, interviewing, buying and reviewing books, taking notes, and writing a report. But it was worth it. I stayed in the fanciest hotel, and lived like a queen, all expenses paid (I also gained weight on the rich food). I got a chance to visit with my good friends, Rose and Hamid, who live in Shiraz. I ran into a friend from Tehran and her husband staying in the same hotel. But the strangest coincidence happened while I was shopping in the bazaar. I heard "Jackie" and turned to see some of my friends from my square dance club. They explained that they had come to Shiraz for a special square dance party that evening which I hadn't heard about. They persuaded me to stay for it, so I spent a hectic 2 hours to get a phone call through to Bahman to let him know I would stay an extra day. It was a great dinner (lasagna!) and square dance. I wore out a pair of shoes dancing for about 8 hours—until 2:30 a.m.!

J: Now after all that, it may appear that I was (am?) hyperactive, but remember, I wanted my Mom to know I was enjoying an active, happy life in Iran.

B: Of course! Of course! You had to make sure it was authentic when you told her you were happy!

Teaching, Learning, and Driving

Oct. 7, 1976 My new school opens the day after tomorrow. From the time I returned until this week, we've been having teacher's conferences and special training to help us prepare creative programs for gifted children. The building for the school is really an apartment building with about 24 apartments. We'll be holding classes (about 15 students each class) in the living rooms of the apts. The building is new—today men were laying linoleum, hooking up the electricity, and moving in furniture. I'm excited about starting teaching gifted children.

My other job seems to be 'driver." The kids started school about 3 weeks ago. But the school said that we are the only ones who live so far south, and they won't send a school bus to pick up the kids this year. Since we haven't yet found another way to solve this problem, I (and sometimes Bahman) have been doing a lot of driving. I'm glad Bahman has installed the seatbelts in the front seats at least.

Oct. 11 Well, if I don't finish a letter at one sitting it takes me several days to get back to it! Anyway I've been teaching 3 days now and so far it's OK in spite of being a bit disorganized still. The class that's the most fun for me is a group that knows no English at all. I found that I *can* teach in Persian, and they learned the whole English alphabet from me in 2 days (1 hr. per day).

B: Well now, the time span between the last two letters is a mere four months. It was during this period that we spent our summer vacation in the U.S. In your June 6 letter to your mother you're telling her that your university sent you to Shiraz to participate in an English teaching program (and you enjoyed it!). Then, a few months later, in your first letter after your return, you're talking about "a new school." Lady, you've got a lot explaining to do!

J: Ah yes! I did change jobs. I wonder if the letter with that news got lost? I remember that in Tehran we had monthly dinner reunions of the University of Wisconsin. At one dinner, I met an American woman who said her husband was opening a new school for gifted children. I didn't think he could entice me to leave the Farah Pahlavi University, but when he offered me significantly more than my university salary I decided to change jobs! The University sent me to conferences and raised my pay a bit, but they couldn't match that salary figure. So I embarked on the new adventure of teaching kids--256 geniuses!

Oct. 29, 1976 I've been pretty busy since my school started. It hasn't really got a name yet. We just call it the Center for the Gifted and Talented. I teach four classes a day and have been getting out at 1 p.m., so it's really like a part-time job. We haven't gotten our paychecks yet but I hope the salary isn't like a part-time salary, too! Most of our students have never studied any English, so we're busy teaching a lot of ABC's. I'm surprised that I'm enjoying teaching kids. This age group (11-yr.-olds) seems pretty easy to get along with, except that sometimes they get a bit noisy.

Feb. 3, 1977 Some of the counselors and teachers at my school have been asking for English lessons, so I decided to teach them before school 8:30-9:00 and after school 1:45-2:15. So far three of them attend regularly two or three times a week and five others have expressed an interest. They make interesting students. I enjoy it and I earn extra money too.

March 4, 1977 My job is going along pretty well, though the students seem to get noisier all the time. I've heard that next year there will be two Centers for Gifted Children, one in East Tehran and one in West Tehran, both very inconvenient locations for me. I imagine that I'll have to choose one of those Centers (and spend *hours* in traffic every day!).

March 17, 1977 This past week I've been attending meetings of the annual conference of the Association of Professors of English in Iran. I enjoy conferences and I think I learn a lot too. This year the conference was held in Tehran at Farah Pahlavi University where I worked last year (and 4 ½ yrs. altogether). So I was recognized and greeted by everyone from the chancellor of the University down to the students and the servants!

Here are a few letters she wrote him about her job activities in the U.S., while he was in Iran.

She: 6/22/77 Early Monday morning Carol phoned to tell me what subways to take to Columbia Teachers College and I've been to the conference 3 days now. (Some of our group arrived in NY one day late for the conf., and two others don't start the conf. until tomorrow as they are due in today!) There was a rumor that Mr. Kamali was bringing our summer pay to us—so I delayed writing you to see what pay it was. Yes, he did bring 2 months pay (in American dollars) but today he assured me that it is pay for Tir and Mordad, so that my Khordad pay should be in the bank to cover the check I wrote to Central School.

She: 7/4/77 We finished up our seminar in New York last week, and I handed a term paper, which I stayed up to one a.m. to type (just like the old days of student life!). On Sat. the kids and I took an all day bus trip to the Canadian border where Carole [Weller] picked us up in her new little car.

She: 7/11/77 The classes are going well and we're getting lots of information. Now we really have to get down to the business of designing lesson plans and workshops for training the new teachers. Iraj has postponed the training in Iran until Aug. 20 but I don't think that means 2 weeks vacation since he has said he wants us back there to interview and choose the new teachers for next year! Iraj himself should come to the U.S. around July 15, but we probably won't see him until the conference in San Francisco on July 27.

She: 7/21/77 I got a great compliment from a trainer (our main teacher in fact) named Sandy. She said my lessons were fantastic but she couldn't praise me too much in front of the group because they would attribute it to my English, so she told me privately. She said I'm a 'natural teacher" good enough to teach *with her* in the Leadership Training

Institutes. That's the highest praise, really. And if I ever need a job in the U.S., I know where to look!

B: I sense a need for some explanation here. In your above letters to me, you're talking about classes you were attending in the U.S., and later below you would be telling your mother about university courses you're taking in Tehran. Could you explain all that in a nutshell?

J: The classes we were taking in Pasadena, CA that summer were basic information on how to train new teachers and more specifically how to train teachers for gifted children. Our trainers were educational consultants and faculty members from the University of Southern California. Later in the fall, our training became more formal and degree-focused as others (new teachers) joined us in classes led by USC professors, who came to Iran for a month at a time to give us classes in gifted education.

Oct. 27, 1977 Thanks for going through all the trouble to get my GRE scores sent to me. They are certainly high enough to qualify me for the doctorate program. If the University accepts the scores, you have saved me the money and time involved in retaking the test. Technically the Univ. could still require me to retake the test, since they prefer test results to be less than 5 years old—but I'll try to get them to make an exception for me.
My school is opening two more branches in other areas of Tehran. As head of the English Dept., I am supposed to assign the English teachers to the various schools, arrange their contracts, etc. Things are pretty hectic now and it keeps me quite busy.

Feb. 18, 1978 The professor who is teaching the university courses I'm taking now is an enthusiastic skier—and that's about all he really seems to like about Tehran. He's not as friendly or concerned about students as Dr. Yoshida, our first professor. One course is on Education Programs for the Gifted, and that's easy because I already know it. The other course is dull and boring Educational Administration, which is mostly history. I'm still doing OK though, my midterm exam mark was 100% and highest in class again (I'm sure to get unlucky one of these days and miss a few questions!). Next week is final exams. Six weeks for a course sure passes fast.

Our Organization has two schools in Tehran this year. Last week the members of the English Dept. in the second school got into a squabble over rights and responsibilities. I arranged a meeting and went out there to bring peace today. After negotiating with those teachers and getting a tentative agreement, I really feel I deserve a medal now!

March 21, 1978 I think I mentioned that I was going to get a medal from the Iranian government for outstanding services to education, and two weeks ago our director handed out the medals to the 25 winners in a ceremony at our school. The medal winners were also handed two invitations. One was to a party at the Golestan Palace, which we all expected would be a dinner. But it wasn't! All we had were a few small sandwiches and lots of speeches in a crowd of 1,600 writers, artists and journalists. I did get to shake hands with Prime Minister Amouzegar and Court Minister Hoveyda (former P.M.). But we were so hungry afterwards, that we persuaded our director to take the 25 of us to dinner at the Sheraton Hotel. The second invitation was for the next day to a ceremony marking the 100th anniversary of the birth of Reza Shah the Great (the Shah's father) at his tomb in south Tehran. But that day it snowed! (And we have had almost no snow this winter!) We were driven in special buses (beginning at 8 a.m.) to the tomb but had to walk a long way from the parking lot in flooded streets, snow, rain and freezing wind. I had only a light coat over my long formal dress and I was *so* cold. At least the reviewing stands we sat in had canopies over them. The Shah, Empress, and the Crown Prince came about noon, had a 20-minute ceremony and left again by helicopter. At least the sun had come out by then! I got home by 3 p.m., cold and tired and wishing I hadn't gone at all!

The day after that (March 16, Thurs.) four other English teachers and I left for the Eighth Annual Seminar of the Association of Professors of English in Iran. This year it was held in the northeastern city of Mashad, the holiest city in Iran, where many Moslems go for pilgrimage, especially at New Year's time. We had registered early for the conference, and were lucky enough to get rooms in the luxurious new Hyatt Hotel. The conference was held at Ferdowsi University, and I saw so many old friends I used to work with in different places. The conference ended at noon on Sunday, and we then had a tour to the library and museum of the Holy Shrine and a 20-mile trip out of town to the tomb and memorial for Ferdowsi (the great epic poet of Iran). We flew to and from Mashad in Iran's new Airbus (280 passengers).

Unfortunately the conference was at the same time as the first official visit of the Shah and Empress to our school. We had been preparing for weeks for their visit and then we weren't there when they came. But the teachers who were there said he got a very good impression of our school and was quite pleased with it. He talked to the children and the teachers. He has ordered more gifted schools built throughout Iran and things look good for our future development.

J: Reading about medals reminded me of the medal you got from the Shah after you graduated from college at the top of your class. And it was so nostalgic to find in Fereshteh's storage, a framed picture of the medal ceremony in our trip to Iran in 2001.

B: Oh yes, I had forgotten all about that. It still surprises me to see myself in the picture in the presence of the Shah and the Queen without a tie! I must have been very unorthodox back then. I'm not that stubborn anymore, am I?

J: I guess not. Nowadays, you wear a tie to weddings and funerals and that's an improvement! (Or, were you talking about other kinds of stubbornness?)

May 14, 1978 *Next* year I might buy a car in the U.S. If all goes as planned and I pass all my admission tests, etc. etc. I might have to spend next summer on campus in Los Angeles. Then I really will need a car to get around.

Teaching, Learning, and Driving

The university course is really work! We have seven assignments and two tests in the next three weeks! At least I'm still getting fantastic grades—lots of encouragement.

My Organization is like a big family—so many cousins, brothers, wives, etc. work in it. So it was only natural that Bahman should join, too. He is directing an electronics lab for gifted students, and they're so enthusiastic, they come for 3 hours after school on Wednesdays. It's nice that we can eat lunch together again even though now it's in a noisy cafeteria.

June 20, 1978 At least my University classes are in recess now (until Aug. 19), and I get to spend my evenings at home for a change. I finished the last courses same as usual—top student, straight A's. In fact it turned out good that I took the Graduate Record Exams again. I got quite unbelievably high scores—99 percentile verbal, 93 percentile math and 92 percentile analytical—even better than 13 years ago. I got the first acceptance letter from the Univ. for enrolling in the Ph.D. program of anyone in our class. My scores arrived on the day we gave our professor a big good-bye dinner party so I got lots of congratulations.

I'm still working even though classes are finished. I spent some time interviewing applicants for English teaching positions. Next week I start teaching them in the Teacher Training Program. Bahman will have a 2-week course in the Electronics Lab for the children as part of our Organization's Summer School. He has found out, as I did last year, that these children are more fun to teach than college students.

Sept. 9, 1978 I'm getting ready to take exams in my USC Educational Philosophy class. It's quite interesting. But today I heard that there may be *no* doctoral program with USC because they couldn't arrange a suitable contract with our Organization. That's rather disappointing, but there's some hope that another university may offer such a program. Anyway I'll probably get a Masters in Education this winter at least.

Sept. 30, 1978 The opening of school last week was pretty hectic—I mean the school where we work. Sorting out students into classes took a long time. Then there was buying books, ordering new equipment, etc. etc. The school where Ramin and Susanne go seems more organized. The only thing that bothers me there is that Susanne's teacher is untrained and inexperienced, but Susanne likes her and that's important. The teacher also likes Susanne and says she works so quickly she has time to help other students in class.

* * * *
* * *

Learning the Persian language (Farsi) by Jackie started very early in their relationship. From the very beginning of their meeting each other in October of 1964, she expressed interest in the language. Of course there is nothing special or unusual about this. When two members of the opposite sex (or even same sex) meet and continue the relationship, each would be usually interested in anything and everything that the other has been and done; especially if one happened to be from Mars and the other from Venus in a more real sense than normal!

By the time Bahman returned to Iran more than two years after they met, she knew quite a few Farsi words and could put a few short sentences together. Her ambition for seriously learning the language sharpened after he left for Iran and she was expecting to follow him in a few months time. Here are a few passages from her letters to him in Iran.

She: 6/19/67 Thanks for checking on the teaching job—it's nice to know there is some job possibility I could take without having to know much Farsi.

She: 6/27/67 Your letters have been more encouraging (especially about job possibilities for me) lately, and I am much less depressed. In fact, enough optimism has returned that I have gone back to my study of Farsi again, after a long break.

She: 7/30/67 You can find out if any of the American firms in Iran use much English or totally Persian in their business. I think it would be good for me to begin Persian lessons immediately when I arrive in Iran. Do you know a professional tutor?
Finally, last week, the set of Persian records that I ordered while in Oregon arrived here. One set got lost in the mail. These records teach the usual things a tourist ought to be able to say. Do you have a record player so that I can bring them with me?

She: 8/20/67 I play my Persian records every day. I can say such necessities as "Mostarah kojast?" [Where is the bathroom] and "Lotfan neshan bedahid," [Please show me] among others.
Just think, in three weeks you can sing to me in Persian in person.

So, she was trying to prepare herself in advance and for good reasons. Not only was she concerned that her future job in Iran would require her to know a lot of Farsi, she also knew that knowing the language and being able to communicate with her (hopefully) future in-laws, would make a good impression. And here is his response to her last comments.

He: 8/26/67 My goodness, you have learned only things like "Mostarah kojast?" (I guess it *is* a necessity!) and so on? (I am kidding.) This reminds me of what Joy [a mutual friend in Wisconsin] used to learn (swears, etc.).
Yes dear, I am practicing that song over and over in the bathroom! [shower] And I guess I have a pretty good voice now!! So, hurry up. I want to sing for you: "Since you are my love, I will come to you. I will search for you all over . . . . . ."

J: That song is still in my memory and I remember that you used to sing it often after we met.

B: Yes, that song was one of my favorites even before I met you. Not that I could sing a song by any stretch of imagination, but I liked to utter it a lot! It was one of the best songs of one of the best singers in Iran of the time, Ms. Delkash.

J: OK, but didn't you use to tell me that you used to play that song while playing your violin?

B: All right, now you are stretching it!. Well yes, I started going to violin classes for a couple of years after graduating from college in the hope that I had some talent. But it turned out that nothing was farther from the truth than me having musical talent! Anyway, it was really surprising to find the old musical notes and lyrics of the long past when we traveled back to Iran in the summer of 2001. Real nostalgic!

Going back to the events of 1967, she arrived in Tehran and landed a job teaching English. This obviously meant that she really didn't need to know Farsi. As a matter of fact, they usually discourage the use of Farsi in English classes. OK, but still knowing the language was really advantageous if she was going to become part of an Iranian family. That is shown in the following letters to her parents.

Oct. 3, 1967 Today I began going to a once-a-week class in Elementary Persian at the University of Tehran. The quicker I learn the language the better. It's kind of funny not to know what everyone around you is saying—all day long!!! Being on the English faculty gives me people to talk to though. Last week Bahman and I went to see a Persian movie—I had seen the movie in English so I understood the action, but it was boring not to be able to understand the words. We saw an English movie at the Iran America Society on Sat. night and that was *much* better.

Oct. 12, 1967 I'm taking two hours a week of Persian at Tehran Univ.—it's a nice class. Also I have a conversation book from the Iran-America Society and Bahman is teaching me from that.

Teaching, Learning, and Driving

Oct 30, 1967   I'm learning Persian little by little. All the teachers where I work speak English of course, so I don't *need* to use Persian. I enjoy my Persian class every Tuesday though.

March 6, 1968   It seems that I am not learning to speak Persian very fast, so I have signed up for a conversation course at the Iran-America Society beginning next week, in addition to the course I'm taking at Tehran Univ. (I got an "A" last semester). Bahman speaks to me in English and to his family in Daree (the Zoroastrian language) so I don't get much practice in speaking or hearing Persian at home.

J: This seems to be the right place to reminisce on something. I always found it easy to begin studying a new language—Latin, Russian, and German in school. But the second year of a language became *much* more difficult for me. I had trouble remembering all the vocabulary and I was much too shy to just plunge ahead, conversationally, making mistakes right and left. Much to my dismay this language learning pattern of mine persisted in the case of learning Farsi. Fluent Farsi would have been so useful— and an incentive for our kids to learn, too.

Sept 13, 1968   I've had more time for reading, violin playing, and writing letters lately. Next week I start back on my four hours a week of Persian conversation classes at the Iran-America Society. Then the following week University classes start again and I should be very busy once more.

Sept. 27, 1968   University classes are late in starting, but I expect them to begin tomorrow (maybe). At least I signed a contract last week. I also signed up for more Persian lessons at the Univ. of Tehran, so now I have 4 hours a week of Persian conversation and 2 hours a week of reading and writing.
Dec 8, 1968   Did I tell you that I started taking Persian classes at Tehran University, but that the Iran-America Society classes have ended. However the students from my IAS classes now come to our house and we are continuing Persian lessons with Bahman as our teacher.

B: This seems to end the reporting to your Mom of your struggle with learning Farsi. Do you recall anything more that happened after that?

J: I just remember getting much too busy to go to Persian classes any more. I was also quite discouraged by the second-year classes at Tehran University. The students were not the same ones that I had studied with in year one. Most of these students were quite fluent in spoken Farsi and just needed to read and write it. I was lost!

B: But of course you gradually learned a lot more Farsi for the next ten years by "immersion" as is called. Right?

J: Yes, immersion works, but two things worked against me. One was my shyness or reluctance to speaking incorrectly, and the second was the fact that almost everywhere I tried out my Farsi I was answered in English by people trying to improve their English! Even *you* spoke to me exclusively in English, remember?

B: Right. But why do you think that was the case? How about other mix-married friends; did they speak Farsi to each other or English?

J: As a matter of convenience and ease, I think most of our mix-married (good term!) friends did speak to each other primarily in English. Only those Iranian husbands that weren't so fluent in English spoke Farsi to their wives who also became bi-lingual more easily.

B: Come to think of it, I guess that your lack of *good* knowledge of Farsi (especially in the beginning) probably played a big role in the relative peace and good feeling between you and my family. As you are well aware, usually hard feelings between relatives starts with small things that could escalate to real conflict when they start using sharp tongues in emotional states. What do you think?

J: Sounds reasonable. And of course you were always there to smooth things over!

* * * *
* * *

They had to go to work like most others, by bus or on foot. Cars were luxuries, but even then Tehran's traffic wasn't so good—to be very generous! Here are some samplings of Jackie's thoughts and expressions to her Mom.

Oct. 3, 1967 I can read Persian numbers so I am able to take the right busses (two of them) to and from the University. I commute about one hour in each direction. Busses are cheap—3 or 4 cents a ride!

April 11, 1968 It will probably be many, many years before Bahman and I can afford to get a car, since cars here are about twice as expensive as in the U.S. (!) especially the second-hand ones, since cars don't depreciate here as much as they do in the U.S.

Feb. 28, 1969 With the terrible traffic here in town, I thought something would happen to us sooner than it did. But last night we were in our first traffic accident. We got out of the movies ("Thoroughly Modern Millie") at midnight when buses don't run and taxis are scarce. So we accepted a lift from two fellows in an old car. In Tehran, drivers always fight for the right of way at intersections. Since the car we were in had poor brakes, it ran into a car crossing in front of us. The cars crashed fenders but I guess the shock of the crash was less than if our driver had been able to slam on strong brakes (as drivers usually do). Certainly it was gentler to go crashing into the next car and no one got hurt.

B: So, we were involved in a traffic accident without even owning a car, huh? Believe it or not, I had completely forgotten about it!

J: Yes, I really still have no memory of that accident. I am remembering how the lack of transport led us to use those "private taxis" that were so common in Tehran.

B: OK. Now, I bet it would be a surprise to the readers to read the following letter only a year and a half after you told your mother that it would probably be many, many years before we can afford a car.

Sept.27, 1969 Big news! We bought a car! After years of waiting for taxis (sometimes ½ hour or more) or standing in long hot bus lines (can you imagine 100 people waiting in line for a bus that arrives after 20 minutes and is full!) we decided to take the big step and buy a brand new car. Used cars here depreciate very little so they're almost as costly as new ones. Our car is a *Peykan* which is a locally-assembled model of a British compact car. About half the cars here and most of the taxis are *Peykans* since they are relatively cheap compared to imported cars. Still, we are paying close to $3,000 for this car, including taxes and insurance, which is more than my yearly salary! We picked up the car at the factory on Thursday. We ordered a red one, and it looks very much like my first car—about the same size too—but this one has a lovely "ivory" interior and bucket seats. We took Ramin out for a ride and discovered it's an easy way to put him to sleep!
We decided it's an especially good time to get a car so that when school starts (today) Bahman will have an easier time getting to work. In addition to his bakery project and his part-time position at Tehran Univ., he has accepted two other part-time teaching jobs, so he'll have a lot of travelling around the city.

J: Getting our first car *was* a big deal. And we were lucky not to have had to wait much on a list to buy the car because it was a new factory and the waiting list was short. But a year or so later our friends Hamid and Rose would have had to wait *much* longer to get their car if we hadn't used the "help" of the father of one of my private students to "jump" the line and get them a car sooner!

B: All right. Now what are we going to do with that "bakery project" that inadvertently came up in the letter. As you may know, I have very mixed feelings about the whole thing and don't know how to treat it in this writing.

J: I suggest we defer the explanation to a later time and a better place.

B: Good idea. That at least creates some temporary relief!

Oct. 19, 1969 Now that we are riding around in our *own* car, I'm about as nervous about Tehran's traffic as I was when I first experienced it two years ago. You wouldn't believe the wild traffic here. Few people obey traffic laws and there is no politeness on the road at all. I loved to drive in the US, but I've more or less lost that desire here. Anyway it will be convenient or necessary for me to drive our new car sometime, so we've inquired about getting me a driver's license here. Seems it will involve a lot of "red tape" and a couple of tests—what a nuisance. I really shouldn't say "new" car anymore, since it's beginning to look old already. The first day we had it someone stole the trademark off the grill, about the fourth day some thief stripped the chrome off one side and the back, and about the tenth day a taxi ploughed into the left rear fender. I get so frustrated when I consider how much time we worked in order to buy that car.

Nov 14, 1969 Nothing else has happened to our car, thank goodness. I was able to get an international driver's license but I'm a little afraid still to drive in Tehran's crazy traffic. Yesterday Bahman gave me my first "driving lessons" in city traffic. We drove up north of the city to Isabel's house. She and her husband, Ahmad, moved last summer into a new house they built. It's huge—like a palace to me—with a swimming pool and everything. Also this past month they bought *two* brand new cars!

Dec. 2, 1969 We were planning to go to a Thanksgiving service but at the time our car was in the service garage for battery charging and replacement of the voltage regulator, which was faulty, so the car wasn't starting. Now the car is fine, it even starts in the cold mornings with no trouble. On the mornings Bahman doesn't need it I drive it to work. I think it's easier driving in Tehran than riding because at least I know I have the brake pedal right there under my own foot for quick stops. But pranksters have struck our car again! One night they smashed the rear-view mirror, which we had only recently installed on the front fender. I think we need a garage.

B: I have two questions and I put them together here. First, do you think the reason that nowadays you want to drive while I am the passenger is the result of your driving experience in Tehran and your desire to have the brake pedal right under your own foot?! Second, do you want to explain about needing a garage, was it a serious thought or just rhetoric? I honestly don't remember!

J: Second idea first—a garage was simply a "pipe dream." Who had garages? Around our neighborhood everyone parked in the alleys with the exception of those few whose yards were big enough to hold a car. The answer to your first question is no. I have always enjoyed being in the driver's seat. Driving was also a way to insure against motion sickness.

Jan 26, 1970 I'm in the middle of a cold now—good thing it's final exam time now at school and I don't have to teach. Our other problems involve our car again. Thieves struck for the 5th and worse time—they stole the front grill and both headlights (our neighbor suffered the same thing last month). Our car looked like a second-hand wreck. Even worse, insurance won't cover partial theft and Peykan supply stores don't have anymore headlights in stock these days. We finally had to buy replacements on the black market (where the thieves probably sold them) at inflated prices. Then last week someone with a sharp instrument scraped a line of paint off the left side of our car. How disgusting.

Teaching, Learning, and Driving

Feb. 17, 1971 The traffic policemen in Tehran have been spot-checking drivers lately to be sure they have licenses. So now I'm scared enough to start planning to take my driver's test here. The test is supposed to be extremely tricky and difficult, and I've heard of people failing it up to 14 times!

March 8, 1971 Last Sat. I took a driver's test (in English) for an Iranian license and passed easily, so tomorrow I can pick up the license. This testing process is long and more complicated than in the US—usually you have to wait 3 months for an appointment even, and even after that most people fail the test several times ($20 for the test, $4 for the license). However, we knew the uncle of the head of the licensing dept., so the process was simplified for me. Apparently the only efficient way to accomplish official business here is to know someone, unfortunately.

J: "Knowing someone" or *parti bazi* was a common way of doing business. Although hard to accept, I did get used to it, as you know.

B: That and "gratuity." Do you remember the time right after we got married when we went to get your *shenasnameh* (Persian ID)? If I remember correctly, because of a very small typo that *they* had made in it, we went back to make a correction and they gave us a real hard time. Later we learned that a little gratuity would've gone a long way to solving the problem.

J: Yes, and I was (am) surprised that *you* didn't know that much!

August 22, 1973 Bahman's latest project is Rausti Electronics, an electrical and TV repair shop which he opened last month. He has one young man working with him and so far their repair jobs have been for our friends. Bahman wants to teach part-time during the school year and supervise the shop too. He is now teaching summer school two mornings a week, but he's had enough free time to design a product he calls Auto-Switch. It's a hidden switch which the driver must push to start the car's engine and is designed to prevent car thefts. Bahman's shop will sell these switches. Anyway, Bahman has been pretty busy this summer.

J: Here you have a chance to tell us all about Rausti Electronics.

B: Do I have to?! That is another thing I'd rather forget, or at least defer! On the other hand, maybe it is better to go over it real quickly here and put it behind us. I had grand plans to create a very competent and honest electrical repair and service business in Iran, but it failed. And I'm going to tell you why before you ask. I was *not* a businessman by any stretch of the imagination, and if one doesn't know how to run even a technical business financially, it is doomed.

J: Well, I'm glad you cleared that up. I really didn't know exactly how you felt about it until now. It is good that we're writing these things down!

Oct. 5, 1973 Yes, we did recover our stolen car. Police found it outside the city four days later. It was stripped of everything that could be sold even the dashboard, the back seat, and the windshield! We didn't have theft insurance so it cost us about $600 and two weeks in a repair shop to put it together again. Now Bahman has designed a *new* ignition lock and burglar alarm system that really ought to be foolproof. We can't afford to have another clever thief take advantage of us.

B: OK, some explanation is due here. First of all, I don't see any mention in your previous letters to your Mom that our car had been stolen. On the other hand, in your letter to your Aunt Jo on August 26, you write, "Yesterday our most expensive possession, our car, was stolen from a well-traveled street in broad daylight! Worse yet, Bahman had just recently equipped the car with a special electrical switch that he designed to prevent car theft!!" What is going on?

Teaching, Learning, and Driving

J: When you look at the letters of this period you'll see that my correspondence with my mother is different because of the fire in her home in May, 1973. She had a grease fire in her kitchen which destroyed her kitchen and burned her severely. She was in intensive care for weeks. My first news of the fire was a telegram my brother sent to the American Embassy, thinking they would be able to reach me the quickest. That took a week to arrive! Trying to get an open phone line to the U.S. to check on the news took me eight hours! Communication was never easy. It was during this time that I started sending her audiotapes with us and the kids talking as a way to cheer her up. We still have the tapes!

B: So your mother learned about the theft of our car from your aunt. It is good that she had given the letter to your Mom to read and now we have it for reference.

Feb. 9, 1974 We've had more excitement than we'd care for here the last few weeks. Our car was stolen again! Can you believe it?! Bahman's special ignition lock and alarm system developed a fault and he was waiting for a snow-free day (and boy have we had lots of snow this winter!) to repair it. It took only 3 days without that lock and the thieves grabbed it while Bahman was in a movie theater. This time it was gone for 2 weeks before the police found it abandoned in Tehran. The thieves had driven it 4,000 miles until the clutch broke down, and they stole tires and parts off it. We figure they must have been smuggling drugs or something. Anyway, it's repaired and running again, and we are going to keep that ignition lock on it in good repair.

B: Here we go again with that infamous "Auto-Switch" or ignition lock. It never became a success partly because, again, I wasn't a businessman, and also because it was my own design. Now that I think about it, if one really wanted to sell a product successfully, one had better import and sell.

91

Chapter Four

The Fruits of their Labor

After any marriage usually come children and there was no exception here. The first time Jackie wrote to her Mom about this topic was on Nov. 13, 1968.

Nov. 13, 1968 Bahman and I have decided to surprise you with a combined birthday-Christmas present, but you'll have to be patient for about 7 ½ more months. It should be all set and ready to deliver next summer, and I really mean "deliver." My doctor says he's about 99% sure that I'm pregnant, and the baby's due at the end of next June! So Bahman and I are going to make you a grandmother! How about that!?! Aren't you feeling *old*? We're so very happy about the whole thing.

Actually, this past week I've been *quite* sick with nausea and vomiting. Finally, I went to a gynecologist recommended by a British teacher at the university. Dr. Tavacol speaks English and has studied medicine in England. He prescribed some pills and some injections for the vomiting. (It seems strange—doctors in the U.S. never *prescribe* injections, do they? but here it's very common. One usually finds a clinic to give the injections. I'm lucky that Bahman knows how to give injections.) Since the injections, I've been feeling quite a bit better, and I can eat almost normally. But I wonder if it will be necessary to keep on taking daily injections. I didn't think that "morning sickness" was such a horrible all-day thing.

It's nice to be expecting a baby, and it's also nice to know that the baby should arrive exactly when we want it to. I'll be free of classes and able to rest in June, and then I'll have two free months to stay home and take care of it. Do you want a grand-daughter or a grand-son?—we haven't decided! I'll probably work only part-time next year so I can spend a lot of time with the baby. First babies seem so special, I guess.

Well, now that I've told you, there doesn't seem to be anything else important to say. So, I'll go write letters to other people and wait for a note from you.

Jackie: I remember pregnancy as a completely happy time— apart from the morning sickness. I was completely awestruck with the fact that we were producing a new human being. It was also amazing to me that we could have such luck in planning this pregnancy so that I could give birth during my summer vacation.

Dec. 8, 1968 I've been real lazy about writing letters lately, so that's why you haven't heard from me in a while. Most of my "free" time is in the evenings and for the past month I've been feeling sick in the evenings. At least my "morning sickness" comes only in the evenings now. And I've discovered that I can keep from vomiting if I keep my stomach full! So I eat a lot. Last week I saw the doctor again. I seem to be in good health. He prescribed Dramamine for the vomiting and iron pills for good measure. My women friends are so happy and excited when I tell them I am expecting. And they are full of advice! I'm gaining weight already, and I wonder how big I'm going to get.

Jan. 3, 1969 I was the one who told Bahman's mother about the expected baby. She smiled and seemed surprised. Later she said something about children being trouble but I didn't understand everything she said. Surprisingly, she and Bahman have never even discussed the subject, so I don't know what she really thinks. I usually find out her thoughts from Bahman's translations.

Bahman: So you told my mother about being pregnant, ha!

93

Jackie: Somebody had to tell them, you know! Now, you tell me why you didn't talk to your mother about the baby?

B: I don't remember any specifics at all. But I can vouch that what you told your mother was very likely true! We didn't talk about these things, you know.

J: This in spite of the fact that not only did you have to talk to your folks about getting married, but you had to fight for it. Why not talk about children, what was the difference?

B: I don't know, you caught me red-handed here! All I know is that we usually didn't talk unless it was really necessary. Maybe because we usually didn't get along and any discussion could often degenerate into squabbling or worse.

J: At any rate, do you think your mother was happy that I was pregnant?

B: I am sure she was. Any Persian (or anyone else, for that matter) would be happy to become a parent or grandparent. And if she told you something about children being trouble (which is true!), well it was just small talk.

J: I remember her preference for a boy, though!

B: Yes, as you know, that is true of many cultures and societies.

Jan. 23, 1969 We haven't gone skiing this winter because I'm not sure whether a pregnant woman ought to; I forgot to ask my doctor. In fact, I've thought of something you can send me. Can you find some paper-back book that tells what a pregnant woman ought to do and ought not to do? I've got about 5 months and 5 days left to wait, and I'm not sure what I'm supposed to do during this time. I borrowed one book from my doctor called *The New Childbirth* by Erna Wright (which you probably won't be able to find, since it was published in England) which includes lots of exercises to prepare you for "natural" childbirth. I think it would be grand to stay awake and see my child born, in fact my hospital specializes in natural childbirth. Sometimes this method is called the "Lamaze method" since it was developed by Dr. Lamaze. Can you find me a little book about it (maybe you want to call and ask Linda Scotch, since she's used this method and loved it). I have a copy of Dr. Spock's baby book already, but I'd like to read about what to do *before* the baby gets here.

Bahman and I expect our kids will be Iranian citizens. Anyway, they can always change citizenship later if they want to emigrate. But it's quite impractical to fly off to the U.S. every time I am going to have a baby. I'm surprised that you talk about the baby as "she"! Grandma Uzwiak and a couple of my friends have predicted a boy. This first baby doesn't make any difference to us, though Bahman says he wants a little girl who looks like me, and I tell him I want a little boy to look like him. I seem to be developing "maternal amnesia"—which means I think about this baby more than anything else these days!

B: Do you remember what your mother wrote you about children and American citizenship?

Jackie: Not exactly, but I suppose she thought only children born in the States could be citizens. Apparently, even I, at this early stage, was unaware of the great advantage U.S. citizens had in being able to pass their U.S. citizenship to their children no matter where the children were born. And only one parent had to be a U.S. citizen for that to be true. My British and German friends had different laws to contend with, and their kids didn't automatically receive their mother's citizenship.

Feb. 28, 1969 Now and then I can feel the baby moving inside, and it's quite exciting. I'm getting rounder and rounder little by little. I have two jumpers and one loose shift that fit me comfortably now. Yesterday I asked Morvarid (sister-in-law) if she could make me a new dress using the shift as a pattern, and she said yes. So I bought some inexpensive spring-weight material for her to try on. Already she has it cut and basted together. It already looks

95

so nice that I might get some fancier material and ask for another one!

March 13, 1969 I tried to remember what I wrote in my last letter that made you think I was "gallivanting around." Was it going to late movies? Well, we only go out at night when I can sleep late the next day. I don't expect to miss my freedom, as you say, when the baby comes since probably the best thing about living with in-laws is having an always-available set of baby-sitters. I even expect to work part-time at the university next year. I know it's important to get more rest these days though, and I've begun to sit down while teaching most of my classes, though the students are awfully noisy that way.

I found some books in the American library which tell about prenatal and baby care, and there is a friend (American married to a Persian) who loans me books on "natural childbirth." In fact, she is a nurse who teaches at a nearby hospital, and I've begun to attend her Thursday morning classes in order to practice the breathing and relaxation exercises involved in "natural childbirth." But I haven't yet received the book you sent. Did you send any patterns? Morvarid finished my new green dress, but it'll be the only Spring dress I have to wear for the next 3 months unless she or I make more.

B: Finally something good to say about in-laws, they make good baby-sitters! Have you discovered anything else good about them?!

J: Well, you notice at this point they are also willing and capable seamstresses, at least Morvarid was. I remember doing some sewing myself and came up with a maternity bathing suit—something that may have been a *first* in Iran!

By the way, my La Maze teacher was Susan, who remained a friend for years afterward and kept in contact when we both moved to California—different cities. She was also married to a Zoroastrian, but it seems their marriage, in the U.S., was easier to arrange.

April 13, 1969 I should be careful with all the delicious lunches I've been getting lately. I've already gained more than 20 lbs., and the doctor warns me to cut down on carbohydrates. I had some blood and urine tests today, so tomorrow I'll find out if I'm really healthy.
We bought a book last week which lists several hundred Persian names for boys and girls so we hope we can choose some suitable names before the baby comes.

B: Oh yes, choosing names, quite a project! I bet you have a lot to say about it, right?

J: Yes, I remember what seemed like hours spent together with you pronouncing the names from the Persian name book and me trying to decide if I liked it *and* if it was a name easy enough for my American relatives to relate to. One complicating factor was that you said we could not have any of the common Iranian names that were Islamic, so we were limited to the ancient Persian names. We finally came down to two good names. Ramin for a boy (from the ancient Persian love story of "Vis and Ramin") and Susanne for a girl (meaning "lily").
I remember you saying it was a common custom for a boy to be named after his deceased paternal grandfather, and I feared your relatives would insist on your father's name "Kaykhosrow" if we had a boy. Thank goodness that topic never came up!

B: I'm sure one of my mother's worries was that her grandchildren were going to be Americans with foreign names, and I bet she was relieved when we chose good ol' Persian names for our children.
J: Yes, I'm sure she was relieved. I remember suggesting that, like many of my friends, we could give our kids American middle names. But no, you said Persian kids didn't have middle names, so the names we chose were as close to American names as we could get, and easy to pronounce.

May 8, 1969 I've got 7 weeks left to delivery date, and I've become quite large (it seems to me, anyway) around the middle so that it's a little hard to find comfortable positions for sitting or sleeping. I prop myself with several pillows. I haven't gained much more than 20 pounds so far. I finished sewing myself a maternity blouse and skirt, and Morvarid finished another dress (in bright pink, yellow, and orange colors!) so I have 3 suitable outfits. Actually I've been feeling quite healthy lately, until last week when I caught a cold which has made me feel miserable this week. I'm trying to rest a lot, hoping this awful cold will leave quickly. Bahman caught the cold too, but it has mostly affected his voice.

Next week is supposed to be the last week of classes for my students but since they never come during the last week, I suppose we finished classes yesterday (thank goodness!). Now we have only to give final examinations to students until about the middle of June. Yesterday my students asked me what I would do if I went to the hospital before their exams were corrected! I said, "Don't worry I'll take the exams with me!"

Actually I've been waiting for classes to end so I could concentrate on getting things for the baby. So far, all we have is 6 diapers and a plastic baby chair. I hope it doesn't arrive early, or we'll be quite unprepared.

May 29, 1969 If everything happens on time, our baby should arrive in just one more month. I think the Iranian birth rate is one of the highest in the world. Last week, two of my Persian friends had babies, and I went to visit them in the hospital. *I* am planning to produce the most beautiful baby in the world, and I'm sorry you won't be here to see it! Two weeks ago I bought some cheap but lovely material and made myself another pretty maternity dress. This past week Bahman and I made a long curtain for our storage room so that part of it can become the baby's room. Now all our storage has been pushed behind the new curtain. There is another curtain which divides our room from the baby's room.

Bahman also had another good idea last week. Since none of our windows had screens, we were getting a lot of flies and mosquitoes inside. So he put up inexpensive tulle curtains as screens and we have practically no insects now!

I got rid of that cold I was suffering from, but this past week I've been miserable with diarrhea. I think it was something I ate in a restaurant last week. Unfortunately, this is the week our landlord has chosen to rip out the toilet and tear up the toilet room and shower room for pipe repairs! My doctor prescribed pills though, and I'm almost better.

J: Imagine being pregnant and having a torn up toilet! That was also the time when I learned much to my amazement that between the bricks and mortar of our building was dirt—plain old dirt—and our torn up bathroom was full of dirt.

June 17, 1969 With less than two weeks to wait until the baby's expected arrival, I'm getting impatient for it to come. The last time I wrote I think I had diarrhea . Well, that went away and I developed painful hemorrhoids. The hemorrhoids have become small and don't bother me, but now the doctor says my blood pressure is "slightly low" so I'm taking extra medicine with my iron pills. At times I'm a bit dizzy, but usually I feel quite good. The baby has turned with his head down—I expect a normal delivery.
At least my university work is finished. I cancelled my full-time contract and will probably work part-time in September (I seem to be worrying that the six of us won't have enough money to live on, but hopefully Bahman's inventions and projects will be successful). We bought a new crib and mattress and a new rug for the baby's room. I also have yards of material from the bazaar to make into diapers, crib sheets, and baby clothes.

July 2, 1969 No, this is not a birth announcement—not yet. The baby was "due" last weekend, but it still shows no sign of coming. I'm not worried though, since I read a few news articles in which some doctors say the traditional method of predicting a baby's arrival produces a date usually a week or so too early. The prediction method needs revision. Anyway, my doctor said if it didn't come by July 4th to come see him again. It would be nice if the baby waited as long as July 5th, so that I could go see the 4th of July fireworks at the American Embassy! But I am so bored and impatient with waiting and waiting. I hope by the time you get this letter, the baby has come.

Tehran's present heat wave has been miserable, especially for fat, pregnant ladies like me. For over a week the temperature has been between 95 and 100 with expectation for it to reach 104 soon. I miss swimming, so I take frequent showers, rest, read, drink cold drinks, and keep the fan going day and night. We often go for walks in the evening to look for a cool breeze and give me some exercise. With this big, barrel belly of mine, I guess I waddle when I walk. Bahman calls me his penguin!

Sunday, July 13, 1969 Well, this *is* a birth announcement, at last!!! We have an 8 lb. 15 oz. (1 oz. less than 9 lbs.!) son who was born about 1:30 a.m. this morning. He is 21 inches long and has black hair, of course. We are calling him Ramin (pronounced "rah-meen"). I'll write at least to Grandma Uzwiak and Grandma Martin, but you can have the pleasure of announcing your grandson to the rest of the relatives anyway you like.

As of yesterday, the baby was 2 weeks late and showed no sign of coming, so we went to the hospital anyway and the doctor decided to induce labor. I had a hormone solution dripping into my arm from 10 in the morning until the delivery. The solution really worked, and I had contractions so thick and fast I could hardly rest in between. Even with these, the doctor still had to rupture the membranes and even cut me in the delivery room to make a space large enough for the big baby to come out. Unfortunately the contractions got the best of me, so that my childbirth training only helped about half the time. I'm ashamed to admit that just before going to the delivery room I was really screaming. Once in the delivery room however, I started getting violent *pushing* contractions which were a little easier to control. So I pushed the gas mask away and insisted on watching the baby being born. A fat nurse helped me push it out, and finally they laid this warm wet baby on my stomach for me to see. I just touched his leg and said "My baby!"

Bahman was so helpful all during labor, encouraging me to relax and giving me light massage. At the delivery room door however, they sent him home to get some baby clothes (which the hospital doesn't provide)! So he just missed seeing his son born. They showed him the baby right afterwards though. When they wheeled me out of the delivery room, we talked a while. Then he went home for a few hours sleep and came back this morning with a basket of roses.

I didn't manage to sleep at all, but I feel good today and the head nurse says it hardly seems like I just had a baby this morning. The stitches across my bottom bother me a bit, but otherwise I can walk a bit, etc.

This letter was interrupted by visitors, and the nurse actually brought the baby in for me to show off (even though she had said I couldn't have him until tomorrow morning). He sure has a head full of hair. His face is rosy pink and white and chubby. His fingers are still grayish and seem long. At this point he doesn't seem to resemble Bahman or me or anyone!

Last week Isabel came over our house carrying a huge nylon net playpen which she said was a gift from you! What a lovely surprise! It's the nicest one I've seen in Iran. We certainly thank you.

I don't know what else to tell you now. Bahman and I are very happy.

Tell Lois she's an *aunt* now!

B: This business of the hospital sending me home to get baby clothes sounds fishy. Are you sure that was the real reason?!

J: I still find it incredible that a hospital wouldn't have sets of baby clothes or why they wouldn't have informed you of this well in advance! Do you think they just didn't want you in the delivery room? My guess is that, really, you didn't want to be there either!

B: Well I don't think I ever volunteered to be present in the delivery room, and I can sense elements of conspiracy in place here!

August 2, 1969 In your last letter you sound as excited about Ramin as we are! I was surprised to see that you opened such a large account for him. Thanks so much, but really *$8.15* would have been generous enough. Now what are you going to do for my next dozen children!? You'll go broke.

Actually, right now I don't see how anyone can care for 2 children when one is so much work. I am nursing him, for a few months anyway. One of my big problems started when my milk "came in." I developed hard, painful, engorged breasts, and it was a lot of hard work to get the milk out at first. Now one breast still bothers me. So every 2 hours I have to relieve my breasts and every 3 ½ to 4 hours I feed the kid. You can see I don't get much sleep this way. Also, I don't know what Ramin's problem is these days, but it often takes him 1 to 3 hours to get to sleep after a feeding! It's fine if he lies in his crib quietly, but very often he starts crying. It drives me crazy trying to find out what to do to make him sleep. On Friday night we were going to a wedding reception and Ramin decided to cry on and off for a couple of hours!

Ramin is 3 weeks old now and every time I look at his long dark hair, I'm reminded of Lois as a baby. When Ramin was born he had a face like a triangle; his head came to a point and his face was swollen from the eyebrows to his chin. Now he's changed and looks much more like a normal cute baby. I guess Isabel has met you by now and given you his picture. The triangle isn't so noticeable in that picture.

In the hospital I only had time and energy for one long letter and that was to you. I don't even remember what I said. Did I explain that in a Persian hospital, people that visit you are treated like guests in your house and you are supposed to offer them soft drinks, fruit, candy, etc. So in a room a little more expensive than the one I had, you have a telephone and a miniature refrigerator for the guest's food! Also all the private rooms have an extra bed so that the patient's mother can stay overnight with her—another Persian custom.

B: So you had already decided that taking care of even one child was too much, ha?

J: I remember telling my university colleagues, when they asked how many children I would like to have, that three or four seem a good size for a family. What a naive answer—when I didn't have any idea how much work even one baby would be!

B: Yes, but it is also said that the next ones would be easier! Now, I don't remember about the $8.15, and I'm surprised at the figure. Why that?

J: My Mom started a bank account for her grandchildren, of which I had the first, with an amount signifying their birth weight. So the 8 lbs. 15 oz. have been $8.15 in the bank. She deposited $81.50 and I thought that was a *lot* of money!

Sept.5, 1969 Sorry I haven't written sooner but I've been incredibly busy lately. I feel like I'm running a race but never reaching the end! I thought Ramin was taking up 99% of my time, but now I've had to go back to work at the university to proctor and correct makeup exams. (So far I haven't signed a contract for part-time work next semester.) Ramin is almost 8 weeks old now and growing fast. He drinks so much milk, but is always ready for more; so I've started giving him tastes of baby cereal. When he is on his stomach, he pushes with his arms and lifts his head and chest up for several minutes. He has flipped himself over on his back 3 times that I know of, so far. Also he's started making cooing noises. Everyone says "What a lot of hair!" Bahman says he didn't know little babies were so cute and so much fun. He loves talking to and playing with Ramin, and I think he's ready for more kids! But when Ramin cries, all the family here runs to pat him or pick him up—so he is going to be so spoiled.

Sept.27, 1969 We took Ramin for a DPT shot last Monday (age 10 weeks) and found that he is already 14 ½ pounds (and quite healthy). He gains more than half a pound a week. We're trying to finish our roll of the film so you can see how cute he is. In the pediatrician's waiting room a little girl came over to pat Ramin on the head, and he's so pretty that the doctor even thought he was a girl (or maybe it's just his long hair). He smiles a lot and laughs and makes baby "noises"—we think he's irresistible. But of course he's not *all* sweetness. He stays awake most of the day and most of that time he's hungry! I spend hours feeding him. For about a week now he's been taking cereal happily from a spoon. It's pretty messy especially when he sneezes. But what can you do with a kid that takes both breasts, an ounce of cereal, and four extra ounces of formula at a typical feeding? Also last week he learned to suck his thumb. It took him less than a day to learn that, but he learned it so well that he won't even accept a pacifier in place of the thumb now.

Oct. 19, 1969 Yes, I have a copy of *Dr. Spock* already. They sell it in Tehran, but I was foresighted enough to buy it in the U.S. last summer. I follow Dr. Spock religiously , and Bahman teases me about it since I'm always quoting "Dr. Spock says . . ."

In fact we followed Dr. Spock just yesterday in bundling Ramin off to the doctor. He seems to have developed diarrhea or at least watery bowel movements. The doctor prescribed several medicines, one of which looks like cocoa which we are to put in his formula. Incidentally, about two weeks ago I stopped breast-feeding Ramin. He was already getting more from the bottle than from me anyway.

Ramin doesn't act sick though: still smiles, gurgles, and plays. Last week he discovered that he has hands which he can use to reach out and touch things. He spends lots of time playing with his hands—but this new "talent" makes feeding him cereal difficult when he tries to grab the spoon (he eats 3 kinds of cereal and strained apples now). He manages to gurgle out most of his cereal too, if it doesn't have a little extra sugar. He's about 16 pounds now, which is just two pounds less than my friend's 10 month-old baby!

As one can imagine, in every letter home, Jackie would inevitably write something about "the baby." But since most of it would be familiar things (his first or third tooth, his first word, etc. etc.!), it is only reasonable to limit our reporting to the very special events.

Dec. 11, 1969 The doctor says we can start feeding Ramin meat this week. How I wish Gerber's Strained Meats were imported here! We have only the fruits and vegetables and the little jars cost 63 cents!! I'm looking around for a good blender to help me make baby food.

May 26, 1970 Ramin is on the brink of taking his first step (my in-laws, in fact, say he stepped last week) but he much prefers to hold on with at least one hand or to sit, then crawl. People tell me so often that he's a beautiful child, that I get a little embarrassed. One said yesterday that I could "put him up as an advertisement for mixed Persian-American marriages," he's so cute. Another lady said her son (2 months old) looked really like a baby but Ramin already looked like a little boy. Unfortunately I hear that beautiful children often become spoiled, and Ramin already gets an extra lot of attention.

June 26, 1970 Ramin enjoys the beach apparently. We went to the Caspian seashore in the North and stayed 2 nights in a motel on the beach early this week. It takes 5 or 6 hours to drive there because you have to go through the mountains, but the North is lovely and green. I'd never been there before but I love it; it reminds me of the US. Bahman and I got sunburned, but we kept Ramin covered better. He didn't especially like the noisy waves, but he loved playing in the sand. I hope we can go North more often.

* * * *
* * *

Let's leave the first baby on the side and meet the second one in the coming. The unexpected news appeared first in a letter as suspicion, and later as a fact.

March 8, 1971 I myself have been feeling uncomfortably pregnant lately. I certainly hope *not*, since this would put my second child seven months too early on my planned schedule. However, we have been careless with our birth control precautions so it is quite possible. Let you know for sure next letter.

April 9, 1971 I thought it was a long time since I had heard from you, but then I got your letter and noticed it took nine days for it to arrive here! Anyway, it seems that you can expect your second grandchild to arrive the first week in November, there seems to be little doubt about it now. I've been "evening sick" for weeks and weeks now (which didn't help me to enjoy my No-Ruz vacation). I guess I'm getting used to the idea of being pregnant again, but I dread the moment I have to tell my "boss" that I have to quit my job.

Would you check on the price of maternity girdle (large size?) for me. Maybe it's cheaper to order one from the U.S. than to buy it here. Also see what prices there are on maternity bathing suits if you see any.

It's been so springy and beautiful lately with the weather high in the 60's. We took Ramin to the park the last couple of days. He's younger than most of the kids there, but he enjoys running around after them. He's quite an imitator now. How he loves to "wash dishes," and today he tried "frying eggs" with an empty frying pan and spatula. He's putting up some resistance to toilet training though, usually he'll tell us *after* his pants are wet, not before. If one kid keeps me *so* busy, how in the world am I going to manage two?

B: I think we owe the readers an explanation. How come our plan didn't work this time?!

J: Well, I hate to admit that I am not supremely organized, but that *was* the case with our second pregnancy. Actually, after the first kid we had told the doctor we didn't mind if a second came along, since we did want more than one child. The timing was inconvenient only because of my job. No one ever told me that I was eligible for maternity leave in Iran. I always assumed I'd have to quit!

The Fruits of their Labor

May 30, 1971 Ramin looks good, as usual strong and healthy, and people are *still* telling me what a beautiful child he is. Last week a friend saw him for the first time and said, "Oh is that your little boy? How old is he? Three?" She was quite surprised when I answered, "He's not quite *two*." Ramin communicates quite well with the few words he speaks—sometimes he uses a Persian word when speaking to Bahman and then the English translation for me! He's about half toilet-trained now although we've been working on it for months.

Aug. 28, 1971 The doctor says I'm going to have another *big* baby. It's already good size. Fortunately I don't have any complaints about my condition other than minor ones (occasional hemorrhoids, etc.) and at least my hands and feet haven't swollen up like Isabel's. I'm the only pregnant woman who ever swims at the public pool where I take Ramin and I get a lot of stares and attention from the Iranian women who apparently have never seen a pregnant woman swim before! This pool is restricted to women only (and little boys under five) and all the public pools are segregated by sex.

Sept. 20, 1971 Ramin is getting more talkative all the time, everything now is "big" or "two" (more than one). One of his cutest phrases is "apple juice" which he says very quickly like "abu-joos." Some mornings he surprises me by saying "Mommy, pretty dress." He absolutely loves to eat thousand-island salad dressing, and so we have been putting it on any food he has decided not to eat, and it works like magic. Finally, he is beginning to tell us to take him to the potty *on time*. This is a lesson I've been trying to teach for 8 months or more , and at last he seems to be learning and cooperating.

This pregnancy is making me pretty bulky and awkward and now that the baby's head has turned downward, it is sometimes uncomfortable. I suppose the hemorrhoids are my worst complaint though. Also I'm getting bored of being home so much, and I wish I could go back to work (schools open this week). I suppose that when the baby finally arrives I will be *too* busy. I'm reviewing my lessons and exercises for "natural childbirth" and this time I hope to deliver without anesthesia and do a real *good* job at it!

Oct. 19, 1971 A group of 8 or 10 other wives with Persian husbands and I meet at each others' homes for coffee (and gossip) every other Sunday. Last Sunday they gave me a baby shower! What a lovely American custom I've been missing (Iranians don't have this tradition)! This baby is going to be well-equipped—especially since several people gave me sweaters. I also got diapers, a towel set, a box of Johnson & Johnson products, two sleepers, a baby thermos bottle, a *pink* receiving blanket, etc.

Nov 17, 1971 We got the idea to telephone you about the baby when Isabel had told us about her call, and then it seemed especially appropriate since your first granddaughter was born on your own birthday! It was early morning here (about 6:30 a.m.) on Nov. 15 when Bahman went down to the central phone exchange to put through the call. Happy Birthday!
We got the daughter we both wanted so much, and we were so surprised and happy! Aren't we lucky—a son and a daughter! She came at 1 a.m. on Nov. 14, and weighed 8 pounds, 4 ounces. She looks quite like Ramin did at birth with lots of black hair and a round, puffy face. She was a week late, of course, but labor occurred naturally this time. Bahman drove me to the hospital at 10 p.m., and I was unable to walk much because of the contractions every 3 minutes, but I was using the La Maze Method and managing the contractions nicely. I did a good job with the La Maze Method this time, and I was proud of my delivery. Of course, Bahman was a great help in reminding me to relax, and having a 3-hour labor kept me from getting exhausted. I was up and walking the next day, and today I'm going home.
We've named our daughter Susanne, which is both English and Persian. The middle "s" must be pronounced strongly in order to give it the right Persian accent. In Persian, "Susanne" means "daffodil." It is a very common name for

the daughters of mixed marriages here, but we both like it no matter how many others have it!

My obstetrician is the husband of Dianne, an American friend of mine (my baby shower was held at her house) and his partner is now our pediatrician. This pediatrician is a young, American-trained fellow who is very particular about details. I'm glad he's such a careful doctor, but he's going to make me a nervous wreck! The first day he visited the baby 3 times and ordered a chest x-ray because she was breathing too fast. They finally traced the rapid breathing to hyperventilation from the rapid breathing I used in the La Maze Method! Breathing soon became regular, but the 2nd day he noticed a fever and ordered antibiotics for the baby, and he decided she was too jaundiced and ordered blood tests! Well the baby looks much less yellow today, and if I can convince the fussy doctor that she has no blood disease, we can probably take her home today too!

Do you know who else was born on Nov. 14? Prince Charles of England and King Hussein of Jordan—it's quite a day for birthdays.

Nov. 19 – Well, the baby's color turned pink and white so we were able to take her home when I went home on Wed. Ramin was certainly excited. He kept running around the house, and talking a mile-a-minute. He wants to pet and kiss the baby and keeps bringing her his toys. The last couple of days though he seems extra mischievous and disobedient. Part of it is due to the stage of growth he's in now, but part of it may also be due to jealousy, so we are afraid to discipline him just now. He's become difficult to live with anyway.

The baby's easy to take care of. She just eats and sleeps and wets. *Except* between midnight and 6 a.m., which are her most wide-awake hours. We get much less sleep around here now. I phoned the pediatrician last night (as he requested) and he said a test of the baby's mucus shows a slight staph infection. It's nothing to worry about except if she shows signs of fever or acts sick. Then we should give antibiotics again. However, Susanne seems quite well and there's no fever. I'm sure she's healthy.

Dec. 17, 1971 Yes, it does seem pretty hectic around here at times with two kids to take care of. Ramin is sometimes jealous of my divided attention, and he's overly affectionate and concerned about Susanne to the point that sometimes he almost hurts her. Today we took photos of Ramin holding Susanne, and if they come out, they should be pretty cute. One problem we have now is that Bahman's sister doesn't like to baby-sit for *two* kids on those occasions we have to go out without them. Yesterday we went to a wedding and left her with both of them awake for the first time. We rushed home at 6:30 p.m. between the ceremony and the reception to feed the kids and put them to bed (leaking milk is the worst problem I have with breast-feeding). Last week we took Susanne in the carry-cot to the Square Dancing Club, and I suppose we'll have to carry her along to the two Christmas parties we're going to next week. I sewed myself an evening gown (never had one before) of gold and silver lame for the wedding reception and the parties. It cost a total of $8 to make, and I like it more than the $80 ones I was looking at in the department store last week!

Dec. 30, 1971 The American women's Club (700 members!) had a children's Christmas party , and I took Ramin last week. He loved the cartoons and the puppet show, but he was rather afraid of Santa Claus! Bahman and I have been to several Christmas parties too, and since Susanne wakes up frequently at night (colic, I think) we take her with us instead of leaving her with the in-laws. We've been to dinner parties at the Naficy's (my obstetrician), at Isabel's on Christmas Eve, and at the Square Dancing Club. I guess we won't go to a dinner-dance on New Year's Eve (sponsored by the Foreign Wives of Iranians Club) though, it's a bit of trouble caring for a wakeful baby at a party.
I'm anxious to go back to work part-time, but I suppose that means we'll have to find a maid for the kids since I'm sure the in-laws don't want to watch two kids. Fortunately you can find maids here for $30-$60 per month! I'll bet your 6 dogs cost you that much (?)

110

The Fruits of their Labor

Feb. 8, 1972 I was expecting to go back to teaching part-time so we hired a maid! I feel like a real lady of leisure now, though having a maid is very common here. Our maid, Mariam, works six days a week from 8 a.m. to 4 or 5 p.m. and baby-sits 2 nights a month. For this we pay her the equivalent of $53 a month. Believe it or not, that's a very high "American-style" salary. Most Iranian families pay their maids half of that. But we were in a hurry to hire a maid so we paid extra to get one that has lots of experience working for American families. Now the problem is to find a teaching job in the middle of the school year—a more difficult problem than I expected. Most places have full staffs already. I was about to accept a position at Iran Girl's College, when the old teacher decided not to quit after all. So I'm still unemployed and staying home. The maid does all the housework and since our apartment is so small, she cleans the entire place every day (things are going to wear out!). I get to feeling uncomfortable with her so busy and me with so little to do. Of course there's Susanne to feed, etc. and Ramin to entertain while the maid's cleaning; I'm spending as much time with them as before, but now my house is clean too.

March 5, 1972 I don't get as much time to write now. I finally got a job about 3 weeks ago at the Iran Girls' College. The teacher who wanted to leave finally made up her mind and left!
Our maid is quite good and rather *too* clever. She's complained again that Ramin is too mischievous and that in her previous job she had only one child for more pay. So, in order to keep her, we've had to raise her salary to about $60 a month. Now she's happy. Next year I expect Ramin will go to nursery school mornings, and Susanne can stay downstairs with the in-laws, so we won't need a maid.
Already I've checked four English-speaking nursery schools, tomorrow one more. It costs over $250 to send a kid to a half-day nursery for nine months. I want to be sure to find a good one for Ramin. Incidentally, Ramin seems to be less negative these days, so I hope, by next summer, he'll be

tolerable to live with again and won't turn your house upside down.

Susanne is her usual cheerful self. She smiles a lot, and at everybody—it's the most beautiful thing to see. Today she laughed aloud. This week I'm taking her off breast-feeding. She has been an impatient and fussy nurser, though she drinks contentedly from a bottle. For weeks now she's been getting more from the bottle than from me anyway. She's 15 pounds and 25 ½ inches long. Included are two photos—the month-old one is for you and the earlier one is for Grandma Uzwiak. Did you get the three photos I sent, two letters ago? Please tell me when the photos reach you, as I'm always afraid that they get lost in the mail.

I was teaching Ramin to say his age, and I thought he learned it really well. But then he *showed* me what he has actually been saying. He put his hands up to his ears and instead of "Two years old," he says "Two ears hold"!!!

March 29, 1972 Ramin chatters away in three languages—though not perfectly yet. He speaks to me in English, to Bahman in Persian, and to Bahman's mother and sister in Dari (the Zoroastrian language). It's real cute to hear him translate: for example, he will say something to me in English then repeat it in Persian to Bahman to make sure everybody understands! I've enrolled him in an English-speaking nursery school for half-days beginning next September.

May 14, 1972 School ends this week and we've decided to let our maid go. We can't seem to get used to having her around all day especially when we are in the house (our house is too small). Besides she doesn't care to watch two children especially since she can't seem to get Ramin to obey her. Next year Ramin will be in nursery school mornings and Susanne can stay downstairs with Bahman's mother and sister.

B: I was waiting for an opportunity to cut in between the long letters and offer the readers a break. And this seems to be a good place to do it by asking you to comment on the maid situation—I am guessing that you've got something to say!

J: I remember having a hard time finding a maid. The one we had before Mariam would just clean and leave before I got home. Getting Mariam was good for us for a while. I wish your folks had agreed to watch both kids and we wouldn't have needed a maid. At one point, didn't we take Susanne to your other sister's home to be cared for?

B: As usual, I don't remember! And to be fair, I think my folks would've really had a hard time taking care of both a baby and a "terrible two!"

Oct. 11, 1972 Ramin cried when I left him at nursery school the first week but otherwise seemed all right, only being shy, during the mornings. We spent four nice days at the Caspian seashore, and then Ramin went back to school but started crying during class, wouldn't drink his juice or eat his cookies, wouldn't use their toilet, etc. After 2 weeks the teacher had a talk with me and said Ramin had not spoken or smiled in all that time! She said he was very unhappy in school and finally, last week the school asked me to take him out because he hadn't adjusted. Do you remember how long it took him to speak to you and especially to Lois? Well, it was like that in school—not a word to anyone! We kept him home for several days (though my in-laws have a difficult time with 2 kids) until we decided what to do. Well, today I started him in a much smaller school—only 2 classes in a house and only 23 kids altogether. The school is on the Montessori method, and so kids learn lots of practical things like how to button buttons and polish their own shoes, etc. Of course Ramin cried a bit and didn't talk, but the most fun for him was the ride in the little school bus to come home. Ramin still loves buses, and I guess I made a mistake to take him to that other nursery school and pick him up myself, because he always wanted to ride on the bus. We're trying out this school now to see how he "adjusts" there.

Susanne walks pretty well now, though she still plops to the floor quite often. She walks more than she crawls anyway. She really toddles like a wind-up doll. It's a cute stage to watch. She can also clap her hands (when anybody sings), wave "bye-bye," shake her head "no" so vigorously that she sometimes falls down, and imitate certain sounds. What really amuses and surprises me is that she plays with the pots and pans in the kitchen cupboard and then shoves them all back in and closes the door before she leaves! She neatly stores her toys in strange places too.

Oct. 29, 1972 Did I mention that we put Ramin in a new school called "Tehran Nursery and Kindergarten"? Last week he brought a note from the teacher, and I was afraid he'd been expelled again, but *no*! the note said that after 10 days of school Ramin started talking (in Persian) and playing with the other children and seemed much happier. The last few days Ramin has been quite cheerful about going and even asks about the school bus on holidays.

Dec. 8, 1972 Susanne enjoyed the birthday card (and Ramin recognized it as a poodle) in fact, she "loved it" to death!.
I was suggesting that it would be nice to get a pizza to eat at home, when Ramin surprised me by saying "God made pizza." I asked him how he knew that, and he said "God made a fish," pointing to our goldfish, and later "God made sun." So, I'm wondering what else he's learning in that nursery school, since I haven't yet mentioned God to him myself!

Jan. 20, 1973 People who have seen Susanne say she is certainly an "active" child; which means she can climb on all the chairs in the house now! We've had to move the telephone because we can't keep her away from it! She picks up the receiver and says "A-yo." She has two toy telephones, which are not as interesting. She also says "ah" for "hot" when she is near the heater, but still her favorite word is "Daddy"—for everyone! Her favorite activity is going out, and she gets real happy and starts waving "bye-bye" as soon as she realizes anyone is going to take her out.

We seldom *walk* outside though, since it's been *so* cold here.

Aug. 22, 1973 Ramin's school let out two weeks ago, and I'm going crazy trying to find things to keep two kids at these ages busy. Ramin can always play with clay, look at books, or draw pictures (he prints his name without help now) but Susanne can't sit still and she always bothers him. She also knows enough English to argue with him and they seem to enjoy fighting until Susanne ends up crying. It's still too hot to play outdoors much.

I've been taking my kids to visit all my friends' kids, and we go to the public swimming pool about once a week. Just recently we discovered a nice club called the Society for Iranians Graduated Abroad. It has a wading pool and a swimming pool, lots of nice grass (rare in Tehran) and trees to sit under for picnics, and dues are less than $10 per year! We plan to go there more often. We did spend four nice days at the Caspian seashore—a mini vacation trip.

Nov. 10, 1973 Ramin seems to like school more this year. He's learning to put letters together to form words now. He's less shy and in fact, is often mischievous and sometimes gets into fights in school. We went hiking in the mountains yesterday for the first time this Fall and took Ramin. He enjoys it and keeps up quite well. His greatest fun is running down, laughing all the way. Susanne is cute and clever. Her understanding and her vocabulary amaze and amuse us. I imagine she's a bit spoiled though. I think I might give her a *small* party next week.

I took the kids to a Halloween party last week. It was at a club and was held by the Foreign Wives of Iranians. What a mob of kids! There must have been a hundred or more there. We carved pumpkins for the first time this year, but there's no "Trick or Treating" here in Iran.

Jan. 3, 1974 I'm anxious for summer to come so you can see your grandchildren. Ramin is a great deal less shy (and a mischief-maker in school sometimes) and though his speech is not completely clear (can't pronounce "l" or "r") his

115

vocabulary is quite good for his age. And you can imagine the changes in Susanne!—a real doll who's clever, talkative, and affectionate. Sometimes these two are good playmates and then other times - - - ! But you'll enjoy them both, I know.

Feb. 9, 1974 Susanne learns so many new things, it's fun to watch her. She's out of diapers in the daytime now and uses the toilet by herself. She also puts on her own panties and slacks, always asking "This way? This way?" At lunch or dinner she carries in the (plastic) dishes, spoons, and forks and sets the table for us. We bought Ramin a little record player and Susanne very soon learned to use it, even changing speeds for the different records. When she's feeling happy she hugs me and says "I lub you." I wonder why Ramin was never so affectionate. He used to squirm away from hugs or kisses, but now he seems to enjoy them more since he sees that Susanne enjoys them. Ramin has started asking continuous questions beginning with "Why." What a challenge for a mother to answer them all.

B: Did you really expect Ramin, a boy, to be as affectionate (and say "I lub you") as your daughter?! You've had trouble encouraging your husband to do that!

J: Little boys don't naturally resist affection. I think either they learn it somehow or it's a personality thing. I'll bet *you* were an affectionate little kid; our grandson is!

B: Are you saying that boys and girls, or men and women, as groups are intrinsically equally affectionate?

J: Yes, at least potentially so!

B: Well, I don't completely agree, but let's move on and leave the issue to the experts!

April 11, 1974 I took the kids to an Easter party today sponsored by the Foreign Wives of Iranians Club I belong to. They hunted for Easter eggs, played games, and ate as much as they could hold. Last week the Club held a White Elephant Sale and I sold about $10 worth of stuff and bought about $20 worth of American clothes, etc. I have a great time at these second-hand sales (twice a year) because I can buy everything that strikes my fancy, and still not feel that I'm splurging. In fact, I never buy Iranian clothes for me and the kids, and I really don't need to, except for kids' shoes. I can't wait 'til this summer when I can get back to the Stamford and Darien Thrift Shops!

B: There have been several references in your letters about the Foreign Wives of Iranians Club. I think it is high time for an explanation.

J: I remember seeing announcements of meetings of the FWIC when I first arrived in Tehran, and I joined in 1968, right after our wedding, when I was eligible for membership. Of course, any nationality was welcome, and there were women from other countries as members. However, the meetings were held in English at the Iran-America Society, so most of us were American women, which was probably a fair representation of the foreign wife population as a whole.

So many women I knew from the Club relocated to the U.S. after the Revolution and kept in touch with each other. In 1994, the FWIC held its first reunion in Las Vegas. We all met in Hilton coffee shop and burst into loud laughter as one former wife made a grand entrance as she swept into the shop in her *chador*! And we have been holding annual reunions ever since.

May 25, 1974 Even Ramin is getting excited about coming and asks very often when we are going. He says he remembers one time when you were cooking and you told him the food was "Yum, yum"! Another day he said he had a long dream about going to Grandma's house (your mother). I asked "Grandma?" and he said "Yes, that *old* lady."

We've been getting outdoors more now that the weather is nice and the days are longer. The kids are in the sandbox daily, and we got a small bike for Ramin so that Susanne could take over the tricycle. We've been to a horse show, the zoo, and to several parks lately. We ought to be able to start swimming sometime soon. Bahman and I went to another outdoor pot luck supper with the Foreign Wives of Iranians Club and this week our square dance club is having a pizza party dance on a rooftop (rooftops here are all flat!)

I've got both kids on a waiting list to get into a new English-speaking school, Central School, next fall. If they get in, Susanne will be in nursery (every morning she wants to go with Ramin, already) and Ramin in kindergarten.

August 29, 1974 Now it's evening, after the birthday party. The kids had a great time. After Susanne spilled red Kool-Aid down her white dress, I said, "You're a sloppy little girl, aren't you?" and she answered cheerfully, "Yes, I'm sloppy. Nanny told me that I'm sloppy!"

Sept. 25, 1974 Ramin and Susanne have had three days of school. I drove them to this new school (Central School) the first day. Ramin entered his kindergarten class with only a bit of shyness, and I was happy to see that his teacher is a lady that I know from the Foreign Wives of Iranian's Club. Susanne gave me a big, clinging hug as we entered her class, but immediately agreed to sit with the other children (only one was bawling his head off!). Then she put the little purse she insisted on carrying on the seat next to her and began playing with blocks as I said "good-bye." What an easy start compared to Ramin's first day 2 years ago! She says she likes the school, and she's enthusiastic about going in the mornings. Even Ramin likes it. Bahman says it's so nice to see two cheerful kids getting on the mini-bus, smiling, and waving good-bye in the mornings. They both have half-a-day school in English. Today Susanne said she cried a bit because she wanted Ramin to be in her class!

Nov. 1, 1974 Yesterday was Halloween for us "foreigners" here. The Foreign Wives of Iranians Club had a party for the kids which also included a route through the city of houses that would be open for "trick-or-treating." Both my kids wore pillowcases with holes to be ghosts but Susanne took her costume off after the third house (what a lot of driving around the city!). The kids also wore their costumes to a Halloween party at school on Wednesday—I wonder what Iranians thought seeing all these kids dressed up funny? There's no holiday like that in Iran.

Last week was pretty hectic. The Iranian government is taking over almost all schools (5 yrs. and up) to provide free education even in the formerly private schools. So several PTA meetings were held to explain the complications in switching over. (Hopefully Ramin will still be taught in English in a *small* class, but we don't know.) The pre-school section, where Susanne is, was going to be closed completely, but the parents got *very* upset. Most of us agreed to pay extra (about $260 *more*) and to volunteer to help the school. Last week, for two afternoons I watched and "taught" a class of 16 pre-schoolers as my volunteer effort. It was interesting but tiring after a morning of teaching college kids.

Feb. 21, 1975 Susanne decided today that she wanted to learn to print her name though the only letter she could mange was a crooked sharp-angled "S." So she got a pen and paper and sat next to me (I was correcting my students' papers) and kept asking me how to make the letters and then "What comes next?" until she learned to print it fairly well. I didn't think a kid her age could manage it and she really surprised me. She was so proud and happy, she practiced it again and again for about 40 min. and didn't want to stop for lunch!

One of Ramin's projects today was to sew two buttons on a piece of cloth. He wanted to make a collar but at the end he said it was an ant-catcher. He said when an ant walked on the cloth he would turn the button over on top of it! He complained that our house has no ants so I told him he could catch the cockroaches instead! (Do you keep my letters? This ought to make pretty funny reading in about 20 years!)

J: Now that was a prescient comment about reading my letters 20 years later and laughing at them! I tried to give my Mom the feeling of being part of her grandkids' lives by writing her as many of their cute sayings as possible. I even put together a few of them and sent them off to the *Reader's Digest* in hopes of publication (which never happened). One that we've repeated in our family over the years was this:

"Can parents assume their emphasis on cleanliness is taking effect when it pops up at unexpected times? Our 4-year-old daughter arrived home from nursery school and insisted her teacher had said, "Tomorrow is George Washing-hands' birthday!"

B: OK, I don't want to burst your bubbles but remember that everyone can cite funnies from kids and we shouldn't overdo the reporting here!

June 28, 1975 Ramin graduated from kindergarten and the school had a cute graduation program where the kids sang and recited poems. The school might become completely Persian next year, so again I have the problem of finding a good English school with room enough for my kids. Every year a school problem! I put the kids in a "summer school" only two blocks away for July & August. An Indian lady has a kindergarten in her home every morning with kids of several nationalities. In the afternoon I frequently take them to a swimming pool.

August 6, 1975 The kids love to swim (or splash). Ramin learned to swim a short way, but underwater. We go to at least one swim party at a friend's pool each week, and then a couple times to the pool at our club. When Susanne wakes up in the morning she usually asks "Well, where are we going today?" and often she's disappointed to hear it's "Summer School!"

I just remembered a joke. Last week Susanne stared a long time as my friend nursed her baby by the side of the pool. Later when I was changing my bathing suit she looked at me carefully and asked, "Do you have milk too?" I answered, "No, no milk," and she replied "Well, wadda ya got? Coffee?"

Sept. 19, 1975 School for the kids is a big problem for us again. The director of Central School (where the kids are registered) quit last week and the school has been turned over to the government for administration. This means the quality of the school will probably go down and so far I don't think they've found any native speakers to teach the English part of the program (Ramin is entering first grade and should have English in the morning and Persian in the afternoon). They announced that they will not have bus service this year which means a lot of extra driving for me. But the worst part is that they will have classes only for 5 year-olds and up so Susanne is left with no school, especially since every other bi-lingual class in the city is full. It's too bad because Susanne is eager to start school again (and she reads quite well now—first grade level!).

I remember another anecdote to tell you about Susanne. This one I think is funny enough to belong in a newspaper under "Cute sayings." Bahman and I were going shopping and the kids were going to stay home with their aunt. We were saying "good-bye" and Susanne told me, "I'm not going to cry when you leave. Really. So if you don't hear anybody crying, it's me."!!

Oct. 12, 1975 The kids' school started with some confusion as to whether Central School would even reopen. Happily everything has worked out, and last week they even started providing bus service so I don't have to drive the kids back & forth. Ramin studies English in the a.m. and Persian in the p.m. and gets a couple of pages of Persian homework which takes him *hours* (!!) to finish because he hates to sit in one spot and keep at it. It's only copying work. Susanne has only the a.m. program and the same teacher she had last year, whom she likes. So far the government is paying for Ramin's schooling but pre-school for Susanne is about $600, with transport for the two of them about $300.

A couple of weeks ago I took the kids to the dentist for the first time. Ramin bravely got a tooth filled and even seemed to enjoy it, but Susanne said she didn't like the dentist and wouldn't get in his chair. Yesterday we went again and Ramin just as nicely got another tooth filled, and Susanne climbed in the chair and opened her mouth for inspection. The dentist praised her and said he'd work on her next time since it was best to go slowly with fearful children. But as Susanne was getting down she asked me "Why he didn't put silver in my teeth?" The dentist said, "You want it?" she said "yes" and hopped back in the chair for a drilling and filling without complaint. Monkey see, monkey do!

Jan. 9, 1976 Persian schools have examinations and report card marks even for little kids. Ramin got his first report card last week for his Persian lessons and we were proud and happy to see that he got the highest mark (20) equals to "A" in each of his 7 Persian subjects.
Susanne's cute saying of the week: She couldn't put her pajamas on because they were inside-out, so she said, "Mommy, please un-inside-out these for me!"

May 9, 1976 I'm hoping this year I won't have the headache of children's schooling to deal with again—I expect to keep them in the same bilingual school and pray that the program doesn't change much. The only problem I see is that Susanne is already reading 1st grade books and yet she will only enter kindergarten next year.

Nov. 17, 1976 I consulted with Susanne's school about the fact that kindergarten is too easy for her, since she's been reading for more than a year already. They agreed and now each day Susanne goes to the 1st grade class for an hour of reading with them.

March 17, 1977 Susanne enjoyed the letter you sent her in simple language. Did you get her second letter? She's waiting for an answer for that one too! She had mumps last week—at least I was pretty sure it was mumps since she was exposed to several cases of it. But her mumps, like her chicken pox, was very mild, thank goodness. Only pain and slight swelling for three or four days—not even any fever. The hard part was getting her to stay home from school and rest as the doctor had suggested. Ramin had mumps vaccine years ago which apparently is still effective, since he didn't get sick.

Last week I registered Ramin in an American Cub Scout den. After 2 den meetings, he seems to like it. It's such a good activity for boys, and I think the slightly older boys will be a good influence on Ramin.

J: Susanne's early reading and obvious enthusiasm for school led us to believe that she would be more motivated and content by being challenged in a class with other kids reading at her level. She also was advanced in arithmetic. I remember asking the school to move her up a grade (acceleration--a technique I learned in my USC classes at NIOGATE and later used as the basis of my doctoral dissertation). We were told we needed the permission of the Ministry of Education and I actually remember going to the Ministry to present our case. Susanne's test scores were persuasive. She was allowed to skip first grade and start school in second grade with the school year that began in the fall of 1977.

B: That was a mouthful; I forgot to ask for a nutshell!

Oct. 27, 1977   Last week Susanne joined an American Brownie troop. She's so happy—she's wanted to be a scout ever since Ramin joined Cub Scouts last spring. Her first Brownie meeting was one big birthday party for the four girls who had birthdays in October. And next week it will be a Halloween party.

Susanne's class starts ballet lessons in school tomorrow. She has an outfit for it, but the school says bring pink tights and Susanne has every color but pink. People tell me that things get through the mail tax-free if sent in manila envelopes. So let's try an experiment. If you can buy some pink tights size 6X and air mail them to me in a manila envelope, we'll see if they arrive OK, OK?

June 20, 1978   The kids are out of school now and I've enrolled them in a day camp program sponsored by the American Women's Club. It's only 3 mornings a week but they have gymnastics, arts and crafts, woodworking, etc.

they seem to be really enjoying it. They make something new every day.

Sept. 30, 1978 The school where Ramin and Susanne go seems more organized. The only thing that bothers me there is that Susanne's teacher is untrained and inexperienced, but Susanne likes her and that's important. The teacher also likes Susanne and says she works so quickly she has time to help other students in class.

Nov. 3, 1978 Ramin and Susanne have school as usual though. This past week they've had two Halloween parties and Brownie Scouts have a late one next Sunday. Ramin joined a new Cub Scout Den near our new house and Susanne is taking ballet lessons after school. On Halloween we carved pumpkins and I baked a pumpkin pie. The only thing missing this year was trick-or-treating.

Chapter Five

A Place to Call Home

Housing became a problem first for Bahman when he returned to Iran in March of 1967. Then it was Jackie's turn to face housing difficulties when she had to live by herself in Tehran for four months before they got married. Even after they were married the problem didn't disappear altogether. In his first letter to her, he writes,

He: 3/14/67 The first thing I realized was that I can't live in this house for more than a few days—it is unbearable. So, right away, I *declared* my intention of finding an apartment and moving out, which is not very sensible to most of my people because it is free here. But I have the last word anyway, and started to inquire about houses. For your information and comfort I list three things here. My brothers-in-law (one or both) have gas stove (like American's), TV, couch and furniture, beautiful rugs, bathtub and shower, ice box, etc. Almost everything is available here—only needs money! You can guess that I haven't mention you to them yet, but I haven't forgotten (!) it either. I wish we could find a place and move by No-Ruz [Persian New Year starting on March 21]. Then it is the time to break the news and campaign for my second intention [wanting to marry Jackie].

Yes, such wishful thinking, finding a place and move into in seven days! As it turned out it took almost four months to find an apartment and move. But let us not get ahead of events. In his next letter a week later, he is more subdued:

He: 3/20/67 We have been looking for apartments, but so far no luck. Actually, we (four of us and my second sister, her husband and two kids—living here) decided to rent two apartments in a building and move in, to be of help to each other. Of course this shouldn't interfere with our independence. I feel that the more my family can take care of itself, the better is for you (us). Write me if you have any comments. We'll start apartment hunting next Saturday again. We'll be lucky if we could move out by the end of the 2-week No-Ruz holidays.

And a couple of weeks later he writes, "We are still apartment hunting, but the vacation is over and we are not in a big rush." And the hunting would have to continue for a long time to come. In the meantime, she interjects with some of her own ideas and concerns.

She: 4/2/67 I imagine it will be difficult to find *two* suitable apartments to move your family into. I also imagine that if I have *some* small authority in directing my own household, and if we have *some* privacy and independence, that it won't matter how many relatives are around. The hardest thing for me to get used to is having relatives right in the same apartment—but I guess I have accepted and agreed to that much already.

He: 4/22/67 Hearing a couple of suggestions (including Dr. Yaganegi's) and considering my folks' attitude, it seems more sensible to have a "2-section" house. There is a reasonable 5-room 2-story house, but not very modern and fancy. Each floor has its own "services." Would you prefer this over a more modern one-story apt.? Of course we would be sharing things (like food, chores, etc.).

She: 5/28/67 I have a couple of questions: Isn't it unusual that you are not actively apartment hunting for *something* when the place you are in now you described as "unbearable"? Is it going to be possible for you to leave your job for a while in order to come to America to be married? Have you planned that much? When (if?) I see you again you will not be able to say I look like a little girl— I'm wearing my hair now so that I have no more bangs!

As I mentioned in the letter you didn't receive: I very much like the idea of a two-section house. It might be the most peaceful way to exist at least for a while. If I have time I may try to rewrite the letter you did not get.

And so it goes. Many factors contributed to indecision and failure in moving to a better place. He sums it all up in the following letter.

He: 6/6/67 My folks don't like our moving out of this house—with *some* sound reasons. My income is not high enough now and rent is high. I am waiting for some reasonable excuses to start apt. hunting and to convince them about it. These are : 1) The payment of my salary starting this year (I haven't told them yet)--$150 [a month]. 2) I might get a degree of promotion—about $20 in addition. 3) Preliminary steps for the contract of my position as assistant professor. 4) Getting close to summer vacation and having more free time necessary for moving out. 5) My reasons for needing a nicer place to live and receive my friends. Any number of these are enough for me to start apt. hunting again—I hope in a couple of weeks. Yes dear, it is not comfortable to live here, but it is not as bad as used to be in the beginning, and I have gotten more accustomed to it now. Also I should avoid giving them the impression that moving out is for your sake. Also dear, it is easy to get time off for our marriage—such an important event; so don't worry about this point.

Oh dear I liked and will like your bangs. I hope you have not changed your hair permanently!

Jackie: Maybe this is a good point to ask you to tell us a bit about the house your folks, and later you, for a few months, lived in.

Bahman: The house was very old and belonged to Dr. Yaganegi and we were not paying any rent. It was constructed, as was usual in Iran, with bricks and plaster, had several large rooms with high ceilings, but with primitive facilities. My second sister and her husband and two children were also living there at the time and they lived there for a few more years after we moved out. The house was sold after the Revolution and became a shopping center. It is located in the center of Tehran, a very crowded and busy area.

J: Yes I remember that place. Your sister and her family had a large back yard and raised chicken there. The house was old and in disrepair, but their guest/living room had a large beautiful Persian carpet which transformed the old room—as Persian carpets do.

On June 19 he wrote, "Since last Thursday I've started apt. hunting again—no luck yet. My folks have 'necessarily' accepted to move." And her response a few days later was:

She: 6/27/67 So you are apartment hunting again! Now that our plans are changed, I thought perhaps you would wait until I got there, so I could have some choice in our future home. I have fears that your mother will have the new apartment organized the way she likes and will resent my interference even more than if we all moved in together and adjusted together.

What is the young man supposed to do? To move or not to move, that is the question! But not to worry, he's got all the necessary explanation up his sleeves. But before she gets that response, in a letter we saw before and dated 6/29 he declares, "Finally, today we agreed upon renting an apt. It is located on the second floor of the house in which Reza is living on the 3rd floor! It has 4 fairly big rooms, kitchen, phone, etc., and we can sign the contract and move in toward the end of next week—hopefully." Several days later he sends her a postcard with a beautiful view of Tehran, saying:

> He: 7/8/67 It is 2 p.m. Saturday now and I'm resting a bit. We moved out (and in) yesterday—a very busy day. It is a pretty nice place—for 600 tomans [about $75] a month. Now I am going to get some basic necessary households. I'll write you a long letter very soon—when I get a "long" chance!

But her response that we saw previously was not very enthusiastic and was full of questions. Here is a sampling in her letter of July 9, "I hope your family and you enjoy your new apartment. Perhaps I can be more enthusiastic about it if and when I ever see it. . . . Whatever happened to the plan for a 2-section house that you wrote me about? I am hoping that your letter to me this week will explain why you decided it was necessary to move *now*."

And now here is the letter that will hopefully explain everything.

> He: 7/15/67 Now about the apartment. 1) As you know it wasn't easy to live in that house. The living condition was very low and it was a temporary place for me to stay since I arrived. 2) In my calculations (!) postponing your visit from June to Sept. did not mean postponing our moving until after you arrived. In other words I want to receive you in a nice place. 3) Most important of all, in my opinion moving out was the first step toward the rest of our plans—to get the consent of my folks. I have to show them some power, decisiveness, organization, manhood (!), etc. I have to get control over things and be the boss—and this was a big try and a *success*. No dear don't worry, *I* have organized the apt. In the past week I've been organizing and purchasing some *essential* things like a refrigerator, a bookcase, chairs, and so on. And of course I am always having you in mind, there will be so many things and occasions for you to have your choice. The idea of getting a 2-section house was brought up before our plans changed, i.e. I could do that if they knew you would become a part of the family. But under the present condition, there was no excuse to look for

such a place. On the other hand the lease is only for one year, being able to cancel it after 6 months by paying one month of extra rent.

There! This should placate her, and it apparently did because we don't hear anymore complaints after this! And by the way, upon her request, he dutifully enclosed a detailed sketch of the apartment in his letter. Real nice job! Her response was again full of questions, albeit cheerful ones: "I especially enjoyed your sketch of your new apt. Apparently bedrooms are living rooms, but what is the guestroom for? One whole room for storage?! It certainly looks like the plan of someone accustomed to living in one room all his life!" They really have a lot to learn from each other and about their different cultures! So he helps her learn. Here are some bits of comments in their subsequent letters:

He: 7/28/67, 7/29/67 Today we gave a lunch party—like 'your' dinner party. The guests were my sisters and their families and my cousin—about 14 people in all. The get-together was because of our moving to a new place. We had chelo [rice], chicken, and eggplants. And of course "your place was vacant" here.
Well, guestroom is where you take the guests into—it is customary here. Usually one doesn't do other things there unless something like watching TV and so on. The storage room is not only for that and may become for any other thing. Right now, the hall is our dining place, but all these arrangements may change if there is a sensible reason!

She: 8/8/67 The pictures of your new apartment came out fine (so many of them!). The "yard" is more formal than I imagined it and I am curious about that low building at the end of the yard. The light-colored bricks look clean and new though. I am anxious to really *see* it.

* * * *
* * *

A Place to Call Home

We now leave Bahman, his family and their new apartment aside for a while and see where Jackie would live in exactly the four months that she had to live alone before they got married.

She arrived in Tehran on the evening of Sept. 8, 1967 and went to Hotel Sina, which had been reserved for her, and stayed there for two nights. Since there is no written account of the details of those two days, let us appeal to memories of the present.

B: I can only recall one funny thing happening that first evening which was also surprising: The hotel's regulations didn't allow me to come up with you to your room because we weren't married!

J: Wow! That was a culture shock! You did finally convince the hotel that you needed to carry my bags up to my room, which you did. Apparently the few moments in my room of hugging, kissing and greeting each other after being apart was too long for the hotel staff who reminded you of the regulations when you returned to the lobby. Just think if the Islamic laws of today had been in place then, you could have been arrested!

In Jackie's first letter home on Sept. 10, we saw her writing about renting a room. About a couple of weeks later, she wrote:

Oct. 3, 1967   You would really be surprised to see the houses in Tehran, especially the ones in the north near the University. *All* the houses are surrounded by high stone or brick walls. The houses themselves are stone, brick, or concrete too, but all are extra-modern. They all have courtyards and beautiful ceiling-to-floor windows. Everyone has a garden pool and *most* have their own swimming pools! There are many rich people in Tehran (*and* most send their kids to my University if they stay in Iran to study).

Yes, she was describing houses where rich people lived, such daydreaming! Listen to her real life story in her next letter a few days later:

Oct. 12, 1967 I wrote you last week just before I had to move out of my one-room apt. Well, that terrible landlady wanted me to move on Sunday (after *four* weeks instead of the *one month* I paid for). Anyway I couldn't stand living near her anymore, so I decided to move on Sat. Unfortunately there were no apts. advertised in the paper last week or the one that was, was said to be "taken" by the time we got there to look at it. We telephoned Pension Soroya (a kind of rooming house) and they said they had a room open. So I packed all my things, and Bahman went and borrowed his friend's car. I put everything in the car, and then we had one more terrible argument with the landlady about expenses (this landlady was unbelievable— argued with anyone and everyone!). Well, we drove to Pension Soroya but when we got there they said there were no rooms available! How frustrating—I was all packed and had no place to live. It was 9p.m. but decided to try Pension-Swiss. Fortunately they had one room open—their tiniest cheapest room (it was about the size of a large closet) for $7.50 a day, room and board. I stayed there only 24 hours. The next day the English language newspaper had the same ad for the apt. that we had been told was taken! Well, we went to look at it, and I decided to move in right away. It's a bit more expensive than where I was ($80 per month plus water, heat, and electricity) but small furnished apts. are rare, and this one is kind of nice. I have a large living room-bedroom, a small dining area with a refrigerator, and the smallest kitchen and bathroom I have ever seen. They look like they were designed for a trailer. It's much better to have my *own* kitchen and bathroom though, and I also have a real refrigerator. I signed a lease for 5 months.

My new landlord seems nice, but since my old landlady was "nice" in the beginning too, I'm afraid of being fooled again. He speaks a little English and his son and two daughters have all gone to college in the United States. I haven't yet met them.

We all need a sigh of relief here; her housing problems seem to have peaked and passed, as is evident in her letter weeks later:

Jan. 1, 1968 Christmas is not a holiday in Moslem countries like Iran, but my University was good enough to allow the foreign teachers to take the day off. Also they are giving us Jan. 1st off. My students (2 classes) surprised me with Christmas gifts. I got candy, a statue, Persian slippers, and a couple of nice sweaters that they all chipped-in to buy. My landlord also surprised me with a Christmas gift—a pot of beautiful red flowers.

Actually my landlord has reason to be nice to me now. About 3 days before Christmas, he told me that his son (who has just returned from 4 yrs. of college in the US) was not feeling well. They think the reason is living in a *basement* apt. (my landlord lives in a large beautiful apt. in the basement of this house), so he asked me if I would live in the basement and let his son have my apt. Well, we agreed on a reduction in rent, so I said O.K. Now I'm living in a smaller place that had been part of his apt. This makes the 5th place I've lived in since I came here! This place is not so nice (not enough sun for my flowers and no *kitchen* sink) but I'll move again soon anyway.

Ah, that phrase, "but I'll move again soon anyway" is the clincher because it is in this same letter that she writes, "A late January wedding is planned." But as we already know it didn't even take that long for her to "move out;" it happened on January 9,1968!

* * * *

* * *

They officially married on Jan. 9, 1968, had a Christian ceremony and reception on Jan. 19, and her first comment about her living conditions was on the letter to her Mom on Feb. 4.

Feb. 4, 1968 I'm pretty well moved into Bahman's apt. now. We made a lot of changes here, starting about a week before the wedding. Fortunately, Bahman had a huge beautiful refrigerator that he bought many months ago, so we didn't have to get a new one. We did buy a nice counter-cabinet with a Formica top and a big, beautiful modern gas stove with a large glass-door oven. (They used to cook on three little kerosene burners!) Now our kitchen is beginning to look modern. We also got a new modern, but inexpensive wooden bed, and deluxe mattress that is the best one manufactured in Iran. Our printed cotton bedspread is a honeymoon souvenir that we bought in the bazaar in Isfahan, and it's real "Persian looking."

Of course, I've moved in with Bahman's family, but we are trying an experiment to see if we can live together for the few months left in the lease. When the lease is up, we may decide to move to a two-section house and live more separately. So far, life here is better than you might expect. As soon as we were married, Bahman's family seemed to realize there was no basis for opposition any more. They became much nicer, and even gave me an embroidered handbag and a broach as wedding presents. Living in our apt. is Bahman's mother, who is old and sickly and usually stays in bed knitting, his oldest sister, Morvarid (about 48), and Morvarid's 14-year-old daughter, Fereshteh, who is kind of shy and somewhat over-weight. The three of them share a large room where they eat, sleep, and sit usually.

B: I am sure we had extensively discussed the issue of housing in Tehran even before I returned to Iran. But unfortunately I don't remember any of it! So, let's look at it from today's perspective. Reading these letters and going back down memory lane, my first impression about the housing issue is "surprise!" I am surprised that you even considered going to an unknown place and living in *one* apartment with your *in-laws!* Something that hardly any American girl is willing to do.

J: Agreeing to live with my in-laws! That must have been one indication of how much I loved you and was willing to put up with. As for moving to a strange foreign country, well, I know my parents didn't want me to go, but after deciding you were the one I wanted to marry, Iran just seemed like an adventure that was part of the whole package. I do remember you telling me that as the only son in an Iranian family, you'd be the head of the family and your mother and sisters would listen to you. Then of course we had this future plan of moving to separate quarters upon the arrival of our first child, so the live-in in-laws seemed like a temporary arrangement.

Feb. 27, 1970 Lately we've been house-hunting (or apt.-hunting) for a larger place. We've registered with a few agencies and looked at several places so far. But finding what we want won't be easy. Some nice places don't have phones—it takes about 2 years for the Telephone Company to install a phone after you've requested one, and then it is still very expensive (you *buy* the phone number and you can then *sell* it to someone else!)

April 10, 1970 We have been quite busy looking for a new apartment with a yard and one where Bahman's mother, sister and niece can live separate from us. We've finally decided we need *two* apartments, and we saw a place last week only a couple of blocks from our present place. The third-floor apt. is occupied by an English couple but the first two apts. are empty and seem suitable for us. I suppose the worst aspect is that our apt. will be so small that we'll have to use the hall for a dining area so that we can make the dining area into a bedroom, but that's not too bad. We probably couldn't afford two bigger apts. anyway. I suppose we'll move again in a few years. Now we are planning to move on Friday, April 17 if everything goes OK. I'll send you our new address as soon as we move.

April 25, 1970 It has been so hard to find time to write but I must at least send you our new address. When you moved from Ardmore Rd. to Hoyt Street I missed all the "fun" so this is the first time I've moved a whole household—it's quite a job. We've been here a week and still we haven't got the curtains hung, etc. It was a hectic and miserable time just before and during moving. You know we have rented two identical apts.—the downstairs one for Bahman's mother, sister, and niece. But the relatives decided they didn't like the place (really, they just didn't want to move) and refused to move. Bahman had the worst arguments with them since the time he first told them he was going to marry a foreigner. It lasted for days—we moved here and they stayed there. For three days I was without a baby-sitter and had to leave Ramin in a nursery school in the mornings. I was so upset about leaving him with strangers, since I believe so strongly that babies should not be in institutions. Anyway, things were worked out and they finally moved here, before they were evicted.

I like our new place, and it seems so quiet to be separate from my in-laws. Our 3rd floor neighbors are from Hungary but the man speaks English. Bahman is still close enough to walk to work. Unfortunately, it seems Ramin caught a cold in that nursery school, and he fusses most of the day and wakes up a dozen times at night, but I hope that will soon be over.

B: Did we ever learn why my mother and sister didn't want to move, considering the fact that the new place was certainly much better and they had their own apartment?

J: Yes, it was that "having their own apartment" thing that upset them. Your Mom didn't want to be separated even that much from you. I remember that we had to "force" them to move by removing items from their old apartment—furniture, fridge, stove, etc. until they were essentially camping out in the old apartment, where they mainly lived in one room anyway. I don't know why they finally saw the inevitable and moved.

B: In any case, if I am not mistaken our relationship with them gradually improved. Is it fair to say that we didn't encounter any other serious crisis after that?

J: What?! Is your memory fading that much? What about the childcare crisis when our second child born was a girl and they initially refused to care for her. Even with the first one, your Mom would sit in the courtyard and cry over the fact that I relegated our son to his own bedroom rather than let him sleep with us. No, I remember more conflicts than you do.

B: Well, well! Apparently you do remember more. I have no recollection of what you are saying about the problem with

Susanne being a girl, but I have no choice but to accept your words!

May 26, 1970 I really enjoy our new apartment—I feel like a new bride with my own place! We bought a long oval dining room table. The two ends detach and go together to form a separate round table which we use in our hall now. *Before* we got the table we had dinner guests—Isabel and Ahmad and another couple—but we did buy a new set of dishes just a few hours before the guests arrived, so we could serve them on nice plates.

June 26, 1970 Our stupid neighbor on the west has begun building a monstrous addition to his house (without a proper building permit!) which surrounds our house in an L-shape and cuts off the view and most of the sun from the yard and the apts.! The workmen are working day and night and holidays so that by the time our landlady takes this to court, there'll be new tenants there already. So now we've got ugly walls around us and I'm angry. I also heard the neighbor bribed the building inspectors. So much for now.

J: I just couldn't believe that the apartment we so newly moved into became far less desirable only months later.

Nov 14, 1970 Since we moved here, I've given several dinner parties for two to four guests. Most of these are also Persian-American couples. Most of our friends don't know each other, so I have the pleasure of introducing them. I guess the biggest problem, though, is that I don't particularly care to spend time cooking special dishes for a group, so I stick to very simple meals. One time I cooked spaghetti that was so salty it couldn't be eaten! But then the guests didn't show up, which was bad and *good*!!

August 26, 1973 Things are not particularly cheery around here right now though I'm sure they could be worse. First, we have a court summons to appear in court next month because our landlady wants to evict us (what she really wants is a lot more money). Second, yesterday our most expensive possession, our car, was stolen from a well-traveled street in broad daylight!

Oct. 5, 1973 Bahman went to court yesterday but neither the landlady nor her lawyer showed up. So Bahman told the court that it wasn't true that the landlady has no other place to live (she owns another house in addition to this one which she bought last year when she first asked us for more rent!) and she *had* to move into our apt. (she got angry when we refused to raise our own rent and she wants to evict us as revenge). The court said they'd let us know what they would decide but we're not worried now. Thanks for your offer of a loan but $1,000 is just a drop in the bucket, I'm afraid, when trying to buy land or houses in Tehran. I suppose you can compare it to buying land in the heart of NY City. We went house-hunting with Bahman's brother-in-law and saw two ordinary places on land smaller than your yard for $110,000 and $135,000! I was amazed. Also a deposit of 10 per cent for a house is not possible here. Loans are rare and hard to get and charge 12% interest anyway. So a house of our own is out of the question, at least for the foreseeable future.

B: So the landlady wanted to raise the rent after three years but we didn't agree. If I am not mistaken the law was on our side. Right?

J: Yes as I remember it. It must have been some kind of rent-control, so that the only way to raise the rent was when one tenant left and a new one came in. So, naturally the landlady did everything to get us to move. It was 1978 before she succeeded!

Sept 19, 1975 Another problem is that our landlady is threatening to take us to court again to try to evict us. She claims she needs to give one of our apts. to her son who is returning from studies in Germany. But because she does own another building, her attempt to evict us is really illegal. Do you remember she took us to court several years

138

ago and lost? I wonder why she thinks she can win this time.

Oct. 7,1976 Our landlady is still trying to get us to move. We got our third court order (we won the last two cases) to appear in court on this matter. But the court appearance is set for 5 months from now so we have a while to see what happens. I wouldn't mind moving, in fact I think we need a bigger place, but any place we move now would be 3 times our present rent!

March 4, 1977 Bahman went to court a couple of weeks ago in our landlady's third court case for eviction. We're waiting to get the court's verdict—they'll let us know by mail. Actually we're facing the possibility of *two* evictions at the same time! The landlord of Bahman's repair shop has sold the shop and the new landlord wants him out (probably to rent it for three times the present rent).

Oct. 27, 1977 Tehran University has gotten some land to the west of Tehran to build apartments and small houses for its staff. Because we have so many dependents and own no property, we are allowed to buy one of the small houses. Bahman put the first down payment on it last week. It will cost over $70,000 plus interest and will not be ready for a few years. But maybe then we will be rid of landlady problems. We are due to appear in court again next month. This time we will probably get a professional lawyer to represent us.

May 14, 1978 After 6 years of court cases with the landlady, it looks like she's ultimately going to win her case to get us to leave. So we decided to give-in gracefully and leave by the end of August. It would be nice to buy a house and beat the rent racket (Rents are sky-high in Tehran. Small apts. for $1,000 per month, etc.), but both of our life's savings and a huge loan would only get us a small house on the outskirts of the city, and where would we put Grandma and Auntie? It's discouraging. The big loans (70% of the cost) are only available for houses and apts. less than 2 years old, and those are the ones with the shoddiest construction! Anyway, we're looking around now.

June 20, 1978 A couple of weeks ago we began the exhausting process of finding somewhere to move to. We've given up the idea of buying a house because we saw that the only houses we could afford to get a loan on were very small and very old, and not in good areas. We are supposed to move out of here by the end of August. The main problem is to find a 3-bedroom house or apt. that also has a separate section to accommodate Bahman's mother and sister. We've spent hours every day with housing agents. Quite by accident, we discovered just the house we want. (Sometime I'll tell you the funny story.) Now we are in the delicate process of encouraging the present tenant to move *soon*, and encouraging the landlady and her agent to accept us as tenants at a reasonable rent. Cross your fingers and say a prayer for us!

July 4, 1978 We're having bad luck finding a place to move to. That lovely house we almost rented seems to have slipped away from us. It seems the landlady is selling it now. It's quite depressing. We go house hunting almost every afternoon after work.

Sept. 9, 1978 What a job it is to move! We've accumulated so much stuff living for 8 years in that old apt. It took the movers 9 hours of work and 3 round-trips by truck to move us. Plus we made many, many trips by car to transport our breakables and other small objects. We are finally moved in to our nice 3 bedroom apt. (with Bahman's mother and sister in 3 rooms downstairs) but the house is still messy with everything waiting to be put in place little by little. Somehow this apt. seems to have less storage space! I don't know where to store the winter clothes.

B: If I remember it correctly, in the span of about two months between July and September, we found a place to rent, vacationed in the U.S., went back to Iran, and moved. It's a pity that, after all the effort, we stayed in the new place for only five months.

J: Yes, and that was quite a nice apartment. Each kid had his or her own bedroom and the kitchen window had a view of Mt. Damavand (when the smog lifted). But in five months the Revolution was upon us.

Chapter Six

S-E-X

Q: What?
A: Sex
Q: W H A T??
A: S E X!
Q: Why?
A: Why not!
Q: Who?
A: Birds. Bees. Cats. Dogs. . . Humans.
Q: Where?
A: Anywhere. Mostly in bed.
Q: When?
A: Any time. Mostly at night.
Q: How?
A: Different strokes for different folks.
Q: Strokes?!
A: Shhhhh!
Q: Why?
A: Children
Q: From storks?
A: No, from strokes

Jackie: I want to declare here and now that this is all your writing and I had no hand in it!

Bahman: Not to worry! I'll be glad to take full responsibility. For one thing, I wanted to try my hand on something that is standing on its own feet and was not dependent on the letters. Moreover, I thought readers may be expecting some juicy stuff and we had none to offer!

J: And you think that is really juicy, a bunch of very tame made-up questions and answers?

B: Well what do you want me to do? Wait, maybe I can go back to the letters and try to extract something juicy . . . What about the following exchanges between Connecticut and Tehran?

She: 8/10/76 I took the kids to the Stamford Branch Library to see children's films. Another day we got a card for Mom at the Darien Library and spent some time in the beautiful new spacious children's Dept. The kids were fascinated. It was a problem to drag them out of there away from the books. We checked out seven to read at home, including one I chose called *A Baby is Born*. I don't think I mentioned to you that I've been teaching your kids the facts of life lately—and I mean *all* the facts! We started just before we left Tehran when Sue said her kids knew everything already, and at the swimming park Jahan and Keyvan were talking about the bugs on the trees "making babies." I figured then it was time for them to get the information from me before the other kids confused them (or taught them everything!) What's your reaction?

He: 8/21/76 Sex education? I am afraid they come back more informed than their father! Anyway, I guess it is a good idea also to tell them not to discuss these things in public—don't you think so?

J: This sort of talk may have had allure fifty years ago but not in this day and age. Actually, I don't know why you are so hung up on this "juice" business. What makes you think the readers are interested in it?

B: It's human nature, that's all!

J: Well, in any case, we can't really compete with all the memoirs coming out full of juicy stuff. So, let's just stick to the essentials and move on.

B: But wait, we can't just throw in the towel and leave this chapter in disrespect! Now that we can't find anything in the past to qualify for this chapter, how about taking advantage of the present and try to come up with something presentable?!

J: Shame, shame! Are you so engrossed with wanting to have a sexy chapter that you are even thinking of orchestrating something scandalous just to make some readers happy?

B: Well, it's not only for the readers . . . Oh never mind! The sad fact remains that the chapter that could be most interesting is going to be only a page or two long.

J: But it is going to be clean and wholesome. By the way, I've got to repeat the disclaimer that I had nothing to do with this chapter and you've been putting all the words in my mouth!

B: So be it!

Chapter Seven

Out and About

Travelling is a subject on which we can see quite a bit of difference in opinions and attitudes. We have already seen that Jackie visited Europe for a few days before arriving in Tehran. And we've seen how excited she got when she learned that she could visit Europe for little extra cost.

> She: 7/30/67 I also found out something surprising—for the price of the airline ticket to Iran, I am allowed to make as many stops along the way as I want! Here is a great chance to see Europe for only the added cost of hotels! In fact I am surprised that *you* never stopped to tour on your way back or forth (?!). I have pamphlets that tell of hundreds of places to see in Europe—but of course I can't spend a month or a year getting to Iran. How I wish our original plan worked out so we could see Europe together next month. Do you still plan for us to visit Europe? My wild idea now is that I will spend about 3 extra days traveling to Tehran and stop to see at least London, Paris, and Rome. I will preview Europe for us! I would hope that together we could visit such places as Scotland, Sweden, Germany, and Greece in addition. How much time can you get off from work for such a tour?

Well, despite all the uncertainties about her future in Iran, she is planning to have a good time on the way there, and why not! On the other hand, Bahman's answer a week later reveals a more subdued attitude toward travelling.

He: 8/6/67 Yes, I knew it was easy to visit Europe "in route" to the US, but I never had time for it, or never planned! Actually when coming home in March, I didn't plan for it because of the plan we had for summer. *Of course* visiting Europe *is* in our future plans. Well, you may plan for a few days of "previewing Europe." But please try to get here as soon as possible—I am impatiently waiting—I need you.

So she goes previewing Europe and writes about it in her first letter home.

Sept. 10, 1967 I wish I had had time to write to you from each of the exciting cities I visited this past week. It has been quite a week all right! I only had time to send one postcard—to Grandma Uzwiak from Vatican City because I thought she would especially like that. Well, to start, I got to the Air Terminal in New York in plenty of time—had to wait 2 or 3 hours in fact. I met another girl my age and we talked to each other all across the ocean (except while we slept) and even went into the city of London together. She was taking a trip around the world and planned to stay 2-3 months in India where her sister lives. London is like an old-fashioned America where everyone speaks with a quaint British accent. I had a mix-up in my hotel reservations but I managed to find a nice place to stay for the two days. I took a bus tour of the city (as I did also in Paris and Rome). The rest of the time in each city I walked and walked to see as much as possible. In London I saw the changing of the guards at Buckingham Palace, St. Paul's Cathedral, Westminster Abby, No. 10 Downing St., The Tower of London, Soho Square, Piccadilly Circus (circle), the British Museum, etc. The one day in Paris I saw the Arc d' Triumph, the Louvre, Notre Dame Cathedral, and many other places. At the end of the day I was dead tired, but I walked out to the Eiffel Tower and rode up part way to see the city of Paris at sunset. In both Paris and Rome I managed to get taxi drivers who didn't speak English, but somehow we managed to communicate. Rome is such an old city—everyplace, almost. There are lots of ancient Roman ruins, and every effort is made to preserve them. My tour took us to most of the ruins and a couple of cathedrals. On the morning of the day I was to leave I walked out to Vatican City. I got to see St. Peter's Basilica but not too much else because my time was so limited. The next time I visit Rome I intend to see the Sistine Chapel—perhaps the most important thing I missed.

J: Well, my first trip abroad and I couldn't get enough of it! Was this the beginning of my love of travel or did I have the "bug" earlier?

B: Oh, you've had the bug in you all your life, I guess! Do you recall all those business trips you made during the six months prior coming to Iran and wrote me about?

J: Oh yeah. I guess I never would even have considered moving to Iran if I weren't the traveling type! Every new place is an adventure. You can see how that attitude helped me adjust to life in Iran.

Their first travel together was, of course, their honeymoon trip to the south of Iran, which we already heard about. Their next real trip would be a big one in the summer, but before that, came a few small ones.

May 10, 1968   In about a week we will be giving final examinations at the University. Exams last until June 6th and then we have vacation. I don't know what I'm going to do with 3 lazy months of vacation. At least part of that time we hope to visit Europe and the U.S. One problem now is trying to get an Iranian passport for me. When I got married 4 months ago, I automatically became an Iranian citizen. I am supposed to have identification papers showing this new citizenship, but the government offices are very slow and inefficient in processing these papers. I must have the identification papers before I can get a passport. And goodness knows how long it will take them to issue a passport!

J: This was not my first brush with Iranian bureaucracy! I remember the problems getting a work permit as a non-citizen. My university was supposed to do it for me but they let the deadline slip by, and I was summoned to court!

June 13, 1968 After 5 months of marriage, finally I have gotten the identification papers showing I'm an Iranian citizen. Now Bahman and I are going through the red tape to try to get Iranian passports. I'm sending you a couple of copies of our passport photos so you can see what we look like these days. If everything goes well, we want to travel through Europe a bit (what is Gene Cooper's address?) and come to the U.S. probably before July 16. We'll stay in the U.S. 3 or 4 weeks (time allowed by the airlines' excursion plans) and then maybe see a bit more of Europe before coming back to Tehran.

Bahman and I are not the kind to sit around and relax much, so while we're in the U.S. we want to travel to Washington, DC, to Wisconsin (to visit Carole and George Weller), and, perhaps, to see Boston. We had considered plans to visit the Hemis Fair in Texas or San Francisco and Portland, Oregon, but those trips take either too much time or too much money. On this trip we expect to use up the money in my savings account and checking account. It'll probably be several years anyway before we can visit the U.S. again.

We haven't quite decided what kind of transportation we will use. We think it would be more fun to travel by car in the U.S. than by bus or train, and wonder if it would be possible for us to borrow your car for a while and rent a Hertz-Rent-A-Car for *you* to use at home. Or perhaps you and Lois would like to come along to DC, etc. We could even make a camping trip out of it, if you could find some basic camping equipment. (You like camping now, don't you?) Anyway, I'm writing to AAA to ask them to send you a camping guide (list of camps). We'll decide more about this when we get to the US.

Bahman and I have been on a couple of tours with the Iran-America Society. On one tour we went to visit the hunting palace of the royal family and toured the stables where the

Shah keeps his many fine horses. Two weeks ago we visited Qom for an all-day picnic tour. Qom is a religious city for the Moslems, and is about 3 hours drive south of Tehran. Next Sunday we go to Qazvin where we're supposed to see a Zoroastrian temple.

J: A great find for me in my early days in Iran was the Iran-America Society and its local tours. One of the very first tours we took was to the water purification plant, where my fears about the purity of Tehran's drinking water were put to rest. Do you remember stopping to pick cherries along the route of the tour?

B: If you say we did, then we did!

June 28, 1968   So far we have only tentative plans for our summer trip. Everything seems to depend on when we get the passport and then on when we get airline tickets. At least, it seems we can't start now before July 10th. We found out that Iran Air Line gives 40% discount to Iranian teachers, so we are going to fly Iran Air as far as they go (London). Between here and London we hope to spend 8 or 9 days seeing Istanbul, Geneva, Frankfurt, Munich, and the city of London before leaving for the US. In order to save money from London to New York, we'll probably fly Pan Am *Excursion*, which means we can spend only *21* days in the States. The places we'd like to visit in the US, I told you in my last letter. Then on the way back to Tehran we'll probably stop off in Paris, Rome, and Beirut. There's so much planning for such a trip, I hope everything happens just right!
I guess I told you about some of the tours we've been taking lately. Last week we saw Karaj Dam (the sixth largest in the world), and a water purification center. We went on a boat ride around the lake at the top of the Dam, and we had a nice picnic. This Sunday we're going on another picnic at another Dam. I think the water will be warm enough to swim at this Dam.

J: I can't believe I was planning such a long, complicated trip in those days before the Internet. How did I do it?

149

B: That is what I've been trying to tell you. There *really was* life before the Internet and cellular phones and fax machines and even the personal computer!

July 10, 1968   I've got just a few minutes now to write you our travel schedule. We've been going all over town these days getting the proper visas, etc. Tomorrow morning at 6:30 a.m. we leave Tehran by bus (since all of Iran Air's flights were filled) for a long trip through Turkey (where we stay in Istanbul), Bulgaria, Yugoslavia, Austria, and Germany until we reach Munich, Germany. I wrote to Gene Cooper to see if he can meet us in Munich. We will spend 6 days touring Switzerland, Belgium, etc. and then we will leave London on Thursday July 25th by Air India flight 107. We arrive in New York on the same day at 3:25 PM. From New York of course, we'll take a train to Connecticut and see you in time for supper, OK?
I'm sorry I couldn't write sooner so you would have had a chance to answer this letter, but I guess it doesn't really matter. We are planning to spend about 4 days in Washington, DC, maybe 8 days going and coming from Wisconsin and the rest of the time in Conn. or visiting Boston, etc. We still haven't figured out what kind of transportation we'll use in the US. We will be leaving the U.S. on Wed. Aug. 14th in the evening. We'll fly back to London and stop in Paris, Rome, and Beirut before coming back to Tehran. It should be quite a trip, I'm quite excited.
If I find time I'll write another letter or at least send postcards. See you in a few days.

Most of their plans worked but not all. The bus ride through Turkey wasn't all that smooth and easy. For one thing the buses used to break down frequently and they had to wait for repair or replacement. Another problem was that they had to eat at local and sometimes crummy restaurants. And even though the food was delicious, it turned out to be very unsanitary, at least for Jackie. Upon their arrival to Istanbul, she got real sick with a bad case of diarrhea. She went to the American Hospital and they had to change travel plans for the next few days. Finally she got better and they decided to take the train for a long trip through Eastern Europe. One amusing and curious thing was the fact that trains served hardly any food. Most people knew that and had brought food with themselves. One memorable incident was the following, recounted by Jackie.

J: In a small town, you got off the train to buy a watermelon from a street vendor, while I waited on board. Then the train started moving and I panicked, not knowing how to say in the local language, "Wait for my husband to reboard!" Fortunately, however, the train was only pulling onto a siding and you got back in plenty of time before we left. But boy was I scared!

B: I would've been too! In any case, we finally got to the U.S., did a lot of travelling in the U.S. and more on the way back to Iran. However, the only record of the trip available is the following postcard you wrote to your Mom on the way home.

Aug. 24, 1968   Did you get my card from Paris? Well, now we are in Beirut, Lebanon. We saw a lot of the ruins in Rome on our way through, and stayed in a lovely hotel, which cost us $5.50 per night (including breakfast)! I had my second visit to Vatican City. Today we spent a restful day in Beirut. We saw a part of the American University Campus here, but most of the day was spent swimming and relaxing by the Mediterranean Sea, which you see on this card.

J: Now that was Beirut *before* the war destroyed it. It was a nice city and the Mediterranean was so turquoise in color I couldn't believe my eyes. Remember you traveled all these great places with me—and enjoyed them, too. Somehow, though, it was always up to me to plan the travels, and it was only later in our lives that you became more of a stay-at-home.

B: Well of course, I was younger those days!

March 13, 1969   Last Wednesday, Tehran University called Bahman to say that they had 39 students ready to leave on Friday for a week-long field trip to factories and dams in southern Iran but they hadn't found any professors to accompany the students. They wanted Bahman to go and, since I decided a wife shouldn't be a suffocating influence, I encouraged him to go. So he left on Friday (with $1,500 to pay for all of the trips expenses!). I didn't see how he could manage the students, plans for touring, and all that money, but a note he wrote me on Sunday said he wasn't having any problems! This is the first time we've been apart since we've been married, and it has seemed kind of strange and lonely here this week. But tomorrow he comes back!

B: There! The ink in your complaint is not dry yet when we unexpectedly come across a trip that *I* made myself, on my own! And here is more of what I wrote to you in that postcard: "We've been having a great time—no problems. . . I hope you and [unborn] junior are having a good time! The trip is far from being troublesome—the way we used to imagine."

J: Well, that was a trip on your own, but of course you had all those students along to help you!

* * * *
* * *

Jan. 26, 1970 I had been thinking of visiting the U.S. in 1971, but since you say you're dying to see Ramin (and I'm dying to show him off) perhaps we can arrange to come next summer. Would you be able to stand 3 of us visiting you for several weeks, especially a baby who'll be a year old and probably walking?

June 26, 1970 Last week I was going to write and tell you that summer school had been cut to 6 weeks and we could come to the U.S. after Aug. 10 but this is Iran and nothing is ever certain. This week they changed it back to 8 weeks, so (if there aren't more changes) we can't come until Aug. 24 or later. I want to get there before the beaches are closed so we can swim as much as possible. I also hope I can spend one day at Drew University (are you prepared to baby-sit?).

Out and About

My friend Isabel and her husband and baby are in the U.S.
now. Maybe you've already seen them. They'll be there 2
months and I was hoping we could see them there, but it
doesn't seem likely now.

July 9, 1970 Haven't heard from you lately, but I hope you
can answer this letter as soon as you get it. I have some
problems in trying to plan a trip to see you this summer.
First of all, not enough students registered to take my
summer courses, so Pars College cancelled the courses and I
am unemployed for the summer. Bahman was also a part-
time teacher so he, too, will not get summer pay (but luckily
for only one month of "vacation"). According to the travel
agent the cheapest trip we can make will still cost over
$1,000 but next year it would be even more since Ramin
would be 2 years old and he'd have to travel on 50% fare
instead of 10%. Anyway, we can possibly take the money
for the trip from our savings, but then another problem
occurred to me. I don't remember why, but 2 years ago you
didn't seem to want us to drive your car. Now that your car
is 2 years older (and you know I have enough money in the
bank to buy another one if we damage that one) I hope you
have changed your mind. It hardly seems worth $1,000 to
come and sit in your backyard for 3 or 4 weeks *especially* if
you are going to be working some or most of that time. I
would like to go to the beach, or visiting people, or
shopping almost every day and I just can not put my baby
in a bicycle basket to take him along, nor can we afford a
rent-a-car or daily taxi. I hope that you want us to come
badly enough so that you will let us use your car while you
are working. Please let us know—we want to make
reservations to come at the end of July—maybe.
I will write to the Motor Vehicle Dept. to have my
American license "renewed" or to apply for a driver's test
the day after we arrive there. There are two other points
that I thought of: Can you get beach stickers, passes, or
whatever, so we can use Darien beaches? Will you be able
to have any vacation time for yourself during August?—
you ought to be able to spend some time playing with and

153

getting to know your grandson (I'll help with cooking and housework.)

July 23, 1970 Airlines are pretty crowded these days so we had to make reservations some time in advance. Haven't heard any reply to my last letter to you, but I hope we can work out the transportation when we arrive. Really, I think it would be nice for Lois to visit parks and zoos and beaches with us. She must get pretty bored at home while you're working. You ought to sign some sort of contract with your employers so that you get a paid vacation in the summer, but I suppose now that if you don't work, you don't get paid.
We will be arriving at JFK Int. Airport at 6:25 p.m. on Sat. Aug. 1st on Sabena Airlines.
The cheapest way we could fly is by an Excursion Trip that requires a minimum stay of 28 days or a maximum of 45. So we will be visiting you until Aug. 29th.

*   *   *   *
*   *   *

July 24, 1971 We spent four days at the Caspian seashore just before Ramin's birthday. We went with another couple and their little girl, and everyone had a great time. We stayed at two different motels at different beaches, and spent lots of time in the warm green waves of the Caspian Sea. After four days though I was quite sunburned and ready to come home. That is, until we arrived back in Tehran after a 5-hour mountainous ride. The city was just like an oven—it has been 100-105 F in the city lately. I rarely go out of my air-conditioned house these days.

Sept. 20, 1971 Sept. 9-12 we spent at the Caspian seashore. It was probably our last trip for a while. The faculty of Polytechnic Institute (where Bahman works part-time) was invited by the director to the Ministry of Education camp at the seashore. The "camp" is a group of brick buildings like a group of motels built on the sand. During the camping season it holds 600 university students, but now it was empty and had plenty of space for us—3 bunk beds in each room and each family had a private room. Friends of ours were also there with their son, Ali. Ramin and Ali had a great time together playing in the sand, and Ramin loved the water as much as ever. Fortunately the days were all warm and sunny and we swam everyday.

B: It so appears that form this point until we left Iran in 1979, we had a chance to go to the Caspian seashore every summer, at least once and more often twice. Some of the trips were only family type but many of them were in a groups like with my colleagues in Tehran Polytechnic, or others. Your letters home detail all these trips but they sound repetitious and, heaven forbid, boring. So, instead of quoting them here I'm going to ask you if you have any special event or moment in your memory. Do you?

J: The first time we drove across the Elburz Mountains, and I saw the lush greenery of the Caspian shore area, I got tears in my eyes and said it reminded me of Connecticut. I'd forgotten how much I missed the green! So the Caspian shore became one of our favorite vacation spots. Sometimes we went with friends, some of whom had vacation homes there—the Mohajerins and the Forootanpours. The warm green sea was perfect for our kids and us. I remember even setting up a playpen for Susanne right on the beach. We used that folding playpen my Mom sent as a safe place for her to play and sleep.

B: Well that was a mouthful! By the way, your admiration and desire for the Caspian wasn't unique; more and more Persians were going there.

Feb. 8, 1972 It looks like we can definitely plan on seeing you this summer. I put down a deposit to reserve seats for us on an Iran-America Society charter flight, which leaves Iran on June 25th and returns on Aug. 9th.
We're looking forward to seeing *you* of course and also we're looking forward to Campbell's soups (for Bahman), bacon (me), American baby food (Susanne) and bananas (Ramin)! Bananas are an imported luxury here—I bought four of them this week for 92 cents!!

June 7, 1972 We are due to arrive at Kennedy Airport on June 26th at 3:40 in the afternoon. Is traffic still bad at that time? I would really prefer it if you or somebody could pick us up there since we'll probably be exhausted by then, especially the children.

Our stopover in Zurich is 5 hours! What are we going to do in the airport for 5 hours? Right now I'm worrying about taking enough boiled water, milk, bottles, food, and diapers to hold Susanne for the 20 hours or so that we'll be traveling. Unfortunately Susanne is no longer content with just sitting, she's always trying to stand up. We put her in the baby walker and she's just thrilled. With hops and jumps she scoots all over the house—grabbing tablecloths and pulling books out of the bookcase, etc. Bahman says we just got rid of one menace (Ramin is reasonably well-behaved) and now we've got another! Just after I wrote you that last letter, Ramin began talking much more, but all in Persian. He still speaks to me in English though, and apparently he thinks I'm the only one in the world who talks that "strange language," since he even talks to Susanne in Persian now. I hope 6 weeks in the U.S. will help his English.

March 28, 1973 We are all fine and healthy for a change. We have about 3 weeks vacation now to celebrate the Iranian New Year. On the spur-of-the-moment we decided to go to Shiraz for about 5 days of this vacation, so we got plane tickets for tomorrow. We're hoping the kids don't give us too much trouble on the trip, especially Susanne who is getting more mischievous every day.

April 15, 1973 We had a nice week's vacation in Shiraz where the weather was quite warm, almost hot. The kids enjoyed the plane ride and the stay in a hotel—Ramin says "Let's go to Nanny's again." We saw some friends down there and visited the site of the 2500th anniversary celebration of last year. Shiraz is a very pretty town and a nice peaceful place to vacation in.

May 2, 1974 I was just sitting down to write to you when Bahman came in the door with today's mail including your letter! Also in the mail was a letter from the Iran America Society about our charter flight. The dates have been changed slightly. We will arrive in JFK Airport, New York, at 5:30 p.m. on Thursday June 20 (by Iran Air) and leave on Aug. 4th. Also the price of the flight has been raised slightly. Actually, final exams at my school continue until June 26 this year, but I expect to get my own over with earlier. We're allowed 220 lbs. of baggage on this flight so if you happen to see any lightweight cheap suitcases in the thrift shops, buy them, so we can fill them up with 220 lbs. of American stuff to lug back with us!

May 25, 1974 We've paid for the charter flight tickets and now we're going through the red tape to get a passport and an exit visa (costs over $200 for this exit permit now!). If anyone wants to drive to Kennedy Airport on June 20th to meet the Iran Air flight at 5:30 p.m., we'd appreciate the ride. Otherwise, I imagine we can manage the bus and train connections again. Our flight is about 18 hours straight through with only a ½ hr. stopover for fuel in London. We return on Aug. 4th the same way.

August 9, 1974 Well by now you know we got back to Tehran safely, or it would have been in all the newspapers! Did Mr. Kresan tell you all about the miserable afternoon getting to the plane? This time you were right about the miserable traffic at the airport. I think the bit of rain made it worse. Of course I should have checked somehow to be sure which terminal we were supposed to leave from, but I just guessed it would be plainly marked for charter flights. It took an hour and 15 minutes to park the car and get the information from Pan Am (*several* telephone calls) and then we found out we were on the wrong side of the airfield! Traffic was barely moving, so luckily, I hopped out of the car and got to the proper terminal on foot and told them we were on our way and to please hold the plane. They said they'd hold the plane at least half an hour, but as that half hour was coming to an end, one flight controller was trying to tell me that it was getting time to leave, we were the last passengers, etc. I was a nervous wreck and in tears. As I was telling him we didn't have enough money for another flight, Bahman and the kids finally showed up. How happy I was to see them! In the confusion I gave Mr. Kresan the money (but forgot his name!) and took his umbrella with me (I'll pay for another one or bring his back in 2 yrs.) As it happened, the plane took another half hour boarding passengers and 40 minutes waiting on the runway. After 2 hours for refueling in London, we were still on time arriving in Tehran!

So your wish to have us stay in America *almost* came true by accident. We did have a great vacation with you, though. Ramin suggested we go back and get you and have you come stay in Tehran with us. The kids talk about America as if it were around the corner! And every Volkswagen looks like Aunt Lois's car. Thanks for giving us such a nice vacation.

June 28, 1975 We took a nice trip for about a week to Bahman's hometown of Yazd and vicinity. It was my first trip there and Bahman's first in over ten years. He kept exclaiming how small everything seemed! We drove down in 2 days but made the long hot trip back in one day! Yazd is in the center of Iran and near the desert. The weather was the hottest I've been in. Every place we stayed in had no beds, or water, or electricity so it was really a week of "camping out." We found the old mud-brick house Bahman was born and raised in and stayed one night there. Then we traveled 2 hours across desert to a Zoroastrian shrine in the mountains and stayed two days there. This was the time of the Zoroastrian "pilgrimage" to that shrine, so hundreds of people were camping there, picnicking all day long and singing and dancing far into the night. Susanne and Ramin liked it too. Then we traveled in another direction to a little shady village so high in the mountains that you could still see a bit of snow on the peaks! This is the cool place that many [rich] people from Yazd go to spend their summers. We stayed two days and enjoyed goat's milk and *fresh* eggs for breakfast. We watched the neighbor children weaving a

Persian carpet and took hikes in the hills. (Bahman said to tell you *most* homes in Yazd have water and electricity though. It's not all so primitive!)

June 6, 1976 I got your letter of May 24 last week, but was too busy to answer. Actually, I've been putting off writing until I knew more about our flight plans. In the past, the first charter flight announced turned out to be shorter and more expensive than ones announced at a later date. This year I waited, hoping for the better Iran Air charters to be announced. So what happens?!—Iran Air decided *not* to have charters as usual. Of course the first flight for June 20 is filled-up. Anyway, I've signed up for another charter which just now is still in some danger of being cancelled due to lack of interest. Anyway here are our tentative plans: Unfortunately we have to miss Lois's graduation because this flight leaves on the worst day, July 4th! (It arrives in time for the fireworks I hope.) Anyway, the good part is the length—we can stay longer than ever this time, until Sept. 2! Another bad feature is that Bahman doesn't want to leave his work here for so long, so he will travel separately on a 21-day excursion plan. I think he'll arrive about July 1 and leave July 22. We're timing his arrival before us so that he can drive down (with your car, OK?) and meet us at the airport, since no one else seems to like to do that.
Then on July 7 or 8th we can all drive up to Canada (you haven't changed your mind I hope). The Square Dancing Festival is that weekend, and we are eager to attend as we did before. You can relax at the farm with the kids or we could hire a teen-age babysitter to help you on Sat. I'd like to stay there for Ramin's birthday the 13th and drive to Conn. on the 14th, visiting John and Marcie for lunch, or supper, or an odd hour either going or coming back. Do you like that schedule?

B: It's interesting to note that our summer trips to the U.S. up to this point occurred every other year, starting in 1968. However, you and the kids made an extra trip in 1977. But there is no record of it because you seem to have not written to your mother from the middle of March until your return to Iran. Lady, you've got a lot of explaining to do! (Why do I have a sneaky feeling that I've used that phrase before!)

J: Remember when we located the stash of letters my mom saved? They weren't all in one place and some had actually been destroyed by mice. We did have to throw some badly damaged ones away. Maybe some were from this time period (I know I usually wrote regularly!)

B: Good enough, I meant no hard feelings!

J: OK, but I want to add something here about our return trip in the summer of 1974. I really had nightmares about almost missing that plane for years afterwards. We had no money to purchase commercial airline tickets had we missed that charter flight.

B: Well, now follows several letters exchanged between us in the summer of 1977 when you and the kids went to the U.S.

She: 6/22/77 I hope you haven't become the worrying kind and are wondering why I didn't write immediately after we arrived here! Anyway, everything is just fine. The first couple of days were kind of busy with shopping since I knew I'd only have a couple of weekends in Conn. to shop in stores I'm familiar with (and Thrift Shops and tag sales!) We arrived last Thursday 30 minutes *ahead* of schedule! The flight was 747 all the way and I watched two in-flight movies. We took the limousine service to Conn. On Friday night a whole bunch of relatives got together at my uncle's house to celebrate the high school graduation of two of my cousins. Ramin and Susanne had baths and got dressed-up for the party, but fell asleep in the car on the way there and never did join the party.

He: 6/29/77 It is just about 2 weeks since you have left and I haven't got any letter. I finally called Iraj (with my mother's nagging) three days ago and he said everybody is all right. He had not received any mail either!

So tonight I sat down to write a few things before you get back here! I finally got to go to Yazd driving with my uncle and his son-in-law. We left early morning Sunday 19, got to Yazd late afternoon, stayed in Fariborz's house at night, went to Pireh-Sabz next a.m., came back Tuesday evening (weather was too hot), stayed overnight, drove to Manshad (like Deh-Bala) on Wed., came back Thursday a.m., went to Taft for lunch in Fariborz's house, left Yazd Friday a.m. and arrived Tehran by 8 p.m. safe and sound. The car acted like a good horse all the way until I took everyone home in Tehran and was driving home. Then on Abbas-Abad it went wild—shaking and noisy! I drove home somehow and next day took it for repair. The cylinder valves had to be repaired—also generator brushes were replaced.

And her answer to his outline of his trip to Yazd was a mixture of . . . well, here it is: "So now I know about your trip to Yazd. You were really brave (foolish?) to drive our car all the way. Such a long, hot trip! I wish you had treated yourself to a cool, short plane trip there. But I'm glad you got to do some interesting things there. You didn't say whether you enjoyed yourself but I assume you did."

She: 7/4/77 We finished up our seminar in New York last week, and I handed a term paper, which I stayed up to one a.m. to type (just like the old days of student life!). On Sat. the kids and I took an all day bus trip to the Canadian border where Carole [Weller] picked us up in her new little car. We had a late supper and went right off to bed. Two ten-year old boys are also staying with them this week. They have two horses, two cows and a calf now. George is busy building a barn to house the animals for next winter. Carole's as busy as ever doing everything as a farmer's wife. I don't know where she's going to find time to take care of the new baby (due on Oct. 4). But she said they decided to have this third kid only if they could afford it and only if she could spend the time to look after it properly—so I guess things are going OK with them.
On Sunday we got right into the spirit of farm life. Carole and I picked strawberries. Susanne ran around with the 10-

yr.-old boys—mostly kissing one of them! And Ramin spent most of his time fishing (which is what he's been waiting forever since Tehran). He finally did catch a fish—found it flapping around out of water on the ground! So he put it in a plastic container with water and tried to feed it his worm! The kids seemed contented enough when I said "good-bye" at bedtime last night. I said I would phone and write to them. Susanne wanted to call George and Carole, "Dad and Mom." Ramin doesn't want swimming lessons, but Susanne and Wendie will have swimming lessons and ballet lessons once a week. (The day camp in Conn. worked out nicely, by the way. Only one day Ramin poked along and missed the beach bus and had to be driven there personally by the camp counselor!)

That farm is really a great place for kids. I'm glad I don't have to drag them along like some of the Iranian women with us. And poor Mr. Kamali with 4 little ones!

Sunday afternoon the Wellers had a potluck picnic for assorted relatives which everyone enjoyed. And this morning George drove me ½ hr. to Magog where I got a bus to Montreal, then a taxi to the airport (I get so nervous about the possibility of making late connections) and a flight to L.A. via Chicago on a very nice DC10 (which seems to be like a 747). It's warm and dry here—they're wishing for rain. We just had a chance to check-in and then there was a champagne reception for us. This 3 weeks is specialized training tailored to the needs of us Iranians (I heard Farsi being spoken in the L.A. airport. There are lots of Persians here.) I'm rooming with the math/physics teacher from Kerman, Katayoon Karvani. She was Carol's roommate in N.Y., and Carol said she was homesick for her husband and baby.

Boy do I wish *you* were my roommate here. We could have a great time, especially if the kids stayed in Canada! There's so much to see and do. I just hope we are given some free time to see and do it. Actually we're quite a way out of L.A. in Pasadena.

She: 7/11/77 We went to Universal Movie Studios on Sat. and saw movie sets and special effects like how the six-million dollar man lifts up cars and jumps over walls. It was interesting and fun. Most of the group went to Disneyland on Sun., but I stayed behind and went to the hotel pool and had an expensive dinner in the hotel (it's not really possible to eat all our meals in this hotel on the amount of money we've been provided! Some of us including me, buy supermarket food and do some cooking at the cottage where our classes are held.

She: 7/21/77 I did get into downtown Los Angeles last week to shop and visit the ultra-modern Bonadventure Hotel with a one-acre lake on the first floor!! Did I tell you we went to Universal Studios to see how movies are made. $6-million-man tricks were explained to us. I skipped the trip to Disneyland and went to the largest Flea Market in the world at the Rose Bowl (a football stadium). Maybe I wrote that already?! This past Sat. I found a bunch of thrift shops for shopping.   One of the trainees, Mrs. Epply had us over to her home last Sunday for a barbecue chicken dinner. It was quite nice. I enjoyed it. This Friday we're all invited to another party and about 60 other people will be there. You know I love parties. We're going to Magic Mountain Amusement Park on Sat. nite and Sunday to Marineland then a picnic and swim in the Pacific—all arranged by Mrs. Epply.

She: 7/28/77 This might be the last letter I send this trip, at least I hope it arrives in time for you to come to the airport and pick me up! As of now I have reservations on Pan Am flight 2 which is due to land in Tehran on Thursday Aug. 9th at 8:35 or 9:35 (check that) in the evening. . . I thought I'd spend a couple of extra days in Conn. and try to buy myself a winter coat there. The luggage looks like it's going to be impossibly heavy again! I've become a real tourist about buying souvenirs—but mostly postcards to show you where I've been. Maybe I can check in to my work on Wed. Aug. 10, and then I can spend a peaceful weekend with you. Hope you have the patience to listen to all the details of this great trip (at least pretend to listen, OK?).

We had a lovely scenic trip by rent-a-car from L.A. to San Francisco. But first we had to go to a car supply store and buy luggage racks for the tops of our cars (Mr. Kamali drove another car too). But the racks were *unassembled*! So Nasser Ferydooni and I worked about 1 ½ hrs., right in the parking lot, assembling car racks in 100 F sunshine! What a job! We drove to a lovely town called Morro Bay and stayed overnight in a nice motel--the Iranians were impressed by the motel. Next day we continued driving. Stopped at Big Sur National Park for lunch and at Monterey for swimming at the beach (water was freezing—I went halfway in). The worst part was our arrival here—dorms were filled, hotels were filled, etc. I just cried. We finally found one room for 4 of us in a hotel and settled in about midnight. Moved to the dorms the next day. So far the conference has been OK.

I think I forgot to say that last weekend we went to a *huge* shopping center, Magic Mountain Amusement Park, Marineland, (performing dolphins, etc.), and a big picnic in a seaside park at Santa Monica (part of L.A.). My motto has become "Work hard—play hard!" I'm really having fun. The kids would have enjoyed a lot of this stuff—not to mention you. Would you have enjoyed the Pacific Coastal Highway we drove north? Great scenery.

In the next three letters, she's telling her mom of what turned out to be their last summer vacation in the U.S. Their next trip would be practically a permanent one.

May 14, 1978 I'm writing this letter from Kerman, a little town in southeastern Iran. Our Organization has a school here and I've flown down to visit it for a day. I have an idea that I might become an educational consultant some day. So I requested this trip to Kerman to consult and advise the English Dept. on their problems here. I'm staying in a nice hotel across the street from the school. It's so peaceful and quiet here! (Actually, it would be nicer if Bahman had come too—but of course, he's babysitting!) I fly back tomorrow afternoon.

I'm supposed to train teacher again this summer but I expect to get time off between July 18 and Aug. 18. There are 3-week excursion fares to the U.S. so we might come about the last 3 weeks of that time. I've enrolled my kids in a day camp program for 6 weeks here while I'm training teachers. When we get to the U.S., I'll be on *vacation*, and they won't need to be in a camp this year. Don't go buying a car for us to use (Bahman said you mentioned something like that). We can use yours for a few days out of those 3 weeks—mostly for shopping and the beach. *Next* year I might buy a car in the U.S. If all goes as planned and I pass all my admission tests, etc. etc. I might have to spend next summer on campus in Los Angeles. Then I really will need a car to get around.

June 20, 1978 I still have scheduled a vacation between July 18 and Aug. 18. I've reserved airline tickets for July 20 to go to Frankfurt, Germany. I'd like to see Lois Jespersen (Sister Gideona) and Gene Cooper's family if possible. Is he still in Germany?? Then on July 24 we fly Iran Air to the U.S. arriving at Kennedy Airport at 4:45 p.m. We'll stay in the U.S. until Aug. 16 or 17. What I'd like to do this year is spend a day or two in Boston, which I've never seen. Actually the airline tickets cost more than $3,000 (and we can afford it this year) so you please take the $3,000 you have in trust for me and spend it on yourself—maybe for that new station wagon you mentioned. I really mean it—*you* deserve to enjoy that money.

July 4, 1978 Our travel plans are the same as I wrote you before. I wrote to Gene Cooper in Germany that we'd stop by for a day or two to see them, but I still don't know if they are still located in Bensburg, Germany. Maybe we'll find out when we get there.
We're still planning to arrive in the U.S. on Monday afternoon, July 24th. It occurred to me that it would be good to have the kids' teeth checked by a U.S. dentist. Do you know a dentist for children who can give us appointments between July 25-29 or even Aug. 14-15? (The two weeks in between I'm keeping free in case one time or another is better to visit Canada, etc. for 2 or 3 days. Do you want to come with us again?) Make appointments for them if you

165

can, and also a check-up appointment for *me* with a regular dentist during those same days. (Maybe it's already too late for that?)

Chapter Eight

Dollars and Rials

This chapter covers everything financial. What role money played in their lives and how finances were handled. But first here is a bit of a dialogue.

B: I'm inclined to suggest to those who believe that poor people can't be happy to skip this chapter!

J: Oh, come on, you don't mean that.

B: OK, I didn't mean it that way. How about this? Not all rich people are happy and not all poor people are unhappy.

J: That doesn't say much. It is so general that no one can disagree.

B: What can we say then?

J: As you always say, first you'd have to define the terms, in this case rich and poor. These terms are so relative that in my opinion, you can't make a meaningful statement about the relationship between money and happiness.

B: Well now, you've really stolen my line! OK, so instead of chasing the elusive correlation, let's talk about our own situation in those bygone years!

The first time the subject of money comes up is when Jackie mails him an article on "financial planning," to which he responds on June 19, 1967, "I liked the article about financial planning too. I guess we had discussed and agreed upon most of the ideas mentioned. At present here, we just pick up money from a box and spend it!" His cavalier attitude toward money appears to have been a bit too much for her, as is evident in her answer:

> She: 6/27/67 I am afraid your mother (and sister and niece) will also resent my interference in the area of money management. So, I suggest that you begin *now* to institute some more organized plan of spending *and saving* (do you save anything?) money than just "picking up money from a box and spending it." You can be sure that I will insist on some method of a *planned* budget, with planned allowances and planned savings and investment when I am adding to the family income. Money management is very often the source of *much* argument between newly-weds and already it seems potentially very dangerous— especially since I will have so many people to argue with! Can you do something about it? Please.

> He: 7/15/67 Money management? Yes, I had planned to organize this one too, after moving—and we are doing it now. You can be sure that I (and basically they) welcome any organizing, including financial one.

> She: 7/30/67 I'm glad you have begun some system of family financial management, though you didn't explain what it was.

Poor man! He probably didn't know what it exactly was or how to explain it! Very possibly, it wasn't anything like a "system" she had in mind. So, in his next letter he wrote, "Since we moved, we have kept track of the money we spent. But it wasn't a typical month—I purchased some expensive household items. The point is that they are too thrifty!" That ought to do it—for now!

She also expresses hope and another financial advice. In her July 9 letter she says, "I hope your promotion to assistant professor comes through very soon, because the rent seems high for your present salary (financial advisors usually recommend that ¼ of the income be spent for rent, but of course this is for the U.S.)."

*   *   *   *

*   *   *

She moved to Iran, she got a job, she lived alone for four months, and finally she got married and started living with the other four! But it so appears that their "financial management system" never evolved much beyond "picking up money from a box and spending it!"

However, that crude system meant, "not spending money if not in the box!" And the first sign of this attitude appears in her letter home only three months through the marriage.

> April 11, 1968 It will probably be many, many years before Bahman and I can afford to get a car, since cars here are about twice as expensive as in the U.S. (!) especially the second-hand ones, since cars don't depreciate here as much as they do in the U.S. Televisions and other luxury items are *very* expensive too. There are many common things that are as expensive or cheaper than in the U.S., but salaries are quite a bit lower. Our financial situation is not bad, but Bahman and I are amazed at how much money the five of us use up in a month without even buying any "extras". I just hope we have enough money to have a nice trip this summer.

But of course we've already seen that they scraped enough money together to make that infamous (bus) trip to Europe and the U.S. that summer.

> April 26, 1968 Did I ever tell you about his baking machine? He is developing and building a new machine to produce the Persian bread (which comes in long, flat pieces) in a more sanitary, healthful way than it is now. So far, the U. of Tehran has said it can provide him a place to build the first working model but he is still looking for financial

169

backing to pay for labor and materials. It will be a fine thing for Iran when it's finished.

B: It pains me to recall that all the efforts and expenditure that went into making the production of Persian bread automated and more sanitary failed. However, as we now know others did succeed in doing that and some bakeries are now automated.

J: Yes, I remember even taking pictures of a bakery in our last visit to Iran in 2001. But curiously, people are still carrying the long flat bread under their arms! But why do you think your plan failed?

B: In this case it was technical acumen that was missing. Although I had visited some bakeries in the U.S. and studied some books, the design turned out to be much more complicated. I could've used some technical expertise, especially in the field of mechanical engineering, but no one seriously wanted to help. And after a few years of struggling, I had to give it up.

May 18, 1968 A couple of weeks ago Bahman told me that someone wanted to give us a *nice* present and what would I like. After some indecision I finally settled on a TV set (even though the least expensive one is about $250). And yesterday a TV set arrived! I learned that it was from Reza, who lives upstairs. Reza is an old college friend of Bahman's, and I have been giving him English lessons 3 times a week ever since I first came to Iran. He is the director of Dural Company.
All we need now is an aerial and we can watch TV. Tehran has 3 stations, two in Persian and one in English. Most of the shows are from American TV programs, even cartoons. Yesterday the most surprised person in our house was our niece, Fereshteh. She has been watching TV at a neighbor's house. When she saw the TV coming into our house, she was really jumping for joy!

July 2, 1969 Did I mention that Bahman has picked up another part-time job? A Japanese company has hired him to teach technicians for 4 ½ hours a week. So his schedule will be part-time there, part-time at the university (which is now on vacation), and extra spare time on his own projects. Fortunately he can also spend a lot of time at home with me, especially a few hours every day at lunch time. I'm sure we spend more time together than most married couples—and that's great.

Sept. 27, 1969   Big news! We bought a car! . . . Used cars here depreciate very little so they're almost as costly as new ones. Our car is a *Peykan* which is a locally-assembled model of a British compact car. About half the cars here and most of the taxis are *Peykans* since they are relatively cheap compared to imported cars. Still, we are paying close to $3,000 for this car, including taxes and insurance, which is more than my yearly salary!

Nov. 14, 1969   Incidentally, *our* standard of living should go up pretty soon. Bahman will be signing a contract at Polytechnic Institute for more or less full-time teaching. Then, with both of us working, we should have a decent living wage. I'm happy that next spring or summer we can move into a ground floor apartment with a yard where Ramin can play. I think we'll be able to afford a higher rent then.

Nov. 14. 1970   Just now Bahman and I seem to earn enough for anything we want, but we are such conservative spenders! Travel to the U.S. is our only big splurge. Only last week we finally bought pleasant, comfortable living room furniture (but still at a *bargain* price). The cheap "temporary" furniture Bahman had bought before we were married had lasted 3 years and was actually starting to fall apart! Now we have a 4-person couch, which can be divided into two sections, and four chairs. It's not the best furniture, but it's so much nicer than what we had . It's blue and has a nubby (?) texture--it's funny that the old furniture was the same color! (I'm sure you're enjoying your new furniture too.)
Now we feel more comfortable about having guests in our living room.

May 14, 1972 I've been going to several second-hand clothing sales lately and getting a few bargains in "foreign" clothes for me and the kids. It's almost getting so that I enjoy second-hand clothes more than new ones, because it feels good to get a real bargain. I suppose I'll do a lot of shopping in your Thrift Shops this summer!

Oct. 11, 1972 Yesterday as I looked through my clothes I decided that all the nicest things are the "used" clothes you gave me this summer. I wish I could get more of them. Anyway Bahman's niece is getting a nicer wardrobe too, since I've been giving her lots of the clothes I used to wear.

August 22, 1973   Bahman's latest project is Rausti electronics, an electrical and TV repair shop which he opened last month. He has one young man working with him and so far their repair jobs have been for our friends. Bahman wants to teach part-time during the school year and supervise the shop too.

Oct. 5, 1973   Bahman has put about $5,000 into his new business and that's the investment we're concerned with now. But we are both thrifty persons, even on our small salaries, and it's probably possible for *us* to make *you* a loan if you need it. Mostly our friends have been using Bahman's electrical repair shop so there's still lots of room for us to get new customers, but business ought to pick up little by little.

May 2, 1974 I bought the kids some books and toys at a garage sale last week and some other American things at another sale the week before. It seems a lot of foreigners leave Tehran in the spring and hold garage sales, which my friend Joanne and I consider a form of entertainment for us.

The following two items were exchanged between them in the summer of 1976 when they had a "split vacation."

She: 8/3/76 I often stay up late to watch TV. . . On another show a set of news investigators checked up on claims that most repairmen are dishonest and found that was so! About 70% of TV repairmen overcharge. Estimates given for a simple 75 cent cord replacement ranged from $40 to $53! . . . I'm enjoying shopping at tag sales and thrift shops still—last week it was "fill up a bag for $1 and also $.50!" At one tag sale I bought Ramin a bicycle with removable training wheels for only $3. He likes it. I wish we could bring it to Tehran.

He: 8/11/76 If the TV repairmen weren't dishonest they would go broke—like me!

J: As a final comment on our financial well-being. It was at least a good thing we both had the same attitude towards money. If not, there would have been real problems!

B: OK. Now, referring back to the beginning of the chapter, it's fair to say that we were not poor, and we were not rich. But were we happy? No, there is no need for an answer, it was only a rhetorical question!

Chapter Nine

Trying on Zoroastrianism

We read a lot about religion in past pages because that was probably the biggest hurdle they had to overcome before they could get married. We even saw how a simple innocent "typo" could cause mayhem! However, that wasn't all of it. There was a lot more correspondence on the issue in the months prior to Jackie's move to Iran. We'll see a little more of them here. It should also be noted that this issue had been discussed in great detail much earlier when they were both in Wisconsin.

The first red flag was raised early on when she quoted an "article" she had read in the paper, from who else but, Dear Abby!

She: 3/25/67 I happened to read a "Dear Abby" column in a newspaper last week—unfortunately. The first letter was from a teenager who was upset and confused she didn't know what religion she should be. Her parents were Jewish and Lutheran and left the choice up to her. Abby answered that she was completely against inter-faith marriages because of the family problems they cause. She said, though, that when such marriages do occur, the cruelest thing the parents could do is to force the children to choose between religions. Abby says a child's religion should be agreed upon *before* he is even born. Now, I am confused and upset! Does this make any sense to you?

To which Bahman responded, "What did you mean (or imply) when you wrote about the answer Dear Abby gave to a girl undecided in religion, and finally the confusion you got by that? I am confused dear too—this is one among many."

B: There were two separate points in this Dear Abby column. First, she was completely against interfaith marriages, and second, parents shouldn't leave the choice of religion to the children. Now, tell me, What do you think Dear Abby would say today? Better yet, what would you yourself say?

J: I think advice columnists in general have become more accepting of the diversity in America, including interfaith marriage. In fact, it's probably "politically incorrect" to object to them in print nowadays. I don't know about the latest theories on whether parents should pick a religion for their children to give them a sense of certainty in an uncertain world. However, we didn't pick a religion for our kids and I can't say that it hurt them.

B: Right on both points but I'd probably go a bit further. Interfaith and intercultural marriages are becoming more commonplace as the "global village" gets smaller, no matter what. With regard to children and religion, I'd say it all depends on the parents. Wise and reasonable parents can teach their children to be tolerant and self-confident.

J: Now you sound like an advice columnist.

B: As you know I've been an avid reader of advice columnists "all" my life, and that probably has rubbed off!

He: 4/3/67 I learned that our children cannot become Zoroastrian (a point of objection by my people) and I myself . . . well, I have to ask an authority (my folks say not to talk to anybody about these things); the semi-authority said, they'll reluctantly accept me to remain Zoro.! Yes, dear, I'm having a hard time around here. But I hope everything will come out OK. My friends, Mohammad and Reza, and possibly some other Zoro. relatives (if I find them in sympathy with me) might be helpful in my campaign. I know my letters sound more or less disappointing to you, but we have still got lots of time to settle everything, hopefully.

PS: Last night Mohammad called an authority and without mentioning my name, asked the question. The answer was more favorable. He, an intellectual, said I *will* be considered Zoro. and our children might be accepted, if both parents approve of it. Well, this could be good news to my folks, but they are not satisfied with it.

J: Here is a wishy-washy attitude, if I've ever seen one. No one authority could tell us exactly what the fate of such children would be! And this was true all the way through our wedding and beyond.

B: Right. But remember that there are often unresolved issues such as these in many religions, especially Jews who like Zoroastrians don't traditionally accept converts. But times are changing and tradition gets challenged.

J: At the time we were married I believed the kids could be Zoroastrian if you, the father, were. A few years later I heard the Zoroastrian community had decided that women married to Zoroastrians could choose to be Zoroastrian. That amazed me, because if it was a centuries-old tradition not to accept converts, how could a local community just decide something like that! Do you suppose the fact that some prominent and influential Zoroastrians were getting foreign daughters-in-law at that time helped make the decision?

B: Yes, but even ordinary Zoroastrians marrying outsiders, which was inevitable to happen more and more, was cause for rethinking the matter.

She: 4/2/67 How ironic that, the week before, I sent you a letter telling about the problems for children of an interfaith marriage. I suppose your family is right in saying that religion will be a major problem (of course, we anticipated such a reaction from them). However, it did seem a little surprising to me that the objection seems not to be so much a matter of specific religious differences as it is a matter of losing a good reputation among Zoroastrian friends. It would seem to be similar to what my father might say if I wanted to marry a Negro—the family would lose respect from white people.

He: 4/10/67 Last Thursday evening I was invited to an engagement party. A very far relative—pretty rich—had their daughter engaged. There were about 300 guests. We had refreshments—tea, cookies and cakes, fruits, nuts, etc. By custom, the girl's family gave this party—the boy and his relatives came there. Among all the girls attending, I got interested in only one! I think it is too premature now to tell you the details. On the other hand, I'm sure you are pretty curious, so I'll tell you. It is not so exciting as you are anticipating. As a matter of fact it is nothing, forget it!
There was a blond lady with a little girl. Then I learned that her husband was a Zoroastrian whom I know somewhat (she is German). Later my mother said that he had told someone that he wasn't happy with her and regretted the marriage. Of course this is nothing new. The more important thing that I don't know is: What is the girl's religion? I'll find out. So, this is the girl I got interested in, understand sweetie?
Of course, my family's objection *is* on the religious differences too. But the reaction of people is a more tangible and immediate issue to cope with. They emphasize it *too* much anyway.

She: 4/13/67 If I had written this letter yesterday, after I read yours, I think this would be a very sad pessimistic letter, because that is how your letter made me feel. I am so sorry that you are having so much trouble with your family. I really don't see how we can all live peacefully in the same house. I think they dislike me already. And your comments on raising the children Zoroastrian "if both parents approve of it" made me very sad. Are you asking me to make this sacrifice too? Already it seems my children will be almost "strangers" to me with "foreign" names, raised in a different country, with a different culture and schools, and speaking a different language. To ask me more than this seems more than I can agree to. I thought we were going to work a compromise? It almost seems better to have no children at all and avoid these problems.

I'm also afraid that even if your family becomes happier about the idea, they will continually pressure me to agree to raise my kids as Zoroastrians. I think this problem will begin in June when I visit and they are likely to become very angry with me then. If you think this will happen, perhaps you should advise me not to visit at all. I don't know what to say—I want *you* very much but I don't want all these terrible problems.

I still have problems on my family's side too. I phoned my parents last week to tell them I was coming to Portland. My father told me he is unemployed now and looking for a job (every few years this seems to happen). He doesn't want me leave the US, as you know. He says I should stay here and take care of my folks.

He: 4/22/67 About raising the children Zoro. or not, I didn't really ask you for anymore sacrifice. I think you had agreed (or did you?) that I can tell my people that our children may be called Zoro. (if they are accepted by the Organization). Now let me know if I am mistaken. Anyway, on this matter I tend to take it easy and defer it to future, because it is not an immediate issue (for me and not them). I don't want to be too fussy about religion. Am I being unrealistic?

She: 5/1/67 [Lost but rewritten later on 6/19] I remember *very clearly* the time you asked me if you could tell your family the children could be called Zoroastrian, and I did not say anything. I *couldn't* reply, I didn't know what to say. I didn't want to say "no" because I didn't want to cause even more serious problems between you and your family, and still I couldn't say "yes." I thought, that when you never asked me again about it, you had decided that it was a problem that could be avoided, but I see that our problems must be faced directly and not avoided.

The reasons I cannot say "yes" are complicated. I think we agreed that the children would learn about both of our religions. However, it is usually true (and this comes from my sociology) that what a thing is labeled, that's what it *is* (effectively), and what a person is considered by others, that is how he considers himself. For instance, if a child is continually called lazy and stupid by his family, he will think of himself as lazy and stupid and will find it difficult to do well in school no matter how intelligent he really is. Sociologists describe persons as developing their personality in accordance to the "mirror image" that is reflected to them from their family and close associates. Therefore, a child *called* "Zoro" *is* "Zoro." When a child is called Zoro. he can reasonably be expected to learn certain things, do certain things and act in certain ways. Others can say that since the child is "Zoro," he must . . . etc. and the child comes to expect these things himself too. In this way, the child has no reason why he should even learn about or consider Christian teachings and he is not given a *fair* chance to learn about both religions. I cannot see how I can raise my own children as pure Zoro., and labeling them that is really just the same thing.

It is probably true that since our children will be under continuous "Zoro" influence in your society, they will chose to become Zoro, but I prefer that they choose and not become something just because they have always been called that.

Now, about the advice "Dear Abby" gave to the girl from interfaith parents: Abby believes it is psychologically better for the child to have a "religion" or religious label from birth and not be forced to choose between his parents' religions because, to a child's mind, he is choosing between his mother and his father, not just their religions. Also, there is security in knowing what you *are* because that is what you have been from birth. Now, in our case, we will be acting just opposite from this advice, and we are liable to have very confused and insecure children. The ridiculously obvious (though maybe not practical) solution since you are "not too fussy about religion" and I *am*, is that the children should be called "Christian."

Now that I think about it more, we are going to have very mixed-up children no matter what we do, and you will find it rather difficult being married to a sociologist (you should have picked a nurse or physicist?).

Mohammad even mentioned to me that he found out that the children could be called Zoro. if both parents agreed. He thought this would solve some problems, *until* he found out that I strongly believe in my own religion.

B: I have a couple of points to discuss, but the last one first! We didn't get mixed-up children, did we? And I don't think a nurse or a physicist would've done any better. There!

J: Our kids seem to have grown up OK. But, you know, some people would call them "mixed-up" because neither one embraces a religion now. But they're both good, moral adults. My old letters with the assertions and challenges seem to have been my way of testing whether you were really ready to go through with the challenges of a bicultural marriage. Your soft replies—all reasonable and reassuring—confirmed to me that you really were. That made me happy.

B: So, you were testing me, ha! In any case, let's go to my other question. As you know there are always exceptions to the rules of social sciences. Now, how widespread would you say this sociological "mirror image" theory is?

J: Oh that theory still holds water. People often reflect others' images of them.

B: It may hold water but, in my opinion, it's also got some holes! I'm inclined to say that quite an appreciable percentage of cases would result in a "backlash" and may even have an opposite outcome. For instance, in the case of religion, I know quite a few atheists who grew out of religious family backgrounds. Don't you agree that if a child who is "continually called stupid by his family" has in fact the potential of being smart, *may* grow up to be smart?

J: Of course, but we're talking about probabilities here. No theory of human behavior is 100% reliable.

B: Good enough. Now here is a cute piece I found in an early letter of yours.

She: 5/5/67 I bought my ticket to Iran--$734.60--and I hope that is not wasted money. My minister has reserved the church and the fellowship hall for us on Aug. 19. He wrote to me: "If true love binds you two (not blinds) then no mountain wall can keep you apart. My blessing." I'm glad he approves.

After all the discussions and worries about the children and religion, the situation seems to have been concluded, for now, with the following.

He: 6/19/67 If you don't confine yourself (and you don't, at least to some extent) to the narrow meaning of religion and not being prejudiced, but think in terms of human being, then there is no important problem.
Ironically, I heard the other day that there was an interfaith conference for a week here in Tehran. They hold it somewhere each year. Each religion was represented by some people who were supposed to present the principles and philosophy.

She: 7/18/67 I read parts of the *Iran Almanac* before returning it and learned several interesting things: The number of religious minority group numbers in Iran is "Christians 133,768; Jews 76,190; Zoroastrians 18,364; other minorities 69,211; and undeclared 53,538 (1963 figures)" . . .
In fact, it says there are 5,000 *Americans* in Tehran alone. Zoro. are *very* small group, aren't they?

B: Well, I probably didn't answer you then but I'm going to do it now! Yes Zoroastrians still make a very small group— something like 100,000 in the whole world, mostly living in India as Parsees. In Iran they are concentrated in Tehran, Yazd (my hometown), and Kerman. And just for the record, I think we should give a brief description of the religion, which I think an "outsider" like you can do a better job at.

J: Zoroastrianism claims to be the oldest monotheistic religion in the world and it may be, if you count its basis in Mithraism. The religion depicts an ongoing world struggle between good and evil, with mankind's obligation to always search for and choose the good. Most people recognize it from the motto: "Good thoughts, good words, good deeds." But many are confused and believe Zoroastrians are fire-worshippers, when in reality they simply respect fire. They are like the first environmentalists respecting the basic elements of earth, air, water, and fire. Because they considered themselves the "pure race," they forbade intermarriage and conversion. But modern Zoroastrianism is changing, because people are changing.

Now we take a big leap of over a year forward and to an interesting observation she relates to her Mom.

Oct. 31, 1968 There should be some more weddings coming up. Did I mention before that this summer, when college students studying abroad had come home for vacation, we knew several Zoroastrian families that arranged for their sons to get engaged particularly so they wouldn't fall into Bahman's position of meeting and marrying a foreign girl?

Chapter Ten

The Pets among Us

Although this chapter is about pets, no one should expect to read about a bunch of different animals, because the only pets the family kept were a few cats (and maybe a few chicks!) during all those eleven and a half years.

March 27, 1968 Bahman's No-Ruz present to me was a big wrapped package which contained a block of wood, a bunch of old photographs, and finally, at the bottom, a note which said I could choose any kitten I would like! I have been asking for a kitten for a few weeks now, so I guess we'll get one soon.

April 26, 1968 Last week we went to the Humane Society and got a little black and white female kitten. It got used to people quickly, would follow us around the house, and enjoyed being held and petted. Everyone seemed to like it. Unfortunately, it wouldn't eat anything, and seemed continually to have an upset stomach. On the day after we got it, it just got weaker and weaker and then died. We are almost afraid to get another one in case the same thing happens.

Sept 27, 1968 We went to the animal hospital last week and picked up another kitten for ourselves. But in a day, this one showed signs of sickness just like our last one. We took it back to the hospital and the doctor said it had typhus and nothing could be done for it. They had more kittens if we wanted them, but apparently their whole cat section is infected with typhus so we didn't get them. At least humans can't catch typhus from cats. Next time we'll pick up a kitten from some place else.

June 17, 1969 We got another kitten last night—a furry black one with a funny multi-colored face. Bahman's mother doesn't like it because it's black! All day it's been crying, but the former owner says it's not sick only lonely for its mother. I hope that's all.

July 2, 1969 Our kitten is active and playful and apparently healthy except for her eyes. The eyelids are pinkish and produce a lot of pus. Have you ever heard of using tea to cure such a condition? What would you recommend? The eyes, in fact, seem too high in their sockets so that I believe the kitten is at least partially blind.

Jan. 26, 1970 This part of the letter sounds like a repeat of the last one: The baby was keeping me awake nights last week (probably a reaction from his smallpox shot) and the cat was driving us all insane with crying because she was in heat *again* (please, look it up and let me know how often this is supposed to happen—every 3 weeks is too much for us).

April 25, 1970 I like our new place, and it seems so quiet to be separate from my in-laws. The cat has been worrying me by getting lost in the new neighborhood, but I think she, too, has finally settled down.

Sept. 2, 1970 One unfortunate thing happened. Our cat couldn't wait for us to return, and she ran away a week ago. I keep hoping she'll come back some morning with a bunch of kittens.

B: This of course happened right after our return from the U.S. that summer. And in your subsequent letter you write, "Our cat never came back, but I keep hoping." And so apparently we lived "catless" for a few years because any reference to cats appears in a letter nearly five years later. Do you think that is what happened or something is missing here?

J: Maybe some letters got lost but I'm not sure.

June 28, 1975 Before we went to Yazd I wanted to write to you to tell you how happy I was that Bahman finally agreed we could have a kitten on the condition that he could give it away if it made a lot of trouble. A friend had a litter in her yard but then I saw a kitten I wanted even more. My friend Joanne has several cats that she feeds on her back balcony. One of them had two white kittens a couple months old, one was long-haired and reminded me of yours. So we spent several days trying to capture it. It was really wild. I got it home and it spent a couple of weeks hiding and only coming out at night for food. Then a student offered me her little tame kitten, black and white with *very* long hair from Yazd! Bahman said, "OK if it doesn't bother *me*." This kitten (*Panda*) was very playful and good for the kids. Pretty soon the two kittens started playing together and boy were they cute! One night we left the window open by mistake and the wild white kitten escaped. We searched 2 days for it and then it came back by itself! From that moment on it became perfectly *tame!* How amazing! It apparently decided it prefers living with us. Even the kids can play with it now. Our niece fed and cared for the kittens when we went to Yazd, but when we came home they were both *gone* and I was miserable. My sister-in-law opened the window to give them air, and Cayce (the white one) escaped again. The other, Panda, got sick and my sister-in-law said it was dying so she put it out in the alley where it probably did die from one cause or another. I was wishing I had never gone to Yazd, when Cayce at last found his way back to us. So now we have just one dirty but affectionate kitten. The only difference from yours is that Cayce has yellow eyes.

So a year later when it was time for the summer trip to the U.S., they had to again leave Cayce alone, this time for a long three weeks. Right after Bahman returned home ahead of the family, this is what he wrote them about the cat.

He: 7/24/76 Now about your cat: Apparently he has been very lonely and frustrated. He had not been going out except for some recent days—and today he was out for a couple of hours. Although I am now here (and he wants a lot of petting) he is still asking for you! He tried to bite me a couple of times (I was *not* playing) out of frustration. Often, when sitting on me, he looks straight into my eyes, as though asking me where others are! But don't worry, he is quite all right now that I am here. I gave him the catnip— didn't appeal to him. You should write the company and tell them to make catnips to the taste of Persian cats!

He: 7/30/76 Now about your cat. He is much more calm now. He is fussy about food and goes out once in a while for short periods, but I don't know why he does his messing inside. We sometimes literally talk to each other, crazy uh?

She: 8/3/76 Poor lonely Cayce! Give him a scratch under the chin for us.

He: 8/21/76 You are talking of dust? That is not a problem. The problem is Cayce's hair all over the place—in strands and in bundles! I can't get rid of it no matter what. He is all right though.

At the same time, he wrote, "I forgot to buy a lint remover, you can buy one." And of course we know what *that* was for! In any case, days later when she and the kids got home, not only did Cayce become pleasantly surprised to see them again, but . . . well, read the following.

Sept. 6, 1976 The kids were pleasantly surprised when we got home to find *two* cats in our apartment instead of just one! Bahman says our white cat was lonely and brought home a playmate. It's a young, fluffy, orange cat that is extremely friendly and affectionate. He even lets Susanne carry him around, so I knew he was someone's pet. We put a collar on him and attached a note asking, "Does this cat have a name?" After several hours outside the cat came back with an answer attached! It said, "This cat's name is Musa. Please don't frighten him." But it seems that Musa prefers the food, accommodations, and companionship at our house because he spends most of his time here!

Jan. 5, 1977 Took both cats for shots last week. The vet prescribed lotion and pills for Cayce to cure his mange on his face. He really hated the treatment and ran away. We didn't see him for a week and figured we'd lost him, but last night he turned up again! Our other cat, Musa, is such a homebody, he doesn't even like to go down to the yard.

J: The next three excerpts are from letters you wrote while I was vacationing in the U.S. What a sweet way to say you were missing me!

B: You've always been good at reading between the lines and finding compliments! I guess women are better at that than men! In any case, it's more important to resolve the puzzle that Musa was missing in my next letters to you. Do you remember what happened to him?

J: I remember that one day we left the city and spent a day or two in Qazvin. Musa apparently missed us, went out looking, and never returned! I didn't want to think what might have happened to him, but I hope he just went back to his old owner.

He: 6/29/77 Cayce the cat is all right—but it seems that he feels lonely these days—and who doesn't?! I guess it is not so good to have so much "peace" suddenly! Maybe we should try next time to send the kids away or some other alternatives!

He: 7/8/77 I guess that is all I have to say. But wait I forgot about Cayce. He is all right but very lonely-looking. He wants to be played with. As I said before it is too much peace and you know that too much of anything is no good. See you soon.

He: 7/18/77 Cayce is all right. He is very fussy with food. If I coax him (tarof) enough he would eat better. I am waiting to get your next letter which should tell me exactly when you are coming back. I feel lonely.

Finally, here is a report of "pets" other than cats.

Feb. 18, 1978 Last Thursday Susanne and Ramin went on a field trip with their school to a chicken hatchery, and came home with a couple of day-old chicks as souvenirs (all kids whose parents allowed it, got some). We're keeping them in a cardboard box and feeding them ground wheat. They're really cute. When Bahman was a boy, he had a pet rooster, so he likes chickens a lot and was happy to see the chicks. Our cat hasn't seen them yet, though!

Sept. 9, 1978 What a job it is to move!
Somehow this apt. seems to have less storage space! I don't know where to store the winter clothes. Another problem was our cat. He went outside before the movers came , and then refused to come in again because the house looked different with the furniture gone. For five evenings I returned to the old apt. to try to catch him. Finally he came in to get food and I caught him! Then he managed to escape out the window of this new apt. (but came back). Maybe his name should be "Boomerang"—he always returns!

J: Poor, poor Cayce--the cat we enjoyed for four years and had to leave behind when we left Iran. I remember you told me that your sister wrote and said that the cat seemed lonely and depressed after we left. They couldn't take care of him and found someone to give him to. I *hoped* that was a true story, but I kept thinking of how they "lost" my previous cats! Poor Cayce.

Chapter Eleven

The Fun Times

This chapter was not in the plans until the very end when a lot of different points and stories in the letters seemed to be without a home! These points were neither individually extensive enough to make a chapter of their own, nor limited and small enough to be thrown in the chapter called "Leftovers!" But fortunately they had, more or less, one thing in common—they all had something to do with fun and leisure. So, we decided to put them right here!

American Holidays

Jackie's first holiday season in Iran had lots of ups and downs and was sometimes very hectic. She was new in Tehran, had all the problems that have been already detailed with his family, had to move four times in that many months, and in addition her father passed away in November. So, no one can expect a lot of cheerful activities reported in her letters during this period—except for the following.

> Jan. 1, 1968 Christmas is not a holiday in Moslem countries like Iran, but my University was good enough to allow the foreign teachers to take the day off. Also they are giving us Jan. 1st off. My students (2 classes) surprised me with Christmas gifts. I got candy, a statue, and Persian slippers. And a couple of nice sweaters that they all chipped-in to buy. My landlord also surprised me with a Christmas gift— a pot of beautiful red flowers.

Of course, my nicest Christmas gift this year, I haven't mentioned yet. On the evening of Dec. 24th, Bahman and I went to a fancy Tehran jewelry store and picked out a diamond engagement ring!

But of course next year, and other years that followed, was usually happier and more in line with the seasonal atmosphere. We'll be looking at some of the more interesting ones while trying to spare the reader from repeats!

Dec. 8, 1968 Received your Christmas letter today and a letter from you yesterday. How nice that you had a full house for Thanksgiving. Wish we could have joined you. We didn't do anything special for Thanksgiving. I discovered that even a small turkey was too expensive. But I'm saving up for next year because I discovered that I missed having turkey on Thanksgiving.

We celebrated my birthday by going out for supper to the American Embassy Restaurant where I had steak and French fries—delicious! Of course, I baked a cake too.

Last Thursday we went to see the musical play "Guys and Dolls" presented in English by the Little Theater of Tehran. It was funny and enjoyable. The next day we went to see "Gone with the Wind" *in Persian*! Since I've seen the movie twice before and read the book, I could understand most of what they were supposed to be saying even if I didn't catch every word (and of course, Bahman was there to translate).

Dec. 26, 1968 We got a nice Christmas tree for our first Christmas together. All the trees are the kind with *long* pine needles. Some of the stores have imported Christmas ornaments but they're terribly expensive with not too much variety. We bought some lights and a few ornaments. Then I strung some popcorn and cut tinsels from aluminum foil. We put the tree up on the eve of Dec. 24th. It's over 6 feet tall and stands in a corner of our living room, very pretty.

I decided to have a Christmas party, so we invited 5 Persian friends to a dinner party (the first I've organized). I spent hours yesterday stuffing and roasting a 12-lb. turkey and preparing mashed potatoes and cooked carrots. What a job!

190

I was utterly exhausted afterwards. I guess hostesses should expect certain problems: my gravy had a burnt taste so I decided not to serve it, the guests arrived from 20 minutes to one hour late, then we had an extra unexpected guest to find room for. After all that I felt rather sick from eating too much. The guests seem to enjoy themselves so I guess it was a good party. But I was glad to see it get over, and I went directly to bed.

Christmas morning was lovely though. We sat by our lighted tree and opened our presents. I gave Bahman a pair of winter pajamas and he gave me a bathroom scale to keep track of the weight I and "junior" are gaining. (I seem to have a small bulge now, but I haven't gained weight.) The foreign teachers at the university were given the day off, while the others had to work. The day before the holiday I baked some Christmas cupcakes and took them to school for the teachers in my dept. to eat. Everyone liked that.

The American TV and radio stations have had several Christmas shows, and we went to a Christmas service at church on Sunday. So it seemed like Christmas around here even though Iranians don't celebrate the day. We haven't had snow in the city yet, either.

Dec. 2, 1969   Did you have a nice Thanksgiving? Thanksgiving, of course, is not a holiday here and last year I skipped the regular turkey, but I missed it. So this year we invited six Persian friends over and I roasted an 11-pound turkey (which was the way we celebrated Christmas last year—in fact we had most of the same guests). So it was a gay Thanksgiving—and also it was the overdue celebration, Persian tradition, for our new baby and our new car.

I also enjoyed a happy birthday the day before. Bahman gave me some French perfume and in the evening we went out to dinner at "Rasht 29," a dark and cozy restaurant just across the street from us. I had made a birthday cake for the occasion, too.

Jan. 9, 1970   How was Christmas and New Year's? We celebrated Christmas with two parties! On Christmas Eve we went to Isabel's where she had a buffet for about 10 people. The next evening we went to another Persian-American home where 30 or so of us enjoyed a turkey dinner and party. At our house we had a Christmas tree and a few presents. Bahman gave me some hand-painted Persian jewelry and I gave him a wool bathrobe. Ramin is still too young to enjoy Christmas, but our cat loved the tree (knocked it over by climbing it, in fact!). On New Year's Eve Bahman and I went out to dinner at a Chinese restaurant (probably the only one in Iran) and then to see the Sidney Poitier movie "To Sir, With Love." We arrived home before midnight to find Ramin fussy and keeping everyone awake. So as we entered the New Year I was putting the kid back to sleep!

Jackie: I see an opportunity here for an insert! What makes Thanksgiving so special is, of course, the turkey. Turkey, however, is not your everyday meatmarket staple in Iran. But it could be found if you knew where to look. We "foreign wives" shared with each other this valuable knowledge: most butcher shops wouldn't carry turkey on a regular basis, but some would special order it for you. The most reliable place to find turkey near Thanksgiving was Iran Super, which would also have the kind of bread needed to make the turkey stuffing. (Transplanted Americans were truly thankful for Iran Super.) It was helpful that the Farsi word for turkey, *booghalamoon,* was very entertaining to the American ear and thus easy to remember. What we were not prepared for was that the *booghalamoon* still needed a great deal of plucking! However, the turkeys were large and delicious and none ever needed the preboiling for tenderness that some chickens needed (another reason to be thankful).

Bahman: Well that was quite interesting, even to me! Now then, you can't ignore Christmas, can you?

J: Here are a few things I remember about Christmas. Of course, there are Christians in Iran, and Christmas is not a totally foreign holiday. However, the way most Americans celebrate Christmas is different than what many Iranians had seen. Our Iranian relatives were utterly amazed that I wanted to bring a six-foot pine tree into the house for two weeks. How nice it was that the Tehran street vendors anticipated the crazy American need for fresh cut trees. So many street corners sprouted with fresh cut trees that we had the luxury of choosing one close to home. This was our luck, because, without a car, we were in the position of carrying the tree four city blocks to our home. I'm sure the other pedestrians were amused. To complete the holiday, we were in the same position as early Americans in making our own tree decorations and sometimes in creating our own Christmas cards. What about Santa Claus? Our Iranian-American children had to have the same memories we had of sitting on Santa's knee, so one kindly dad dressed up and provided hours of fun for dozens of our bicultural children, while we moms took pictures for the relatives back in the U.S.

Dec. 14, 1970 Thanks for the birthday card-Thanksgiving card. I couldn't make up my mind whether I wanted to roast a turkey and invite people like last year or not. As it happened we finally went to the Iran-America Society restaurant with another Persian-American couple and had turkey there.

I had a big party at my house last week though. I decided to introduce the custom of the potluck supper and I invited all the people that we knew in Wisconsin who have since returned to Tehran (about 20 people). About 14 came and even that many filled up our living room. Everyone seemed to enjoy this reunion (except Ramin who had trouble sleeping through all the noise) and someday I might give another.

Dec. 30, 1971 If this letter reaches you in time for the post-Christmas sales, would you please buy us some *tinsel* and save it for us. Our tree is well decorated except for tinsel, which is quite expensive here.

Jan. 20, 1973 We had a white Christmas this year! In fact it required snow chains to drive up the mountain to Isabel's Christmas Eve party. Our New Year's was even whiter with a fresh heavy snowfall the day before. Imagine you having 70 [degree F] weather! We went to a final Christmas party on Dec. 28th and then an unexpected New Year's Eve party for only 4 couples. As usual, Ramin didn't want to take the Christmas tree down (so I did it when he was asleep) and for several weeks he still expected Santa Claus to come again!

Jan. 3, 1974 The Christmas season was a hectic one, but really fun. Our English Dept. at school gave a Christmas tea for the whole college faculty. Ramin had a party at his school with Santa Claus there, and both kids saw Santa at the American Women's Club party (350 kids went!), the Foreign Wives of Iranians party (91 kids) *and* the Tehran Trotters Square Dance Club party (a dinner party where we had imported American turkey, ham, and bratwurst with all the trimmings!) I wonder what the kids thought of all these Santas?! At least Susanne got used to him and sat on his knee finally. The first time she saw him, she hung around watching while others got presents, but when her turn came, she just grabbed her present and ran! Bahman and I went to two adult parties in the evenings of the 20th and 24th, as well as a New Year's Eve party at a friend's home. I wonder if we've got enough energy to celebrate our 6th wedding anniversary next week? With all this activity, I still haven't finished writing all my Christmas cards! (I got one day off for Christmas and stayed home on Jan. 1st. Ramin had 10 days off so Bahman took him to the repair shop to "help daddy" most mornings).

Dec. 11, 1974 Thanksgiving was nice for us, and I hope you enjoyed it too. Our square dancing club had a turkey dinner in a restaurant and on Thanksgiving day itself, Isabel, Joanne, and I got our families together for our "third annual feast."
Christmas parties began yesterday and will continue for the next two weeks! I think because we have to "try harder" to celebrate these "foreign" holidays, we get a lot more celebrations here than if we were in the U.S. It seems the kids will get to see Santa Claus at about four different parties again this year! I'm looking forward to Isabel's traditional Christmas Eve party, which we missed last year when she was in the U.S.

We had our first snow of the season last Thursday and what a snow it was! Six to eight inches even in the city and a lot of it is still on the ground. Maybe you heard that Tehran's airport's roof collapsed during the snowstorm. What a tragedy. Papers here reported 17 deaths, have you heard any other figure?

Jan. 9, 1976 We had a nice Christmas as usual. The kids saw Santa twice at different parties. Bahman and I went to Isabel's Christmas Eve party again—a tradition for us now. "Santa" brought me what I wanted—a big, beautiful poinsettia plant. And the kids got lots of toys—fortunately they don't yet know the difference between new and second-hand because I picked up most of the stuff at second-hand sales (except Ramin was surprised to find cobwebs in his toy fort!). It's good you sent your cards and letter late. They arrived. But many, many Christmas cards were burned up in a fire at the Tehran post office in mid-December. We got fewer than usual because of the fire I guess.

Oct. 29, 1976 Yesterday was the Foreign Wives of Iranians Halloween Party, and the kids got to use the costumes we got last summer. Along the route to the party, six members' houses were designated as "trick-or-treat" houses and we stopped at each of them. Ramin and Susanne really had a lot of fun, and Ramin even won a homemade cake at the "cake walk" at the party. I'm glad the kids get to enjoy Halloween even though it's not celebrated in Iran. I have so many happy memories of Halloween on Ardmore Rd. (Remember that great red devil costume?!)
Tomorrow the kids take their costumes to school for another Halloween party. We cut out jack-o-lanterns today from the funny-shaped Persian pumpkins.

J: Halloween is a peculiar holiday with a lot of strange customs for Americans. In Iran we could let our children celebrate with a certain amount of planning and organization. Decorations had to be kept to the privacy of our own homes, because who could explain witches and goblins to our Iranian neighbors? A number of foreign wives would agree to hand out candy, and the rest of us would shepherd each other's kids from home to home in costume. This could take some time considering the state of Tehran's traffic. It was a nice coincidence that the No-Ruz holiday celebration also has a custom of going from house to house for handouts! We could certainly identify with that.

Nov. 17, 1976 Isabel and I and my friend Sue (since Joanne, who usually comes, is in the U.S. for a year) plan to get our families together in my apt. next Thursday for thanksgiving. Actually Bahman and I enjoyed turkey and all the trimmings last night at a party put on by our square dancing club. It was held in a restaurant at the American Embassy and all the food was imported from the U.S.!
Susanne had a great time at her birthday party. We blew up the balloons you sent and decorated the place. Eight guests came for cake, ice cream, and games. I think she likes getting presents the best, and she got some nice educational toys. Today she was busy with her new embroidery set.

Jan. 5, 1977 Isabel had her usual big Christmas party— which I always enjoy. I especially look forward to the big delicious ham she always serves (ham is up to $5 a pound now—and we don't buy much). Dianne, another friend, always has a big party too. This year she invited 80 people so they rented the disco room at the French Club. Food, music, dancing—I loved it. Next weekend we've been invited to Dianne's brand new house for dessert and coffee. I'm anxious to see her house especially since I've heard that one prospective buyer has offered her one million dollars for it!!!
Jan. 8 – I still can't seem to finish a letter in one sitting! I'm writing this in my free time before classes start. I drive the kids to school and get to my school about 8:30.
Thursday night Bahman and I went party hopping. First to the Twelfth Night Party with my Scottish Country Dancing Group and then north through the snow to Dianne's "million dollar" house. The house *is* huge and gorgeous and beautifully furnished. It has a swimming pool, but a

million-dollar house ought to have a bigger yard with lots of old trees, I think.

Oct. 27, 1977   Last week Susanne joined an American Brownie troop. She's so happy—she's wanted to be a scout ever since Ramin joined Cub Scouts last spring. Her first Brownie meeting was one big birthday party for the four girls who had birthdays in October. And next week it will be a Halloween party.

In fact we went to an early Halloween party today. The Foreign Wives of Iranians Club had a party with games, costumes, refreshments and prizes. Afterwards we went to some of the members' homes for trick-or-treating. Susanne was dressed as a pink bunny with a cotton tail and Ramin was Boo-Berry again. It's nice that the kids can still celebrate these American holidays and customs that we "foreign" mothers enjoyed when we were children. I remember all those great costumes you used to sew for us— especially that red devil with the long stuffed tail! So far I haven't yet found time to actually sew a costume for my kids (except for one clown outfit I made for Susanne's nursery circus last spring).

Oct. 28 – I've just spent 3 hours helping the kids cut out and clean two pumpkins for their jack-o-lantern contest in school tomorrow. I am glad I only have to do that once a year! Now I have all this pumpkin pulp and no way to make it into pies and cakes since there is an egg shortage in Tehran right now.

Nov. 9, 1978   Anyway I'm planning a birthday party for Susanne and inviting lots of kids to our new large apartment. Susanne is so excited and happy.

I'm also trying to plan a nice Thanksgiving dinner and I hope I can find a turkey somewhere.

Persian Holidays

This section is essentially going to be about No-Ruz, which is spelled quite a few different ways. Naturally, there are bound to be repetitions, but we'll try to minimize that.

March 6, 1968. The first day of spring is the first day of the Persian New Year (for the year 1347) which is called the No-Ruz holiday. No-Ruz is the biggest Persian holiday and lasts for 13 days. People give gifts, go on trips, visit each other, etc. We get a long vacation from school to celebrate No-Ruz. It ought to be fun.

March 27, 1968 We are now celebrating the New Year's holidays here. The first day of the Persian year 1347 came on the first day of spring last week. We bought presents for all of Bahman's nieces and nephews. Guests have been coming to our house and we go out to visit people, too. We have over two weeks vacation from the Universities. This was the time we had planned to come to the U.S. to be married, but instead we have already enjoyed 2 ½ months of married life now.

When the New Year's holidays come, everyone is supposed to clean their house thoroughly—a kind of spring cleaning. We were certainly busy vacuuming and scrubbing, etc. We have pretty yellow curtains for the kitchen, and at the last minute we decided to go out and buy material for new living room curtains, too. We prepared the traditional Persian "Haft Seen" (Seven S's) table for our living room. That's a table on which you put seven different things whose name begins with the letter "s", such as "sib" (apple) and "seer" (garlic), etc. The table stays in the living room until the 13 days of No-Ruz (New Year) are over.

March 24, 1969 As part of the New Year tradition, every day we've been visited by friends and relatives and have gone to see them. I enjoy visiting but these visits are not the friendly informal kind you find in the US. The young people are supposed to visit the older ones first, then you should revisit everyone who has visited you. I'm afraid I still make mistakes in the formal Persian etiquette because I still act like an American at times.

March 29, 1972 We are now celebrating a 13-day holiday on the occasion of the Persian New Year, which began last week with a 2-day snowstorm! We've had lots of snow this year too. Sunday is the 13th day of the New Year (also it's Easter) and it's supposed to be bad luck to stay home, so everyone will go on picnics.

March 28, 1973 We are all fine and healthy for a change. We have about 3 weeks vacation now to celebrate the Iranian New Year. On the spur-of-the-moment we decided to go to Shiraz for about 5 days of this vacation, so we got plane tickets for tomorrow. We're hoping the kids don't give us too much trouble on the trip, especially Susanne who is getting more mischievous every day.
Got to take a bath and pack now.

April 11, 1974 I'm not even sure if we get Easter Sunday off from school (guess I told you that Thurs.-Fri. is the weekend here) since we've just finished a nice long 17-day holiday to celebrate the Iranian New Year. We had a lovely relaxing holiday then, and our weather was something like yours—warm on the first day of spring but turning so cold after a week that we had to put the heaters back on (we use kerosene stoves with chimneys, but the newer houses have radiators). We carried out the custom of visiting all our relatives and having them visit us. We even took a 2-hour drive to a nearby city [Qazvin] to see cousins. We went sightseeing and shopping in the bazaar, ate lunch at the cousins' house and came back the same day.

March 28, 1975 Happy Easter! Easter falls during our No-Ruz (New year) holidays this year, and I'm planning to go to church Sunday morning and take the kids to an Easter party in the afternoon . . . . Also according to tradition, we've set up a table in the living room with a bowl of goldfish and seven items beginning with the letter "S". I set the table with your white crocheted tablecloth and it's gotten *lots* of complements. Exactly when did you make it? It's gorgeous.

B: That just about covers your contribution to explaining No-Ruz and what we did with it all those years! Now, I've got something to add, not exactly about No-Ruz but about what happened at the dawn of two of them exactly twelve years apart. In March of 1967, after a five-year stay in the U.S., I left and arrived in Iran full of hopes and dreams. And twelve years later in the March of 1979, I had to leave Iran to join you and the children; with no knowledge (or even dream) whatsoever of what was going to happen. I see a kind of irony there.

J: No-Ruz, new year, new life. It seems an appropriate time to start a new year on the first day of spring when nature comes to life again. And it seems an appropriate time for *you* to start life anew, in Iran and later in the U.S.

B: All right, now that we are philosophizing let me add that the two "new lives" were diametrically different. The first one was anticipated, planned, and full of hopes and expectations; whereas the second one was unexpected, unplanned, and full of uncertainties. But then again, that *is* life!

Weddings and Parties

Oct. 31, 1968 Bahman and I had a great time last Sunday evening. One of Bahman's friends (a Zoroastrian fellow) got married, and we were invited to the reception. First of all, it was nice for me to have an occasion to get "all dressed up." This is the first big celebration we've been invited to, and the first time for me to be out and seen by Zoroastrian society. The reception was held in a big hotel around the block from our apartment. There must have been at least 500 guests at the reception! There was a band and singer there, and long tables with fruit and other snacks. Bahman kept running into old, old friends whom he hadn't seen in years, and I was pleased to notice *five* other foreign women there (4 Germans and an American whom I had met before). At 10 o'clock we were ushered downstairs where long buffet tables had been set up to serve dinner. I don't think I've ever seen so much food set out before—salads, rice dishes, lamb, chicken, etc.!! (The hotel charges somewhat over $5 per person for a party like this so you can imagine how much money they spent on it!) Then we went back upstairs to hear the singer again. Then someone pointed us out to an elderly couple who came over and introduced themselves as cousins from Bahman's father's side of the family. They were *so* happy to see Bahman after so many years and to meet me. They're the first ones from the father's side of the family that I've met. Well, I've decided that I like Persian wedding receptions, and I hope we get invited to another one soon.

Feb. 7, 1969   A week ago Tuesday we managed to get through a snow storm (by bus) to attend a wedding reception in a large hotel. The richest family we know had a son who was being married. I went to a hairdresser that morning for a fancy hair style, and my sisters-in-law spent days making their dresses and getting ready for this big occasion. We heard that about 1,000 people had been invited. There was a band there and singers and a hall full of people, but not many places to sit down! After two or three hours of talking , etc. we all went downstairs for supper at 10 p.m. It was quite a sight! There were rows and rows of long buffet tables filled with plates of food. Everyone took as much food as they wanted, stood and ate it, and then took more. Most of us hadn't eaten much all day, just waiting for this feast!

Two days later, according to tradition, we went to the groom's house to give them a present. Usually only women are supposed to go on this occasion, but I hardly go anywhere without Bahman, so he came (and there were a few other men there). We gave them an expensive hand crafted picture frame, and I was surprised to see what kinds of gifts rich people get at weddings. They received a TV, a stereo set, crystal, paintings, carpets, diamond jewelry, and hundreds of dollars worth of gold coins. There were over 60 people there and all were invited to dinner. We couldn't stay though, because we had already been invited to a restaurant by some friends of ours.

A week ago Sunday we went to a sort of U. of Wisconsin reunion. A friend of ours was visiting Tehran from Shiraz, and so it was a good occasion for a bunch of us to get together again. We went to another friend's house for the gathering, and it was funny to see that all four of us wives there were pregnant! Another strange thing happened after that. One fellow came in and brought his new bride (one-month) for us to meet. It turned out that his bride is one of my students at the University! I was certainly embarrassed to see her, and the girl was equally shocked and perhaps embarrassed to see her English teacher there!

June 27, 1971 It's quite interesting that our social life has really picked up lately. Just this month we have been to a wedding reception (300 people), a memorial dinner (it's a Zoroastrian custom to remember a death in the family with a huge dinner on the anniversary every year), a 2-day holiday in a mountain hotel with our square dancing club, a Wisconsin reunion party, an all-day picnic in the country, a dinner party, and a kid's birthday party and dinner with a puppet show! For July there is already scheduled a dinner party, another birthday party (Isabel's daughter) and a swimming-party-barbecue! Also July 8-10 we are planning to vacation at the Caspian seashore with friends.

March 16, 1973 We went to our first Moslem wedding ceremony last week. An American teacher at my school (did I mention Nancy to you before? She went to the Caspian Sea with us last Fall) married an Iranian man in a private ceremony in a home. It was interesting, but very short! The traditional large reception party was not held because this month is one of the Moslem mourning periods.

June 14, 1974 One of the most interesting things I did last week was attend a dress rehearsal for folk dancing put on by amateur dancers from 14 different countries all in native costumes at the Hilton Hotel. The performance was presented 2 days later at a charity dinner in the presence of the Empress at $35 a plate, but we got to see it free! Also this week we went to a dinner dance put on by Zoroastrian Engineers Club, a dinner at a friend's home, and a picnic and swim yesterday with our square dance club (kids included). Today Bahman took the kids and relatives on a picnic while I'm staying home to correct exams and get ready for dinner guests this evening. We still have another pool party lunch and a dinner party at Tehran University to attend next week! What an active social season!

Feb. 21, 1975 Bahman and I have been to between one and three dinner parties a week this month, which is unusual in Feb. I finally stepped on the scale yesterday and found out I've gained 5 pounds. I wonder if I should start dieting now or wait until after the Persian New Year next month. One of the dinner parties was at Tehran Univ. for hundreds of professors and their wives. The huge buffet tables were loaded with a tremendous amount of food. It's something I never saw in the U.S.

B: I think it would make a good change of pace to quote the following piece here. It is from a letter that I wrote you after I returned home from our vacation in the U.S. ahead of you and the kids. Is it fair to speculate that it must have stirred some, shall we say, jealousy in you?!

He: 7/30/76 I am sorry dear but I can't help mentioning it. You missed one of the grandest wedding ceremonies yet. The large Zomorod Salon of Sheraton was all made up. There was a special seat decorated for the king & queen, a seven-story cake one and a half the size of Yousef himself on stage. There were four ministers [political *not* religious!] and the mayor among the guests (so they said), etc. The bride is rather slim, shorter than him and were dancing and greeting people all the time the flood lights for films were blinding, the Rock & Roll was deafening (for me at least). The food was served in Morvarid Salon underneath buffet style but everyone sat at many round tables to eat. Hashemians and Nowrasteh and Bahram were there. The rest I'll tell you here!

J: I suppose I may have felt a little jealous, but not to the point of wishing I had returned early to Tehran!

B: Fair enough--back to your letters to your Mom.

Feb. 18, 1978 Also last Thursday evening we took the kids with us to a music-and-dinner-party. The informal quartet I play with decided to have dinner together and play for some of our friends. I think the kids enjoyed "hearing Mommy play violin" but they were the only kids there and got bored after a while.

We'll all go out to dinner again next Monday. It's the annual Cub Scouts' Blue-and-Gold dinner to celebrate the founding of scouts. It's at the American Military Club so we're sure to get some good American food!

It seems there are a lot of dinners lately. On Feb. 5, our Scottish Country Dancing group celebrated "Burns' Night"—the birthday of the Scottish poet Robert Burns—with a traditional Scottish dinner. (I've gained quite a few pounds this winter, which I'm trying to lose. I've started my annual spring diet earlier this year!) A really special dinner is coming up next month though. I got an official letter saying that the Iranian government (the Shah) is awarding me the Pahlavi Medal, third class, for outstanding work in our Organization. It's not such an exclusive honor since out of 200 or so employees, 20 or 30 of us are awarded these medals. The awards will be made next month at a dinner in our honor at the Golestan Palace. I sort of feel like Cinderella, going to dinner at the Palace!

March 21, 1978 Did I mention that my string quartet played at a *second* party 3 weeks ago. The host's wife is from Thailand and so our dinner was traditional Thai food. It was delicious, but some of it was so spicy hot that tears came to my eyes and my nose started running! I wonder how people, and even children, get used to such hot food.

Sports, Dance and Music

March 6, 1968 We've taken up a couple of new "sports" lately. On Wednesday evenings we go to the American military N.C.O. Club for square dancing. Square dancing is not quite as much fun as folk dancing, but I guess it's second best. The group we dance with is small and I think it's the only square dancing group in town.

The second sport is skiing. Every year on Washington's Birthday, many of the Americans in Tehran get together for a big holiday outing at a ski resort in the mountains, 1 ½ hours drive outside Tehran. This year there were two thousand of us on the outing, including Bahman and me. We rented boots and skis and started out on the beginner's slope. It was such fun that Bahman and I decided to go back and try it again the next week. Even the beginner's slope seemed kind of long and steep. My first problem was just to learn to hold on to the *ski lift* without falling down! Tehran's weather is now beginning to warm up, and I wonder how much longer there will be good snow on the mountains. I guess we started this sport rather late in the season

April 26, 1968 Remember when I told you that Bahman had fixed up his old violin for me to play. Well, today Bahman took out some of his old music books and I played from them. He was pretty happy that music is "international," and I can even play Persian music.

Sept. 13, 1968 We've been out to dinner twice this week. On Sunday we celebrated since it was a year ago that I arrived in Iran, and also it was about time for our eight-month wedding anniversary! We went to Café Naderi, which is a restaurant outdoors in a garden, under tall pine trees, with water fountains and a band and dance floor. On Wednesday our Square Dancing group had a farewell dinner for one of the couples (the man had been in the Army for 19 years, and the Army was sending him to Viet Nam for his last year of service).

Oct. 11, 1968 Last Friday we went hiking with the Iran-America Society. It took us three hours to hike to Kolakchal, a resort camping area in the mountains. It's steep uphill hiking on dry, brown, treeless mountains—quite different from the forests I've hiked in, in the US. At Kolakchal we played chess, walked around the camp, ate lunch, took a nap, and then hiked down. The trip down took only about an hour because we ran most of the way. It must be cute to watch us hike—Bahman and I are the only ones who hike most of the way holding hands!

Jan. 28, 1971 Bahman and I have rejoined the square dancing club we belonged to 2 years ago. Now we're even taking square dancing lessons. We go every Monday and I guess that's about all the exercise we get these days, though I'm anxious to try skiing again when we find the time.

March 8, 1971 Last week Bahman and I graduated from our square dancing class and joined the Tehran Trotters Square Dancing Club. The club is almost all American military people, and there's only one other Persian in it. They have dances twice a month with a professional caller.

May 30, 1971 Next week we are going to a hotel in the mountains for a 2-day vacation. The trip was planned by our square dancing club, and we'll be square dancing a lot while there.

Jan. 20, 1973 I've been putting my free time to good use lately, I think. I have a guitar-playing friend who's been urging me to accompany her, so I got my violin out and practiced for the first time since before Ramin was born! The trouble is, and has been, that I can't play when the kids are sleeping and they don't let me play when they're awake (Ramin keeps interrupting and wanting me to play "Ol' McDonald," and then they end up fighting). Also, I'm learning to crochet, and this evening I made my first Devil's Food Cake—which came out *delicious*! Finally I hope to sew a dress from the material I got in the U.S. last summer!

Feb. 9, 1974 Bahman and I started learning Scottish Country Dancing in a class last week. What fun! We still square dance too.

May 2, 1974 Other entertainment I've enjoyed lately: last weekend we spent a day with a couple of thousand other people at a horse show on a farm outside the city. We took a picnic lunch and saw Isabel and other friends there. The kids thought they were going there to ride the horses themselves. Susanne kept saying "look at the donkeys" (ponies)! and both kids were more interested in climbing fences and finding spiders in the grass than watching the horses jump.

This week I saw a musical production in English of *Godspell*, which is based on the gospel of St. Matthew. It was really great and very funny in most parts. I was lucky to get tickets—two weeks of performances were sold out, even though these were amateur actors. I took along the Barnes; an American couple we know who usually stay at home because they have no car and no baby-sitter for 3-yr.-old Christy. We left Christy at our house with Bahman who did a great job of babysitting and even got the 3 kids to sleep with no problem. (Bahman usually doesn't care for musicals in English.)

Nov. 1, 1974 We've had quite a few parties lately. One kid's birthday party had a puppet show (in Persian) which my kids enjoyed. A couple of times we've gone hiking in the lovely fall weather. Susanne had her first two hikes, and she's still asking to be carried a bit of the way, but we walk slowly enough so that she enjoys most of it. We've taken other families with kids along to encourage ours. Ramin's starting his third year at hiking and he doesn't get tired. The kids really love the chair-ride (like a ski-lift) in the mountains though I think it's a little scary.

March 1, 1975 Last week Bahman and I went to a pot-luck supper with the American Women's Club. The entertainment was a professional belly-dancer. She also gives belly-dancing lessons, which would probably be interesting if I had the time! Did I tell you I found a new group for International Folk Dancing. I've danced with them twice so far. Along with Square Dancing and Scottish Country Dancing, I get to dance quite a lot.

Jan. 9, 1976 We spent New Year's Eve square dancing until 2 a.m. at one of the dancers' houses. It was great fun. Some of the military people even brought American chips and dip, strawberry shortcake, and party whistles!

Feb. 13, 1976 Last week I saw and heard the Prime Minister of Iran [Amir Abbas Hoveyda] in person. He spoke for the American Women's Club. I also went to a luncheon-lecture on women's liberation, and a dinner-dance at our Scottish Dancing Club. Bahman and I took a British businessman out to a fancy night-club with a 4-hour floor show! One night we went to the Opera House for Persian dancing and music. I also gave a ladies' Koffee Klatch, at my house. Aren't we busy!

Oct. 29, 1976 Last week I took Ramin and Susanne ice skating with Isabel and her kids. Isabel has become a member of a club called the Ice Palace which is the only place in Iran with an indoor rink (outdoors seldom gets cold enough for good ice). After two hours Susanne had managed to control her double-runner skates and Ramin was doing surprisingly well on his single blades. I was tired—I hadn't been on skates in over 9 years!
I discovered that some of the people in my square-dancing club play instruments and have been getting together regularly to play. So I took out my violin today (after I-don't-know-how-many-years!) and joined them. We had a string quartet—and it was really fun. I was surprised to see I can still play, and about as good as the other members of the group! I plan to play regularly now with them.
I'm still doing Scottish Country Dancing once a week too. That's the most exercise of any of my activities.

Nov. 17, 1976 Last week I took the kids ice skating with Isabel's kids again. Even Bahman came along and got out on skates for the first time in at least 10 years. Ramin does quite well and really enjoys it. The next day in school he wrote a composition about his ice-skating.

Feb. 3,1977 I guess I told you that I joined a string quartet a few months ago. We play a couple of hours every Friday and sometimes all go out for a pizza supper. It's great fun.

Bahman does a fine job of supervising the kids' bath and supper on Fridays so they're pretty much set for bed when I come home. Two weeks ago the newspaper had a classified: "Amateur string orchestra looking for more enthusiastic members" so I called the phone number given and found out it was a group directed by the music teacher at The German School—the same orchestra that several of my quartet members already belong to. So I got the address and went there last Sunday evening. But what a surprise I got! I walked into the middle of a big party—they had canceled practice in order to celebrate the director's birthday. The dinner was fabulous—spread out on a cloth on the floor in traditional Persian style with about 3 kinds of rice and 6 or 7 different main courses plus dessert. And I met some interesting people, German and American, including three English teachers to "shop-talk" with. So next Sunday I'll go back to actually start practicing with their small orchestra (I was the only one who answered their ad!)

The next night I went to another dinner party! My Scottish Country Dancing group was celebrating the birthday of Robert Burns (born 1759) the famous Scottish poet. We had a bagpiper, poem-reading, special ceremonies, and the traditional Scottish meal of Haggis (a kind of chopped meat) in addition to dancing. I sure hated to get up at my usual time of 6:30 a.m. the next morning!

March 17, 1977 A couple of weeks ago my Scottish Country Dancing Group was having a party, when we noticed an American wedding reception being held across the street. So, as the newlyweds were driving away for their honeymoon, we brought our bagpiper outside and had piping and dancing in the street as a "send-off." This resulted in the father of the bride inviting us all into the reception for champagne and more dancing—what fun! I'll bet the Iranians in the neighborhood thought we were all *crazy* foreigners.

Oct. 27, 1977 The German School Orchestra that I play with is now practicing for a concert the first Friday in December. Did I mention we gave a concert last June in the German

Embassy? I'm also still playing with a quartet once a week quite informally.

B: The silence is killing me! We should at least have a farewell ending for the chapter, no?

J: Silence?! Well, there was music, dancing, and parties. I was obviously having a great time--part of my philosophy of always being open to new experiences.

Chapter Twelve

Touched by Revolution

Theoretically, there shouldn't be a chapter about politics in this book because neither Bahman nor Jackie was involved in Iranian politics. Although he was a student at the University of Wisconsin in early 1960's, and lots of Iranian students in the U.S. were politically active against the Shah's regime, he wasn't among them! Actually, he was a firm believer in the Persian saying, "Quiet you come, quiet you go, and the cat won't stalk you!" And he had a "good" excuse to be apolitical! He was on a four-year full scholarship program from the Iranian Government to study abroad; although this excuse didn't stop some other students to be outspoken against the regime. All that said, however, there is enough material available to make this chapter anything but blank! Especially, considering the fact that it *was* a political upheaval that uprooted the family in 1979.

Of course being apolitical doesn't mean lack of interest in social and political issues. Just a couple of days after he returned to Iran, she wrote to him:

She: 3/11/67 In yesterday's paper I learned that [former Prime Minister Mohammad] Mossadegh died on March 5 at age 86. I also found out that Iran has a female director-general of water and power, Mrs. Effat Nahvi (who is now visiting in Washington).

And just a few days before leaving the U.S., she wrote to him:

She: 8/28/67 I guess you know the Shah was here in Washington last week and of course there were demonstrations by the Iranian Students Association. I clipped out most of the news about the Shah to bring with me to show you what kind of newspaper coverage he got here.

After she arrived in Iran, and for quite a few years, the country seemed pretty stable and the social-political horizon looked rosy. As a matter of fact, her arrival coincided with a huge celebration in Iran and she wrote about it to her folks.

Oct. 12, 1967 Have you seen the October 6 issue of *Time* magazine (maybe you can find it in a library now)? There is a long article and 6 pages of color pictures about Iran. Most of it is about the Shah and the plans for his Coronations on Oct. 26. The Coronation is really going to be something! Streets and buildings are already decorated with thousands of colored light bulbs. We get a 10-day holiday from the Univ. to enjoy the celebration. I wish all my American friends could see that issue of *Time* and learn something about Iran.

Oct. 30, 1967 Last Thursday was Coronation Day for the Shah and the Empress Farah. Bahman and I went to a friend's house and watched the ceremony on TV, in Persian. We saw part of the procession on TV too, but then we left quickly and took a taxi to Ferdowsi Square so we could see the coaches passing. I tried to take a picture of the procession but there were so many people in the way I'm not sure I got a good one. The day was sunny and nice as usual (the weather is still in the 70's though it gets cold at night). I think *Newsweek* and *Life* magazines are having special articles on the Coronation. Have you seen them? The city is decorated everywhere—millions of colored lights—and it's just beautiful here.

And four years later she reported to her mother about another extravaganza!

July 24, 1971 Why don't you come visit Iran next October! The whole country is preparing for great celebrations on the 25th Centennial Anniversary of the founding of the Persian Empire by Cyrus the Great. Tehran streets are being decorated with fancy lights and it ought to be as pretty as the Coronation 4 years ago. Then of course you can be here for the birth of your second grandchild too!

Oct. 19, 1971 This past week Iran has been celebrating the 25th Centenary Anniversary of the Founding of the Iranian Monarchy. You've probably heard about it—did you see anything of it on TV? The lights and decorations on the streets are quite beautiful.

B: The next recorded item to report, having any relation to politics, is your letter of March 1978. But if we enter that here and now, without any intervention (!), it's going to create a gap of over six years with respect to both time and content. Instead, let us take this opportunity for a good lengthy dialogue. What I think we can do is to discuss *our* understanding of why the Revolution occurred. Are you ready?

J: Well, here goes. The previous letters just hint at the celebrations and extravagant events that the Shah was planning and holding for himself and his family. I think we were erroneously under the impression that *everyone* liked these displays, but that wasn't so.

B: OK, your "hints" are good for a start. I think we can explore at least three different areas for discussion. One is the economic factor, which caused dissatisfaction among the masses. The oil revenues of the seventies created quite a few rich people, and instead of having a positive effect, created a much larger gap between the rich and the majority poor. There was no need for the populous poor to be prodded by any opposition group to show discontent; they were already in it.

J: Yes, and every ostentatious display of wealth or major improvement in northern Tehran, or rich sections of other towns, increased their discontent. There is even a report of our visit to

South Tehran a few weeks after my arrival in Iran that is relevant to quote here.

> Oct. 30, 1967 A week or so ago Bahman and I went touring in South Tehran. South Tehran is like a completely different city. The poor people live there and there are lots of slums and everything is dirtier. I began to really appreciate living in the north part of Tehran where it's rather nice. I still like my new apartment.

B: The second area of discontent, which I think was probably more serious than economics, was cultural/sociological. We can say that the Shah's regime wanted to modernize Iran very fast and without regard to tradition, culture, and religion. Nothing can exemplify this more than the occurrences of the Shiraz Art Festival every year for many years. Some of these "art shows" included shows of nudity and sexual displays in public. Forget about the devout religious, even for the educated, the intellectuals, and the so-called "western-stricken," the avant-garde art was too much. (Just between you and me, I cringe at it even now!)

J: I think the Shah wanted to bring his nation into the Twentieth Century, but his view was based on western ideas not always compatible with tradition. There were a lot of incompatible elements in existence then.

B: Right, and finally we come to politics and how the Shah and his family were controlling and running the government of the country. Now of course books are written about this subject but we have to limit ourselves to a page or two! No one can question the lack of democratic principles in Iran such as lack of freedom of speech and the press. And on top of that there was the existence of the secret police, SAVAK. Lots of individuals were arrested, executed, or disappeared.

J: I remember saying I could only live in Iran ignoring the government. Looking back, I think that was a "head in the sand" way of living.

B: By the way, do you recall that even *I* had a brush with SAVAK? Not being cynical, I think it was a case of mistaken identity. In any case, a couple of agents stopped me in the street and wanted to search our apartment. Actually what they mostly did was to go through our bookshelf to see if they could find any subversive books. And since they didn't (I think they missed a couple of *English* books on Communism we happened to have!) they left. I also remember, after they learned I was a Zoroastrian, they became more forgiving. The whole episode must have taken two to three hours.

J: That apartment-search incident was the most terrifying incident that happened to us in Iran--not for what happened, but for what might have happened had the agents recognized the English books (*Mein Kampf*, etc.) that they pawed through!

B: So, the seeds of dissatisfaction and dissent had been growing for years. But the year 1963 can be considered a milestone in Iran's history. It was during that year (while you and I were both in the U.S., not that we knew each other yet) that Khomeini came to national, and even international, prominence. Shah's White Revolution, which included land reform and women's rights, had angered powerful people including the clergy. There were widespread demonstrations and violence in the spring of 1963 that led to the arrest of Khomeini and many others. He was released a few months later but more unrest followed and led to his deportation to Turkey on November 4, 1964.

J: Are you saying that the resistance was "fire beneath the ash" for all those years until we saw its manifestations in 1977?

B: Exactly. The flash point occurred when in October of 1977 Khomeini's son suddenly died and some saw the hands of SAVAK in it. The second flash point happened on January 7, 1978 when a slanderous letter by the regime against Khomeini appeared in a newspaper. And that ignited what was to become the Revolution a year later.

J: Well then, that brings us to the following letter to my mom, which mentions a possible postal workers strike.

March 21, 1978 Actually, I haven't received another letter from you yet, but maybe it's taking another 24 days! So I thought I'd write anyway. Rumor was that postal workers were unofficially on strike here, so that's why mail was so slow.

I think I mentioned that I was going to get a medal from the Iranian government for outstanding services to education, . . . The medal winners were also handed two invitations. One was to a party at the Golestan Palace, . . . The second invitation was for the next day to a ceremony marking the 100th anniversary of the birth of Reza Shah the Great (the Shah's father) at his tomb in south Tehran. But that day it snowed! (And we have had almost no snow this winter!) We were driven in special buses (beginning at 8 a.m.) to the tomb but had to walk a long way from the parking lot in flooded streets, snow, rain and freezing wind. I had only a light coat over my long formal dress and I was *so* cold. At least the reviewing stands we sat in had canopies over them. The Shah, Empress, and the Crown Prince came about noon, had a 20-minute ceremony and left again by helicopter. At least the sun had come out by then! I got home by 3 p.m., cold and tired and wishing I hadn't gone at all!

Unfortunately the conference was at the same time as the first official visit of the Shah and Empress to our school. We had been preparing for weeks for their visit and then we weren't there when they came. But the teachers who were there said he got a very good impression of our school and was quite pleased with it. He talked to the children and the teachers. He has ordered more gifted schools built throughout Iran and things look good for our future development.

Sept. 9, 1978 Now don't phone us just because of the news you may be hearing about Iran lately. We are quite all right and we live and work in the north (safer) part of Tehran. There has been fighting and shooting in the southern streets and the Army is everywhere. Yesterday Tehran and 11 other cities were put under martial law—which means everything is controlled by the military—for 6 months. They also imposed a curfew, no one is allowed outside between 9 p.m. and 5 a.m. so the streets around our house are perfectly quiet all night long. But people in Tehran are used to an active nightlife with lots of parties, so it'll be hard to get used to. No more dancing for me for awhile. Pity the poor movie theaters, restaurants, and nightclubs! Anti-government demonstrators started all this.

Sept. 30, 1978 Haven't got any letters from you yet, but that's not surprising considering that my mailing address is not so reliable. One of the letters Bahman mailed to our new home address was returned to his office address, after 4 weeks, marked "address unknown!" My office address is still the best place to write to me though it might take 2 months to arrive. I wonder if you received my last letter; this is the second letter I've written since we got back.
Part of Iran had a tremendous earthquake with thousands killed. Someone said the U.S. news reported the quake was in Tehran. Well, it wasn't. Some people in Tehran felt a slight tremor, but I was out in traffic at the time and didn't feel a thing. Iran is certainly having more than its share of problems.
We're still under martial law, but we haven't heard of any new incidents. Things are so calm that the curfew now is only from midnight to 4:30 a.m.

Nov. 3, 1978 Hi! Hope you haven't been too worried about not hearing from me in a while. The Iranian postal workers have been on strike for several weeks and no mail has been going out or coming in. even now that the strike is over, they have mountains of mail to go through and there's no telling when mail will be regular again. But a friend's cousin is leaving for the U.S. in two days so I hope she'll mail this for me when she arrives. Of course, now Iran Air is on strike so I hope she has tickets on another airline! I haven't tried to call you because international lines are full of people calling home and calls must be reserved days in advance. Also, there are three on our party line and we've informally agreed not to call long distance because it would be impossible to figure out the phone bill. (We just get the *total* to be paid.) Of course, in any great emergency, I'll call you. Anyway the best address for me is still NIOGATE (National Iranian Organization for the Gifted and Talented Education).

I've heard that U.S. TV had an hour-long special about "Our Crisis in Iran" and that there are frequent bulletins about Iran. So maybe you've been informed on things here. It seems that lots of Iranians want a purely Moslem government, and there are demonstrations by thousands of people in the streets of Tehran and other cities almost every day now. There is only violence when the Army or police try to disperse the crowds (traffic becomes impossible!) or the demonstrators get angry and break windows. Fortunately our new house is far from all these demonstrations and none of it has affected us. In fact, all we know about it is what other people tell us or what we read in the newspapers and hear on the news! It's just the many strikes that seem to be affecting us. The postal strike was annoying (I haven't gotten *any* mail from the U.S. since I got back from the U.S.!). Tehran University is closed by strikes. Our bank was closed for a few days, and our school (NIOGATE) was closed one day.

Nov. 9, 1978 Last week I wrote you a letter and a happy birthday card which I'm not sure my friend remembered to give to her uncle going to the U.S. So I'm writing again and sending this with Barbara and Jeff who are going back to the U.S. this week. I actually tried to call you to tell you not to worry (most of my friends have *very* worried relatives in the U.S.) but the lines were busy of course.

We are still completely fine. The riots in central Tehran got worse last week, and I was so very happy that we moved when we did. Bahman drove through our old neighborhood today and said the banks had broken windows. Lots of workers were on strike and we had to wait an hour and a half in line for gasoline (something like your gas shortage of a few years ago!) They closed the schools and won't open them for another week according to today's news. So we're enjoying an unexpected holiday. It's nice that Bahman and I are both teachers and can stay home with the kids this week.

Things are quieter in the city now that the Shah has installed a military government and the curfew was extended 9 p.m. to 5 a.m. If there are any demonstrators on the streets we don't know about it, because we don't have any newspapers this week.

Dec. 14, 1978   Another friend is leaving for the U.S. tomorrow so I'm sending another letter. Did you get my Christmas card? It was nice to get your phone call. That was the night we began hearing demonstrators shouting at night, which was a little scary. But the two days of deep mourning for all Moslems have passed (did your news report tell about the hundreds of thousands of marchers on those days?) and things seem quieter these days. We still have frequent electric blackouts though. That's the way the electricity workers show their protest against the Shah. The oil workers' strike is resulting in a shortage of cooking gas, and I hope I get some soon or we won't be able to bake Christmas cookies. Otherwise things seem to be getting better. They even started selling Christmas trees on the street corners today (which I didn't expect to see this year!).

Susanne and Ramin's school opened again this week after two further weeks of closure. Ramin went back to school, but Susanne had just burst out in chicken pox. I suppose it's an average case, she doesn't feel especially sick. But there are pox in the strangest places: on her scalp, her eyelid, between her toes, etc. I expect she'll be better by Sunday and can go back to school in time for their Christmas party.

Bahman and I expect to start school again on Saturday. Our school has been closed a total of 5 weeks so far. What an unexpected vacation! We've been doing a lot of reading and cleaning the house, fixing things and finding things to entertain the kids (no radio or TV the past two weeks). It's nice to have some American neighbors to visit and have the kids play with. One neighbor wanted to have a small tag sale last week, so I joined her and made about $25 in one morning of selling old kids' clothes and toys.

The American Women's Club had a Christmas bazaar last week and I went and bought a few things. I bought one ticket in their Grand Raffle, and this week I got a phone call saying I had won a prize! It's dinner for two persons at the Polynesian Room of the Intercontinental Hotel (a fancy, expensive place). I think I'll use it to celebrate our 11th wedding anniversary on Jan. 9th.

We had fun this morning. We went to another sale by an American who is leaving (I've been to lots of these lately— so many Americans have panicked and left) and bought over a $100 worth of American food. I'm going to have fun eating corn, blueberry muffins, canned salmon, Brussels sprouts, etc. and Bahman is in 7th heaven with so many cans of Campbell's soup! We also bought an American toaster-oven so we can cook when we run out of cooking gas (provided we have electricity—which we do most of the time).

Jan. 13, 1979 We're still OK but things are getting more uncomfortable here. Right now we have a power outage (we've had them everyday for over a month) so Bahman's reading the paper (they began printing again this past week after a 62 day strike!), the kids are doing homework, and I'm writing, all by one light bulb that Bahman has rigged up to an old car battery. In fact, Bahman has been very inventive and creative these days. He's figured out a way to heat a lot of water electrically (when we *have* electricity) so we can take shower. About 17 days ago we ran out of fuel oil so we've had no heat or hot water. We do have one small kerosene heater and a bit of kerosene to keep at least one room warm in the evenings. The other rooms stay about 48 F. We also have a very small amount of gasoline so we don't go anywhere (School for Gifted and all public schools are closed again) but we haven't had to get in one of the gasoline waiting lines that stretch for miles. All of this is because the oil workers are on strike until the Shah resigns. I suppose you hear it all on the news.

But Susanne and Ramin went back to school this week after a *long* Christmas vacation. At least their school does have heat and teachers. We did have a nice Christmas and a really fun potluck supper at our apt. on Christmas Eve (even though everyone had to leave before 9 p.m. because of the curfew). We had a real big Christmas tree as usual with lots of lights and decorations. Ramin got chickenpox the day before Christmas, but he's fine now.

I'm really considering coming to the U.S. if things get worse here (or even if they stay the same!). at least it's not dangerous here, just inconvenient. But I'm getting papers, passports, etc. ready just in case.

J: All during January 1979, we ex-pats were advised to call the American Consulate daily for news on what parts of town to avoid and updates on evacuation plans. The military and their dependents were evacuated first, then the American business people, and finally us--assorted wives and other U.S. citizens living in Iran. I was told I could take my kids by military transport plane as far as Germany and then find my own way to America. Those planes had none of the comforts of commercial airlines, not even real seats or food. In addition, the U.S. government would not take my Lufthansa tickets in exchange but required U.S. dollars in payment, either right away or later. But I had no U.S. dollars, so I declined and decided to wait until Lufthansa was flying again.

B: Now, we owe the readers (or somebody) an explanation of how things are at present in Iran. I'm going to limit myself to a short paragraph, starting with the popular assertion that things are worse. The regime can be properly called theocracy with less freedom than before. Repression and violation of human rights is rampant. In short, wealth, power, and abuse of power shifted from one small group of people to another, with a vengeance.

J: What a pity! The Iranian Revolution did not turn out to bring the improvements so many were hoping for. As a result most of the westerners and western-educated left the country. And that included us!

Chapter Thirteen

Ending and Beginning

In this chapter, all the loose ends of the previous chapters are tied up. That is, we are going to see what happened to the family between the time that Jackie and the children left Iran on February 2, 1979, and the time Bahman arrived in the U.S., based on the letters they exchanged during those two months. The main reason for his staying behind was to relocate his mother and sister and to dispose of all the extra household items.

She: 2/7/79 Hi Honey! Happy Valentine's Day on the 14th. Wish you were here. I'm writing this knowing perfectly well there is *no* mail service to Iran (except APO!) so I'll save it until the mails are open again and hope that's soon.

I feel good being in America. Everything is so calm and organized and comfortable. The children are happy too. I sleep well at nights and I'm not nervous (usually). I feel like a person recovering from a long illness or waking up from a bad dream—I'm taking things slow and easy for the time being. Everything would be perfect if you were here.

The trip over was quite luxurious. We flew to Kuwait for refueling but didn't get off the plane. We got a bit confused in the London Airport but finally changed about 100 tomans (188 rials per pound) so we could check our bags overnight. Then we found the service desk for vouchers for overnight accommodations. We stayed at the Excelsior Hotel—quite luxurious—with free dinners and breakfasts. We ate dinner at 1:30 a.m., watched some color TV and slept. Our flight the next morning was a British Airways 747 (much better since there was more room for bags and knees!), and they were celebrating their new "Elizabethan Service" so they gave us free drinks, music, and movie just like first class!

We arrived in Darien, ate dinner, and slept. On Sunday the kids watched TV all day! I went to church and spent most of the rest of the day on the phone. I talked to Isabel, Sue, and Joanne (they took her kids' open visa away and gave her 6 months' tourist visa!) and lots of relatives and friends—all of whom are so very happy I escaped from Iran.

On Monday I deposited the check and opened a checking account. I also arranged to enroll the kids in school; we visited and toured it. It is Ox Ridge Elementary School, one of the most beautiful schools I've ever seen. It has plants and pets, large green lawns, music room, big library, gym, cafeteria, etc. I don't see how any child could be unhappy there. Yesterday was their first day at school—both said they liked it. The bus service brought them home and today they went off on the bus. And all of it is free!! All I pay is their hot lunches—55 cents per day per child.

Yesterday I went out and bought the kids boots, mittens, jackets, snowsuit, etc. so we're all ready for the big snowstorm that's predicted for today. I don't think I'll run out of money for awhile, but you should start transferring as much as you can—at least all my savings—before the exchange rate gets bad.

In a week or two, I'll go into New York to try to change my rials and check with the Iranian Consulate on how to certify that the kids are students and you can officially send them money every month.

I don't know what to do with myself yet. Probably go to the library a lot. Probably won't work for awhile anyway. If I can afford a camper van I'd like to buy one and spend a fantastic 2-week vacation driving to California when you come. That means taking the kids out of school again, which Isabel doesn't recommend, but there are very few furnished apts. for rent here anyway so it's better to go to Los Angeles as soon as we can. I'm going to write to Georgiades for suggestions.

223

Feb. 8 – Hi again! Isabel says she knows someone going to Tehran who can take my letter. I hope the mails will open soon. When they do, send me Gesco's address so I can write to you.

B: Yes, that must have been quite a trip. I'm sure you could add here what we've been telling everybody--about how you got out of the airport!

J: Leaving Tehran was dramatic and traumatic! Some friends and I agreed to get airline tickets to leave on Feb. 1 "in case things didn't get better." But on Feb. 1, 1979 the airport was closed for the arrival of Ayatollah Khomeini. On Feb. 2 you drove us, in heavy traffic, to Mehrabad Airport where the kids and I sat on our suitcases, because of the crowd, and waited eight hours for a plane to leave for America. Finally I heard an announcement that British Airways was leaving for England. I jumped to the counter and exchanged my Lufthansa tickets and we boarded the flight to London!

B: OK, that leaves one more question unanswered and that is about the reasons we wanted to go to Los Angeles right away. My reason was L.A's good climate, and of course you had your own reasons.

J: Yes, I wanted to continue my doctoral studies at USC (NIOGATE had even prepaid tuition for one semester for those of us in the program). Add to that the fact that L.A. had lots of Iranians to socialize with, and our good friends from Tehran, Dick and Sharon Brown, had a house to put us up in while we house-hunted.

He: 2/23/79 It is sad that not only you are all away but that we haven't had any communication. I miss you all and I hope I will be able to join you soon. Today I finally decided to start writing about what is happening and look for some means of sending it. You can also write and mail it to Gesco at . . . and keep a copy of it so that in case I don't receive it I can read the copy later in the U.S.! I am so anxious to know what is going on with you all.

As for us here, I won't say any general social thing, assuming that you hear enough. Again we are all safe and sound here—no worry. It has been a week now that strikes are almost all ended and stores are open. I've been looking for a flat and still am. It should be easier this time to find a place—the only big limitation is location. I want to be very close to my sisters. I hope by next Friday we'll be able to move. I've sold lots of things. The only cumbersome thing left is our bed—I have to get rid of it. Also the "moble" is still with us—and the kitchen table and chairs and lots of clothes.

As for NIOGATE, they opened (with other schools) last Tuesday and I went. Teachers had a meeting on Wed. and boy they are really getting their noses into the affairs of NIOGATE. It seems what Tahmineh used to say had some basis. In any case I am planning to go only until No-Ruz.

Late Friday night: When you called an hour ago, it was so unexpected that I forgot I had a list of notes to tell you! 1) I hope Ramin and Susanne are getting along in school. Make sure they will find some friends there even after school hours—I am sure you know what I mean. 2) Any article you read about Iran keep for me to read.

Tuesday night Feb. 27: I am so anxious to settle everything and come. We have not found a house yet. Still are selling things. Sold the kitchen table and chairs for only 600 tomans (a pity!) I hope to get rid of bed too. . . . Lots of clothes are still left—I don't believe that you & children could store so much clothes. Remind me to tell you more about it in person!

Afsar and some other Persians are running the English Dept. She found a copy of "Teacher's Guide" book on your desk. But apparently Joan didn't turn in hers—told Afsar and also me that she left them in her room (can't believe it). We don't know what other two centers are doing.

I finish this letter here and have it ready to give it to anyone leaving. So, take care and my love to all of you.

Feb. 28 – Ahmad just brought your letter when someone was just buying your typewriter and my bookcase. He didn't stay long, after everyone left, now I finished reading the letter. Everything sounds good—I am glad. Hope to settle everything here soon and come.

He: Friday night, 3/2/79 I just finished watching Pink Panther! They are not showing any of the old shows and only a couple of cartoons. Mehdi said someone is going to England and can mail letters. So I am sending this. We have found an apartment very close to Homayoon and tomorrow I'll go to make it final and if so we'll move in next Friday. We are planning to sell our fridge & gas stove too. I sold the bed and kitchen table. Tomorrow I plan to reserve a ticket for the beginning of No-Ruz, and to ask the bank if I can send money for the kids. If I won't be able to send any money, what do you suggest? Were you able to exchange your rials? If necessary, you can call me until next Friday morning. The problem with the new apartment is that it doesn't have a phone. If necessary, you can give message to Mehdi or Ahmad by phone and I am in contact with them.

He: 3/14/79 We finally moved, and to my surprise we had two truck trips and not one! The only big thing we weren't able to sell is the gas stove. The new apartment is on the second floor in an alley very near Homayoon, has a (relatively) large living room and 2 bedrooms with central heating, and wall paper, but no phone. So far everything has turned out good.

The only thing left is to get permission to fly. I have reserved a flight for Friday morning on March 23 at about 9 a.m. on Iran Air. They are still not letting men out of the country but the list of forbidden travelers they are preparing is said to be ready and maybe I can fly on time. If not, I'll put it off as necessary. I hope I can get there for Easter vacation—which I am not sure when it starts. I sent $1,000 to each kid yesterday. They didn't need certificate now—don't send them if you haven't.

I'm still going to NIOGATE. I got all my back pay.

I have talked to my friend (Jabbehdar) at Tehran U. and they gave my course to someone else. Then if I could get a sort of appointment (teaching, research, etc.) at some Univ.

in the U.S., I could ask for a sabbatical for a while and see what happens after that. Love to all of you, I miss you.

He: 3/18/79 I have sent you 2 letters already. First thru someone going to England and second by mail (I don't expect you to get that one). This letter is going first to India (!) and then hopefully to you. Right now the radio said that people (men) can now apply for passport and exit permit. So I am going to start tomorrow but I think I'll have to change my reservation from next Friday to a later date— maybe the following Wed. or even Friday. The point is that banks are closed (like schools) thru Sunday March 25 and I want to be able to get my 2,000 tomans worth of $. And I suspect there will be lots of people waiting in line.
This was my last day at NIOGATE and I got all my money.

She: 3/25/79 So the mails are open now! What a nice surprise to get your March 14 letter last Thursday, just a week after the one mailed in England. I was waiting for the mails to open and then for you to arrive, so I didn't write. We were all sad that you didn't arrive last Friday. I guess that means that men still aren't allowed to travel. Anyway it will also be sad if you *get* this letter, because that means you still haven't come. Isabel knows some people coming to Tehran in a week or so. If you're still there, I'll send another letter with them and report some of the items of this letter.
I phoned on Feb. 23rd thinking that you had moved, and I could get your phone number from the neighbors. But the neighbor lady picked up the phone, said "Nist," [not here] and hung up on me! I was so upset. It was about 10:30 p.m. Tehran time. Were you really out? I'm sorry you don't have a phone in your new apt. You won't be able to phone your mother when you're here. But anyway, we'll save money. My first call to you was over $18!
When you get to J.F.K. Airport, you can phone collect.. . .Or else take the Conn. limousine service (There is a reservation phone in every terminal.) to Darien and phone us from there. I *can't* wait 'til you get here. I miss you so much. I'm anxious to start our new life *together* in America.

Ramin and Susanne seem fine and well-adjusted. They're active in Brownies and Cub Scouts too. Ramin got his Wolf Badge at the Scouts "Blue & Gold" Dinner last week. Susanne went ice skating with Brownies once. Yesterday she had a friend from school visit. I bought them all kites and we went kite flying! I don't know if it's a good idea to uproot them again and take them to Calif. before the end of the school year. We'll decide that when you get here.

He: 3/26/79 It seems that waiting is taking longer than I expected. They have postponed issuing and renewing passports and giving exit permits. So, I am still waiting. Considering evidences, I don't think I can get out before Wed. April 4 and that is when I have changed my reservation to. I am sending this letter thru a passenger (woman and child) going to India. I'll also mail a copy and see what happens. I haven't received any letter from you—other than the one thru Ahamd. Maybe there is some in Gesco mail—I'll check later. You can still mail letters to Gesco. I'll give them the return address to the U.S. for your later letters.
I wish I knew what is going on with you all. I finally found your mother's phone number in my old letters but no area code. If I find that too, I might call you from somewhere when my departure is certain. Otherwise, I'll call you when I get to Darien or Stamford! I love you all and looking forward to see you.

B: I remember I finally left Tehran on April 1st (the day before *sizdeh*, the thirteenth day of No-Ruz holidays). Do you have anything to add?

J: Yes, here is a bit more of what happened afterwards . . .

B: No, no, you can't go into those later events here. Remember, this is supposed to be based on the letters and can only cover the events up to this point . . .

J: You seem to be nitpicking now! All right, maybe we should provide an epilogue for the readers later. How is that?

B: Great idea! I even like the sound of it--Epilogue!

Chapter Fourteen

Leftovers

In order to avoid ending the book with *thirteen* chapters, we put together this final chapter. Aside from that weird reasoning, it so happened that there were quite a few passages that didn't exactly fall into any particular chapter, but were too "cute" to be thrown away. So, we decided to download them all here!

> Oct. 3, 1967   Last week I visited the famous Bazaar—Tehran's huge market place. The atmosphere is like a big department store built in a stable. There are alleys filled with all sorts of merchandise. The rugs are absolutely beautiful.

J: Yes the famous Grand Bazaar! This is probably one of the most exotic sights for a foreigner to experience in Tehran. Parts of the bazaar seemed to reflect enormous wealth while other parts were very humble. The goldsmith shops were dripping with more gold than I had ever seen. Carpet merchants had stacks and stacks of valuable Persian carpets, which, even back then, were too expensive for a young couple like us to purchase. What did we usually buy? I remember that quite well. We got spices and herbs in a shop that smelled of every herb under the sun. We often got herbs for my mother-in-law to boil into a tea to cure a cold or a fever. We shopped a great deal for material: I made my own bedsheets and cloth baby diapers. Even my wedding gown had come from a shop on the edge of the bazaar. My most unusual material purchase was 10 yards of tulle that I then spent hours and hours sewing by hand into a petticoat for square dancing. The last time I remember going to south Tehran to visit the bazaar, I got a strong impression of how the city population was growing. Around and around we drove, looking for a parking space. After 45 minutes of total frustration, we gave up and went home.

B: Maybe that is why I didn't want to go to the Tehran Bazaar in our trip back two years ago. But you went with some relatives anyway. Was it worth it?

J: Oh yes, a bazaar is endlessly interesting. I took a great photo of a wizened old man with a triangular wooden support on his back, ready to carry some heavy appliance or piece of furniture.

Oct. 30, 1967 Remember I told you my friend from Drew (Keir Holtzel is his name) was in the Peace Corps in Shiraz, Iran? Well, he came to Tehran to see the Coronation parade, and so we got to see each other for the first time in over three years! On Thursday evening Bahman, Keir, and I went to a nice restaurant for supper, and the next day we went hiking in the mountains with the Iran-America Society. This was my third hiking trip and the second time we've hiked to Kolakchal (a beautiful scout camp high in the mountains). Sometime after our marriage, Bahman and I plan to visit Keir in Shiraz.

March 27, 1968 We went to the Tehran Zoo a couple of days ago. Fereshteh [niece] was very impressed, she had never been to the zoo before. Lately, Fereshteh has been curious about everything I do. It's kind of cute to see her standing around watching me beating frosting for a cake, or vacuuming furniture, etc. Yesterday I washed my hair and set it with rollers, using beer and lotion. Fereshteh stood and watched—she must think I'm very strange.

J: It's interesting to remember the small, old, Tehran Zoo. The new Zoo which we saw in 2001 bears no resemblance. It's so much larger. But the new Zoo's most surprising exhibit for me was a cage of white domestic cats—just like our old cat Cayce!

B: So what you are saying is that the new regime has improved the Tehran Zoo, huh! Well, to be fair, some other things have improved too, but . . . (Those readers who are looking for more than just "dots," can go to Chapter Twelve!)

May 18, 1968   Yesterday was a particularly nice day. Bahman and I went to visit Dr. Yaganegi and his wife in the morning. Dr. Yaganegi is a very rich man who was Bahman's former landlord and is a friend (Zoroastrian, of course) of the family. He is also a member of the Iranian Congress (called the Majlis). He had returned a few weeks ago from his annual trip to the U.S. and Europe. It is an Iranian tradition for people returning from trips to bring back presents for friends. He gave Bahman a tie from France and me some French perfume. This was the first time I'd met him. They have a nice house and more servants in the house than family! Bahman knows the servants too, and when we were leaving the servants gave us two potted plants to take home.

June 13, 1968   You asked about our TV shows (incidentally, I'm surprised about your *color* TV!). Well, the Persian stations have shows like Ben Casey, Peyton Place, Lost in Space, Beverly Hillbillies, Mission Impossible, etc. (many of these have the English soundtrack on the *radio* at the same time so you can listen in Persian or English). The Armed Forces TV station, in English, has Lawrence Welk, Red Skelton, Ed Sullivan, The Fugitive, Bonanza, etc. Of course there are movies, afternoon and evening.

Oct. 31, 1968   Also, our bachelor neighbor, Reza, from upstairs, has both of his parents moved in and living there now. They're all busy trying to find a wife for Reza! Even a foreign girl would do. But Reza is fussy—he wants one educated *and* beautiful!
Marriage in Iran makes an interesting study.

Feb. 28, 1969   What kind of automatic washer did you get from Sears? I'm tired of washing things by hand and decided I certainly won't like washing diapers so we've been looking around for a washer. There are a few automatics made in Iran, but they are so small compared to American ones and so expensive ($250--$350). But we know of some American military personnel who are being transferred back to the U.S. after their 2 years of duty here. People like these usually sell their used household things and get very good prices since they're American-made. Well, we looked at a nice Kenmore model 600 last week, which is about a year old. But the people aren't leaving until July 1st and they asked $250 for it. The Sears catalog says this machine costs *$184* so I thought they were expecting too much profit and I said I'd think about it. Just by luck, today we found a Kenmore model 70 machine which we can get *next week* for $200 (what they paid for it). It's 2 years old, but we saw it and liked it, so we put a down payment on it immediately. I'm so happy about it. Of course, now we must buy a transformer to fit it to our electricity, and tear out a sink in the shower room to make space for it!

March 13, 1969 Well, we got our washer too—and all the problems that go with it. The stupid fellow we bought it from delivered it in a big truck that he was afraid to back into our alley, so Bahman went down (this was 1 ½ weeks ago) to help carry it. They dropped it in the alley! So now it has several more chips on it. It is about twice as huge as the little Persian machines here, and what a monster it seems to be. First of all we discovered it wouldn't fit through the door of the shower room where we had planned to install it (so we shoved it in the kitchen). After we paid the fellow, he informed us that the cycle-timing mechanism doesn't work with Persian electricity, so all of the cycles must be set and changed by hand! The next day Bahman had to buy a $20 transformer just to hook it up to our electricity. He bought special connections and made an extension hose to hook it up to our kitchen sink faucets, but it leaked terribly and then the hot water burst the extension hose. So we have just given up on the monster until Bahman returns from the trip. It seems that American machines just don't fit very well into Persian households.

J: Now there's a philosophical statement! It could be expanded to explain the whole Iranian Revolution: Western ways don't fit very well into Persian traditions!

B: Well, and I thought I had the bad habit of philosophizing! Anyway, you are right to some extent, and we saw this in some detail in Chapter Twelve. However, one can't easily generalize— *some* "western ways" could and should be adapted and others shouldn't.

March 24, 1969 I told you about our washing machine last time I think. Well, Bahman made an extra extension cord to our new transformer, added a longer hose for drainage, and bought new kitchen sink faucets and had a friend come in to help install them. So then we were finally able to hook up the machine and do a wash load. But since the timer didn't fit the Persian electricity, all the settings had to be dialed by hand and changed every two minutes. I said at least it was easier than washing by hand, but Bahman wasn't satisfied. He removed the timer, took it apart and put it together again a couple of times and after a couple of days of playing with all the little pieces, he discovered a way to make it work on our electricity! Lately the washer has been working wonderfully and we can even get some spray-and-spin rinses we couldn't dial by hand. I'm quite proud of my inventive husband. When I was a little girl I used to think my father could fix anything, and now I believe my husband can fix anything!
We were able to wash everything in time for No-Ruz (the Persian New Year) and that's a Persian tradition (to be absolutely clean). Thursday night at 10:38 PM, we watched the New Year come in on TV while the Shah gave a Happy New Year greeting. Bahman's present to me was some lovely French perfume, which smells like Lily of the Valley. I gave him an electric mosquito-killing machine which I hope will solve some of our mosquito problems. The machine is supposed to produce a vapor for about 8 hours.
As part of the New Year tradition, every day we've been visited by friends and relatives and have gone to see them. I

enjoy visiting but these visits are not the friendly informal kind you find in the US. The young people are supposed to visit the older ones first, then you should revisit everyone who has visited you. I'm afraid I still make mistakes in the formal Persian etiquette because I still act like an American at times.

April 13, 1969 Incidentally, our washer is still working fine. Bahman seems to enjoy watching it work, and asks almost every day if we've got anything else to be washed. But practically all our washable things are quite clean now!

April 25, 1970 Apparently you sent Ramin a monkey *and* a teddy bear!? The postman brought a package last week described as "a bear and some ornaments." Well, he wanted $12 in customs duties and we decided to send it back to the post office until we could go there to try to haggle that price down. Don't send Ramin any more toys—I guess we can't afford it. We got a little monkey and that was under $2 customs duties and not so bad.

J: It was so sad that the bureaucratic and cumbersome customs taxes took the joy out of receiving gifts from abroad!

May 26, 1970 Your letters arrived OK at our new address. We were able to get the teddy bear for about $6, since some of the taxes could be subtracted under a law that allows each of us $13 in gifts through the mail each year. Taxes on toys, we found out, are set at 200% of the values! So when you marked the teddy bear worth $5, they taxed us $10 plus delivery charges, etc. Books, marked *Books*, ought to arrive tax free, and clothes are not highly taxed especially if mailed in plain envelopes. Hopefully we can bring Ramin to see you in September and you can spoil him for three weeks so you won't need to send him things.

Sept. 23, 1970 Our 16-year-old niece, Fereshteh, is supposed to enter a hospital-nursing school today for a 2-year program to become a nurse's aide. The students live at the school for 6 days a week, and this was considered the ideal way to stop the constant arguing between Fereshteh and her mother and grandmother.

Feb. 21, 1975 We're having an interesting time getting our 21-yr. old niece, Fereshteh, married off. The traditional Persian method of marriages arranged by parents has changed a little to fit modern times but it's something like this now: A young (or old!) man sees a young girl and asks his mother or another intermediary to talk to the girl's parents to arrange an introduction. If the first meeting goes well, he might propose (through the parents again) right away or after a few (usually *chaperoned*) dates, and the girl can say "yes" or "no." Well, this week a fellow proposed after seeing Fereshteh only once! . . . What's more, he wanted her answer before he joined his ship (he's in the Navy) at the end of the week. Of course, Fereshteh replied that she has to get to know him before she can say anything. I think this whole thing is very interesting.

March 17, 1977 So many people are traveling abroad for the New Year's holidays. My friend, Sue and her family are going to Rome and Tunis for these two weeks. So when she phoned me on Monday I thought it was to say "good-bye" but it was to tell me that when she and her husband got home from work, they found their home had been robbed— carpets, clothes, everything. She has no hope of getting any of it back—but they left on their vacation anyway since the airline tickets hadn't been stolen.
Another shocking item: This week a huge dump truck rammed into the front of the kids' school knocking down the iron gates and part of the brick wall. Thank God no children were in the front yard at the time. The driver admitted that he knew he was driving with bad brakes! Since no one was injured, he wasn't even arrested!

There is a point here that seems to be in need of a comment. In his July 8, 1977 letter to her, we come across, "Fereshteh and Bijan and some in-laws went to the Caspian this weekend. Remember to bring something (s) from 'Farang' [abroad] for them." And in a subsequent letter he requests, "bring some wedding gift for

Leftovers

Fereshteh." Obviously Fereshteh had gotten engaged to Bijan D. (*not* the Navy man) before the summer, and as obviously some letters to Jackie's mother must have gotten lost before and after the summer of 1977. In any case, we are happy to report that they did get married, and they have a daughter and a son.

Epilogue

This portion was added just to briefly tell the readers of what happened to the family since their arrival in the U.S. in the Spring of 1979. If you remember, Jackie was going to address this point at the end of Chapter Thirteen before Bahman interrupted her! So now he graciously lets her have her way!

J: Thank you Professor! Here is a synopsis:

In mid-April we moved from Connecticut to Southern California. Driving a Chevy Vega station wagon (!), it took us two weeks to cross the country, camping and visiting friends. We finally settled in a suburb of Los Angeles.

Your mother passed away in the spring of 1982, and you were unable to get your passport renewed in time to go there. My mother passed away in August of 1983, and we all flew to Connecticut for her funeral.

Ramin is single and lives in his own condo nearby. He is an artist and a sculptor.

Susanne, husband Ted, and son Jayse live fifty miles away and see us often.

You and I are still married and living together. At this writing that amounts to over 35 years of married life!

B: Not bad Goldoon! Now, there is something else. We have so far had a few short references to our trip back to Iran in 2001. Do you think the readers can stand a bit more of the details of the trip?

J: Possibly! Why don't we end this with what I wrote and sent to our friends after our return?

B: OK, that would make a good ending.

Iran Revisited!

Years ago, on Sept. 8, 1967, I set foot in Iran for the first time in my life, and stayed on to live there for 12 years. On Sept. 7, 2001, 34 years later, Bahman and I set foot in Iran again, for the first visit back since the Iranian Revolution of 1979. It was a "Rip Van Winkle" experience to see this land we had known so well—so familiar yet so changed in our 22 ½ years' absence. At first I strained and strained to recognize landmarks and make out where I was, but after a while, I gave up. The only constant geographic landmark is that, with Tehran being on a long hillside, north is still always uphill.

Almost all the pre-Revolutionary street names are changed to eliminate any references to any Shah. I did recognize the miles of tall sycamores that line ValiAsr (old "Pahlavi") Avenue, but most of the little shops are changed. The Sorrento Restaurant is still there. The bakeries are automated (!) but people still carry multiple fresh loaves of flat bread home in their hands or wrapped in cloth.

And the streets! Now there are long, wide highways that cut swaths through the city. At times, cars can even get up to speed on them. But the traffic is worse than ever! Why bother painting lines on the street, I wonder, when drivers pay no attention to them, weaving across the center line at will and squeezing into six lanes where three are marked. It is still true that traffic is a large game of "dodge-em," and pedestrians step out into oncoming traffic seemingly risking their lives at every step. The car with its fender edged in front of another is always the one with the right of way. Bahman wanted to keep his eyes closed as we were driven about. The only thing scarier than traffic was when our driver answered his cell phone while driving with one hand! (Lots of people have "mobiles" as they call these phones!)

We were met at the airport by almost all of our Iranian family members, even though we arrived well past midnight. They carried flowers for us and videotaped our arrival. There were lots of tears of greeting. Bahman is an only son, and his three sisters all have grown children with children of their own now. The "kids" we knew are now middle-aged adults. The only ones we had seen at all in 22 years were a nephew (Bijan N.) and his family who came to the U.S. last January. It was at Bijan's house that we mostly stayed while in Tehran.

The first five days we stayed in a Tehran hotel that had once been fancy but was now a bit frayed. When Bijan's guest rooms were painted and ready, we moved in there. That was Sept. 11, and we saw the horrifying events of the U.S. on BBC television in English. Iranians we spoke to were horrified and sympathetic for the most part, but also some weird conspiracy theories were circulating. We were glad no Iranian was among the terrorists, and the President of Iran publicly expressed sympathy. My American friends e-mailed me, worried because I was in the Middle East, but we felt no threat there.

We took several internal flights and toured the cities of Shiraz (including Persepolis), Isfahan, and Yazd, where Bahman and I made our last trip to his old, old family home. He and his sisters have decided, finally, to sell it. It has been deserted for years. As we walked around his old childhood neighborhood, it was amazing to run into old friends and acquaintances who still lived in the old Zoroastrian neighborhood and remembered him!

The Iranian rial is now worth about one one-hundredth of what we remembered it to be, so paying for things was always a challenge. Imagine tipping a hotel clerk 20,000 rials—which, in the old days was about $275 but is now less than $3! Shopping in the bazaar in Shiraz, Bahman inadvertently paid the seller 10 times what he had asked. (The seller was honest enough to say so.) My old savings accounts were still in the bank, but so reduced in value that my twelve years of saved Iranian salary barely covered the few days of our hotel stay! Our dollars did go far though. A good hotel meal was never over $5, and taxi fare between city and airport ran less than a dollar.

Of course we visited all the relatives in their homes. One niece, Fereshteh, had stored some old mementos of the past for us, including my wedding dress! We also visited tourist sites including the Carpet Museum, which I had never seen, and the Bazaar. What a grand outing we had to visit the Sa'adabad Palace to see how the Shah and his family had lived! It is actually a compound with 18 palaces, and we had time to visit only four, which are now museums. Each of the Shah's children had their

240

own palace on the beautiful wooded grounds, which resemble the regional parks we are used to in the U.S.

September is really too hot for touring in Islamic dress, which is what I had to wear anytime outside the house. I wore a scarf and a shapeless dark cotton coat over my clothes. This is what most Iranian women seemed to be wearing in preference to the all-encompassing black "chador" that many elderly women wore. Being so covered up meant I was dripping in sweat wherever I went. Hot, hot, hot.

We spent two days at Amol on the Caspian Sea coast, and I had the unique experience of swimming under Islamic regulations. The women's part of the beach is a piece of sand and water surrounded by cloth barriers, like large tablecloths, tied to large poles. Inside the barriers, the women wore all sorts of bathing clothes into the water, and one woman even wore her large gold earrings, bracelets, and necklaces into the sea. The female lifeguard seemed almost panicked that the barrier cloths were being whipped about by the wind, and men might be able to catch a glimpse of the women swimming! The men, of course, had the whole rest of the beach to themselves.

We returned on Sept. 30, as planned, and Bahman decided to come back with me rather than stay on longer. Security measures were strict, but not too bad. The worst part was waiting for Ramin to pick us up at the airport, not knowing that he was not allowed to get closer than the remote parking area. After an hour and a half we took a Super Shuttle home, but he waited for us at the parking lot for 5 hours!

I asked Bahman how he felt about being back in the U.S. He said, "Sweet, home-sweet-home." And what is his prediction of Iran's political future? He quotes an old Persian proverb, *Hamin aash ast va hamin kaseh,* which translates to "the same soup in the same bowl." In other words, no change for the foreseeable future.

ABOUT THE AUTHORS

Bahman, born in Yazd, Iran, met Jackie at the University of Wisconsin, where he earned a Master's and Ph.D. in Electrical Engineering while on an Iranian government scholarship. He was employed as an Associate Professor of Electrical Engineering at Tehran University and later, at the California State University at Long Beach, California.

Jackie, born in Stamford, CT, attended Drew University in NJ and the University of Wisconsin, for an M.A. in Sociology. She later earned her Ph.D. degree in Education from the University of Southern California. She taught English in Iran, and is currently on the staff and faculty of the University of Phoenix, Southern California Campus.

Bahman and Jackie have a son, Ramin, and a daughter, Susanne, both born in Iran. In 1979, during the Iranian Revolution, the family relocated to California, where they continue to reside.

ISBN 141201231-7

9 781412 012317